Lin Tianmiao

Bound Unbound
Lin Tianmiao

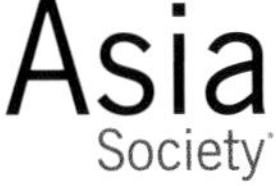

CHARTA

This book is dedicated to

Vishakha N. Desai

whose passion, vision, and creative energy
have inspired Asia Society Museum
for more than twenty years.

Design
Fayçal Zaouali

Editorial Coordination
Filomena Moscatelli

Copyediting
Emily Ligniti

Translation
Sun Yue

Copywriting and Press Office
Silvia Palombi

International Editorial Director
Francesca Sorace

Promotion and Web
Elisa Legnani

Distribution
Anna Visaggi

Administration
Grazia De Giosa

Warehouse and Outlet
Roberto Curiale

ISBN 978-88-8158-853-4

Printed in Italy

Cover
Focus, 2001

Photo Credits
All photographs © Lin Tianmiao, courtesy of the artist.

Page(s) 13: Photo by Yang Yuguang; 14-15: Photo by Wang GongXin and Lin Tianmiao; 16, 19: Photo by Wang GongXin; 20: Photo by Yang Yuguang; 22: Photo by Wang Peng; 23: Photo by Yang Yuguang; 26–33: Photo by Wang GongXin; 34-35: Photo by Yang Yuguang; 36–37: Photo by Wang GongXin; 38–39: Photo by IT Park Taiwan; 41-43: Ni Haifeng; 44-47: Photo by Yang Yuguang; 48–57: Photo by Wang GongXin; pp. 58–71: Photo by Wang Chuan; 72-125: Photo by Yang Yuguang

We apologize if, due to reasons wholly beyond our control, some of the photo sources have not been listed.

Asia Society
725 Park Avenue
New York, NY 10021
www.AsiaSociety.org

Edizioni Charta srl
Milano
via della Moscova, 27 - 20121
Tel. +39-026598098/026598200
Fax +39-026598577
e-mail: charta@chartaartbooks.it
www.chartaartbooks.it

Published on the occasion of the exhibition

Bound Unbound: Lin Tianmiao

organized by Asia Society Museum.

Asia Society Museum, New York
September 7, 2012 through January 27, 2013

Major support for this exhibition is provided by The Coby Foundation, Ltd., Carol and David Appel, Artron, and the W.L.S. Spencer Foundation.

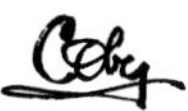
THE COBY FOUNDATION, LTD.

Additional support is provided by Will and Helen Little and Sarah Peter.

Support for Asia Society Museum is provided by the Partridge Foundation, a John and Polly Guth Charitable Fund; Asia Society Contemporary Art Council, whose members include Carol and David Appel, Max and Monique Burger (Hong Kong), Susan Hayden, Joey Horn, Joleen Julis, Yung Hee Kim, Marie Lippman, Helen Little, Harold Newman, and Cynthia Hazen Polsky; Asia Society Friends of Asian Arts; Arthur Ross Foundation; Sheryl and Charles R. Kaye Endowment for Contemporary Art Exhibitions; Blanchette Hooker Rockefeller Fund; National Endowment for the Humanities; Hazen Polsky Foundation; New York State Council on the Arts; and New York City Department of Cultural Affairs.

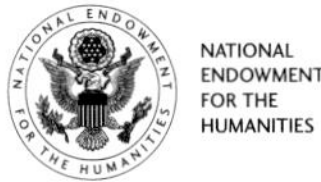

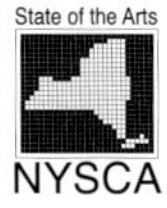

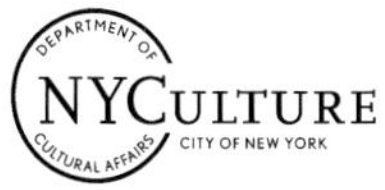

Contents

Director's Preface

Melissa Chiu, Museum Director, Senior Vice President, Global Arts and Cultural Programs, Asia Society

"Bound Unbound: Lin Tianmiao" is a survey of Lin's works from the past seventeen years. She first exhibited in the United States in 1998 as one of three women artists from mainland China in Asia Society's historical overview of the Chinese avant-garde, "Inside Out: New Chinese Art." Her contribution to the show was the ambitious installation work *Bound and Unbound*, which is also included in this exhibition. Since 1998, her work has been shown in group exhibitions all over the world, including the Brooklyn Museum and Museum of Modern Art in New York City. This exhibition represents the first museum survey of her career.

I first met Lin in 1995 when I began researching the Chinese art scene in preparation for my Ph.D. During my visits to artist studios in Beijing, I became interested in why there were few women present, aside from the artists' girlfriends. I published my findings in an article in *Art Asia Pacific* on installation art and women artists, and Lin was one of the three artists I discussed in the essay. Around the same time, Lin began her move back to China after seven years of living in New York. Although it would be another year until she left the United States permanently, this return marked the beginning of Lin's professional life as an artist.

"Bound Unbound" continues Asia Society's interest in and commitment to developing scholarship on modern and contemporary Asian art. Begun in the early 1990s, Asia Society's program has put forth landmark modern, historical exhibitions such as "Art and China's Revolution," "Rabindranath Tagore: The Last Harvest," and "Revolutionary Ink: The Paintings of Wu Guanzhong." "Bound Unbound: Lin Tianmiao" is the continuation of a series of monographic and survey shows that began in 2004 with "Montien Boonma: Temple of the Mind" and have included artists Zhang Huan and Yoshitomo Nara. The decision to focus on Lin's work stems from her approach to the exploration of the human body through different techniques and materials, such as thread and textiles, which demonstrates her consistent development as an artist. Perhaps more importantly, the exhibition provides us with insights into an artist's development over one of the most important periods of change in the Chinese art world, the 1990s through to today.

Exhibitions with large-scale installations are always complex and involve many people. First I would like to thank the artist Lin Tianmiao for being such a wonderful partner throughout this project. We had many exchanges over the years about how best to present her work, some of which were very site or project specific; these conversations were always insightful. I would also like to thank Lin's husband, artist Wang GongXin, for supporting the project and allowing us to include in the exhibition the work *Here? Not There?*, their collaboration for the Shanghai Biennale.

I am most appreciative to the lenders to this exhibition, especially Eve Tam, Chief Curator, Ka-lun Ng, Curator, and Lai-yee Chan, Assistant Curator of the Hong Kong Art Museum; Kingsley K. W. Liu; and Larry Warsh.

I am especially thankful for the support of our generous funders, all of whom are recognized elsewhere in this book. I also thank the members of Asia Society's Contemporary Art Council, who have provided leadership and advice for Asia Society's contemporary art exhibition program.

At Asia Society, I wish to thank Marion Kocot, Director of Museum Operations; Dr. Miwako Tezuka who worked on the project as Associate Curator until her departure from Asia Society; Clare McGowan, Collection Manager and Registrar; Jacob Reynolds, Associate Registrar; Davis Thompson-Moss, Installation Manager; Kate Williamson, Museum Publications Coordinator; Nancy Blume, Head of Museum Education Programs; Donna Saunders, Executive Assistant; and Zixuan Feng, Museum Intern.

I also want to acknowledge the continuing support of Shayne Doty, Vice President, External Affairs and his team Kim Woodward, Kyle Carroll, Judy Chen, Freda Wang, Fran Linton, Wendy Westwood, Alice Hunsberger, and Andrea Petrini for their fundraising efforts; Michael Roberts, Executive Director, New York Public Programs and Rachel Cooper, Director, Cultural Programs & Performing Arts for their work on New York programs; Elaine Merguerian, Director of Communications and Briana Green for their work on publicity and marketing; and Bill Swersey, Executive Director, Asia Society Online and his team.

Finally, this exhibition and its publication are dedicated to our President Vishakha Desai, in acknowledgment and appreciation of her devotion to Asia Society for over twenty-two years. In the early 1990s, as Museum Director, Vishakha was responsible for initiating Asia Society's efforts in the contemporary art arena and we will miss her insight and support.

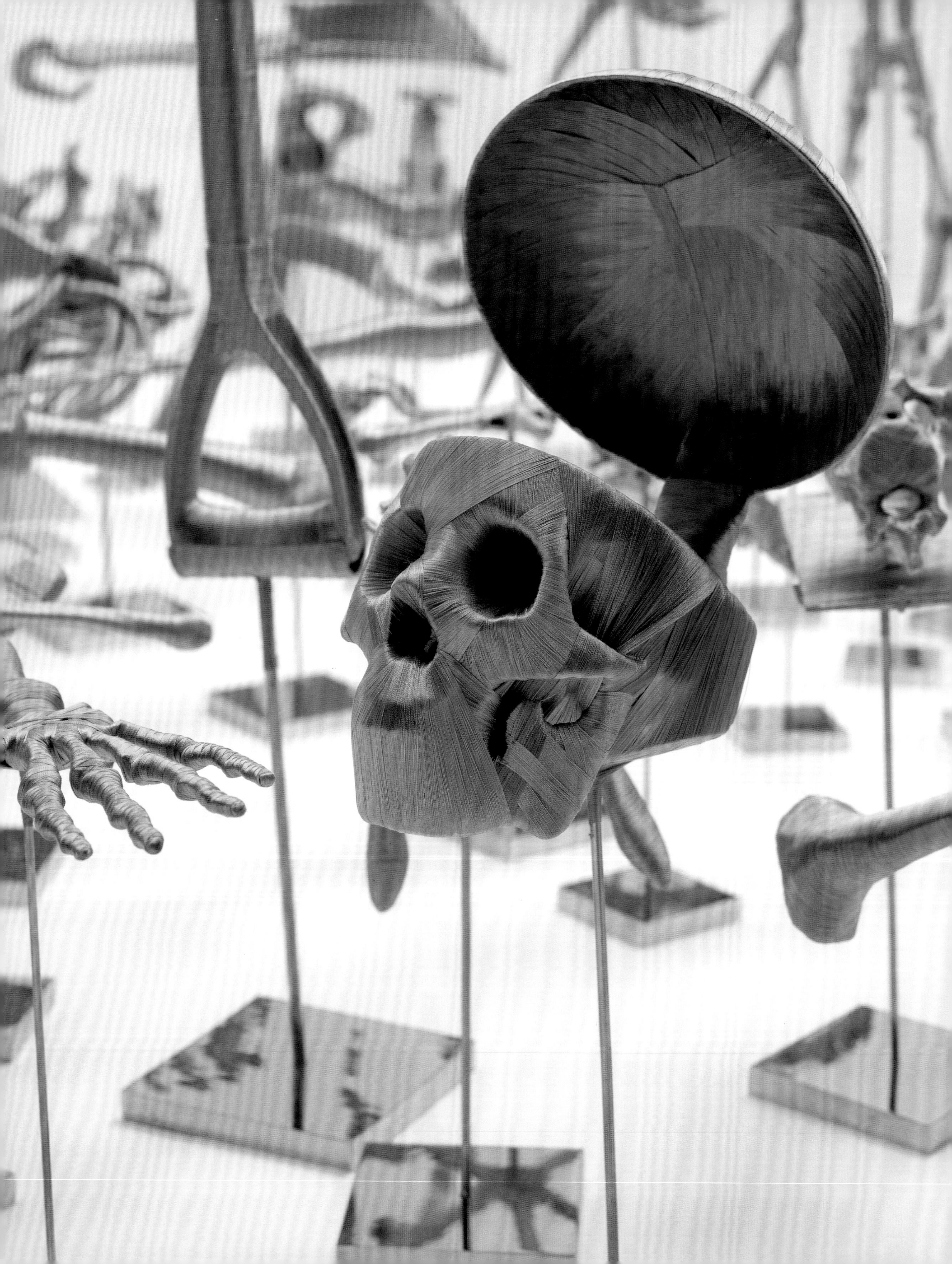

The Body in Thread and Bone: Lin Tianmiao

Melissa Chiu

For the past seventeen years, Lin Tianmiao's sculptures and installations have been about the body. We could say that they are about our own physical experience—a universal one—yet they are often imbued with a gender specificity that sometimes makes them more personal statements with an emotional dimension. Her materials evoke domesticity and female labor which orient the works towards the ideas of feminism, but the feminist principles founded in Europe and the United States do not hold the same value in China where Lin lives and creates her work. In some ways, she resists the label of being a feminist artist because of this difference in cultural context, although at the same time she recognizes that her work may be interpreted this way. As one of only a handful of women artists to have emerged from her generation born in the 1960s in China, Lin's work holds a consistency of vision that allows us to see how her ideas on physicality have evolved and transformed through the development of her own visual vocabulary of everyday materials with a particular emphasis on thread, silk, and felt.

Lin received some art training in China, but she credits her experience living in New York City with giving her an education in what it means to be an artist. When she moved to New York with her artist husband Wang GongXin they became a part of the Chinese diaspora community, an expanding group in the 1980s and 1990s in New York that included some of China's best talent, such as artists Ai Wei Wei, Xu Bing, Chen Yifei, filmmaker Chen Kaige, and composer Tan Dun. In China, this was a time often described as being gripped by "leave the country fever"—if you had an opportunity to leave, you did. Although these artists are all established in their respective fields today, back then they were trying to make ends meet with odd jobs, sketching portraits on the street, or even busking on the subway. Lin worked as a designer for a textile company and describes spending her first three years in the city in "culture shock." She did not create art during this time, but rather took classes at the Art Students League and visited art exhibitions. Her professional career really began back in China when she visited in 1995 and finally settled permanently the following year.

Lin Tianmiao returned to Beijing after eight years in New York, where the art scene and environment for artists had radically changed. In 1988 when she left, artists were still experimenting with diverse art forms that stemmed from the '85 New Wave Movement. When Lin returned to China, the 1989 Tiananmen Square Incident still pervaded government attitudes to art. This meant that artists were largely not able to show their work at any of the state-run museums, such as the National Art Museum of China; and installation art was treated with a great deal of suspicion and performance art was banned. Some artists such as Ma Liuming who performed in Beijing's East Village were arrested during this time. Lin's first substantial work, *The Proliferation of Thread Winding* (1995), was created for "Women's Approach to Contemporary Art," an exhibition designed to coincide with The United Nations Fourth World Conference on Women held in Beijing. The installation has all the attributes Lin has become known for, especially her technique of "thread winding"—the winding of cotton thread around objects or into multiple balls which are accumulated for her sculptural installations. At the time, she enlisted friends and family to help her. In an artist statement published in the accompanying catalogue she states that her interest lies in binaries: "I tried to explore the subtle relationship of things in contrast, the conditions necessary for their shift from one aspect to another, big and small, gathering and scattering, aggression and withdrawal, harshness and tenderness, proliferation and reduction, male and female."[1] The exhibition that included *The Proliferation of Thread Winding* was staged in a series of small pavilions. Lin's work comprised a bed with her thread winding balls streaming from the mattress with an oversized pair of trousers hanging from the ceiling, its elongated legs made from paper extending onto the floor. The overall installation gives the impression of a fantastic bedroom which is made menacing by the 20,000 steel needles embedded into the mattress in place of the body.

Lin continues to employ thread winding in her work today. What began as a nostalgic reference to a childhood spent helping her mother sew the family's clothes was transformed into a technique that has not only become her technical signature, but also has enabled her to address issues related to a gendered experience of the world. The installation *Bound and Unbound* (1997) took this technique to a much more ambitious level. An installation first shown in Beijing at the Central Academy of Fine Arts gallery, one of the few exhibition spaces in the city open to contemporary artists, was an accumulation of nearly 800 household objects around which Lin had carefully wound white unbleached cotton thread, transforming everyday utensils that ranged from pots and pans to tea pots and children's toys into a sea of formal, aesthetic objects. Greeting the viewer at the entrance was a video of a hand cutting threads with a pair of scissors projected onto a screen made up of actual threads. The video image was a strange act of disrupture in what was otherwise a scene of order. That same year she created *Sewing*, an old-fashioned manual sewing machine completely wound in white thread with a video at the needle showing the act of sewing. Again, an everyday object, this time one that she and her mother would have used, was transformed into a sculpture through the act of thread winding.

More or Less the Same (detail), 2011

In the mid to late 1990s, very few artists in China were working with video, and certainly this combination of video and installation was unusual. At the time, Lin's husband Wang GongXin was a leader in video art and is credited with creating one

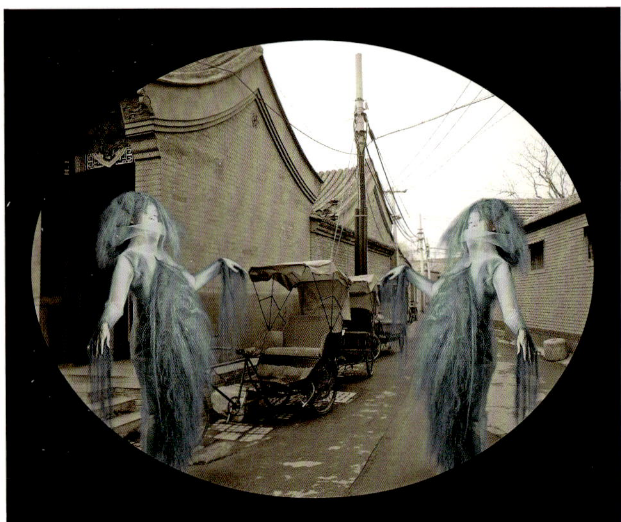

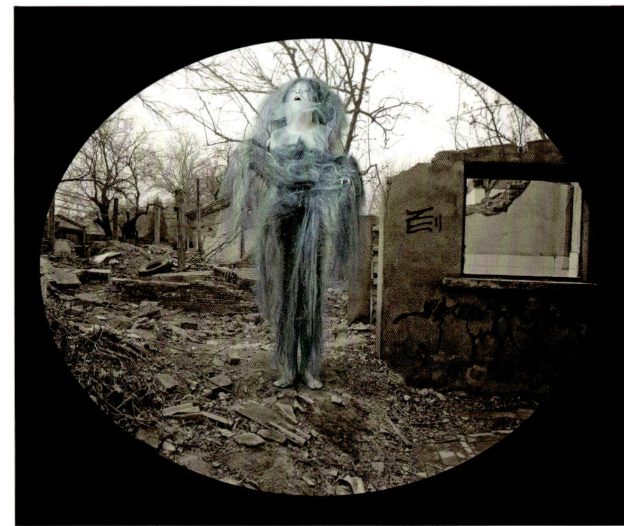

Here? Or There?, 2002

of the first video installations in China, while others such as Zhang Peili and Li Yongbin were also pioneers in this medium. The scale, execution, and vision of *Bound and Unbound* in the context of Chinese art established her reputation and led to her inclusion in Gao Minglu's exhibition "Inside Out: New Chinese Art." Presented by Asia Society in 1998, it was the first major museum survey of the Chinese avant-garde in the United States. Lin was one of only three female artists from fifty mainland Chinese artists.

Following these works and the development of her thread winding technique, Lin began to use images of her own body in her work. *Day-Dreamer* (2000) was one of the first examples. A black and white photographic image of the artist's full, naked body was printed onto fabric and suspended from the ceiling, parallel to the floor. Hundreds of threads were sewn onto the image of the artist's body and strung to a small platform on the ground. The effect is one of tense reiteration through thread. Similarly, *Untitled No.2* (2006) shows two mirror images of the outline of the artist's body sewn in white hair on white felt. The two works are joined by hair sewn across the two figures. *Spawn* (2001) is another image of the artist's naked body rendered in black and white, but this time a series of white thread balls have been sewn onto the body in graduating sizes with the largest at the bottom.

Continuing in this style, *Focus* is perhaps Lin's best-known series of works. Black and white images of herself, her son, and many other people were printed on canvas, then altered by various applications of sewing, embroidery, and thread-winding with small balls of thread sewn onto the surface or other applications of thread and embroidery. These works operate on two levels. On the one hand, we see them as portraits. For Lin's generation, portraits have a significant political reference because in their youth only portraits of Mao Zedong were available and allowed, especially in the 1960s and 1970s. Lin's images of herself and family members are efforts to correct this imbalance in her memory. On another level, the portraits are obscured and made more tactile by her application of embroidery over the surface of the canvas. This has the effect of making them more intimate through the handiwork and detail, an effort to make them about the person rather than a political statement.

In a rare artistic collaboration with her husband Wang GongXin, *Here? Or There?* (2002) brought out a more physical rendering of the body. Created for the Shanghai Biennale, *Here? Or There?* was an installation of nine figures and six video projections. The works were installed in a darkened room with the figures dressed in a manifestation of all of Lin's embroidery and thread winding techniques—one with shiny black braids, another with white balls of varying sizes—it was less clothing and more a series of formal shapes and patterning. On the walls, video images of the figures inhabiting traditional houses were projected in the shape of ovals, as if they were seen through a window or a traditional moon door. On occasion these images are interrupted by a crashing sound, suggesting a disruption to everyday life and tradition that many were experiencing at this time in Beijing with destruction and reconstruction taking place across the city.

Here? Or There? was the first occasion of Lin rendering the body in three dimensions and it launched a series of works that were more about forms of communication and the bonds of community. The two works *Chatting* (2004) and *Endless* (2004) comprised figures made with stretched silk across their physical forms. *Chatting* is six, nude female figures in white silk satin, each imperfect in its body shape, their heads replaced with strange shapes like boxes or receptacles. These bodies, which can only be described as normal rather than society's picture-perfect ideal, attracted the attention of an online Tumblr community with a blog titled, "I love fat! A fat acceptance." Yet the investigation of body ideals is just one element of this work. Each of the figures is linked by white threads and sounds can be heard between them conjuring up a sense of a gendered bond between women. The overall effect is part science fiction, part post-feminist statement. In a similar vein is *Endless* where three aged men, their nude bodies stooped and gaunt, stand around a pool of pink thread on the ground. Its color matches that of their skin which is created from pink silk satin stretched taught across their forms. Lin has stated that with these works she wanted to move beyond sexual desire and have the bodies embody life experiences. Beyond this though, the forms of communication that Lin suggests in these works is a rather narrow one, perhaps also reflecting the limited forms of dissent available to those in China.

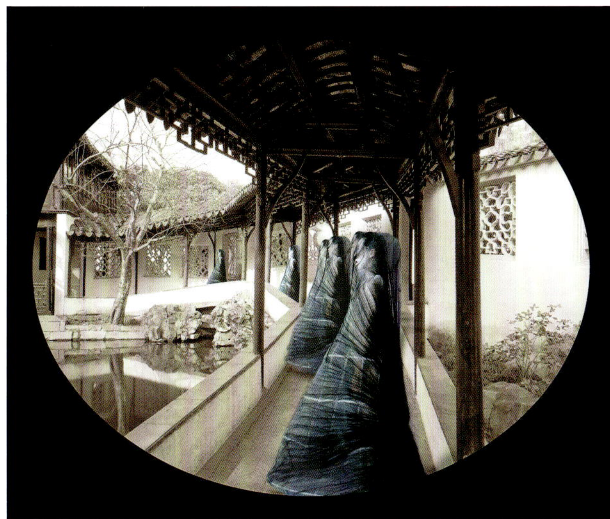

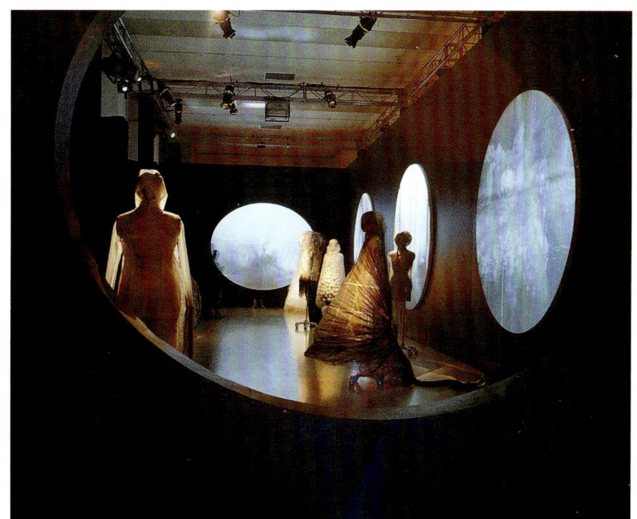

It would be true to say that since 2002 Lin's practice has been successively more three-dimensional, with *Mother's!!!* (2008) being the culmination of this practice. With this installation, Lin created an enveloping environment in which visitors entered an all-white room covered from floor to ceiling with white fabric. The overall effect was that of a surreal dreamscape. Aspects of the installation included a miniature, plump woman's body wrapped in white satin sprouting tubes from her severed neck; two dogs standing over a woman's body with the entire scene covered in wispy white thread like cobwebs; a headless woman climbing onto a mirror; and other figures set up around the room for viewers to encounter. All are visual non sequiturs. This work appears to be less about any specific statement, but rather it is an environment of the artists making, inviting the audience into a personal set of fears recreated through a dream sequence.

One of the surprises with Lin's works over the past year has been the introduction of bright color. In the past she restricted her palette to white and various shades of gray, but recently she has introduced citrus greens, sweet pinks, and sumptuous gold and gold leaf into her sculptures and paintings, along with bones. *The Golden Mean* (2012) is a multi-paneled work which is a formal play on materials and depth perception. Created from gold-colored silk the painting is embroidered with images of flowers and bones. Bones of the human skeleton fabricated in resin and wrapped with gold thread are attached to the panel. The subject matter and play of depth between the flatness of the picture plane and the sculptural objects reference the *vanitas* tradition of Northern European painting of the sixteenth and seventeenth century when skulls were paired with flowers in still life in order to conjure up a sense of mortality.

Color is used to even greater dramatic effect in *All the Same* (2011), a work of synthetic human bones wrapped with different colored silk thread and arranged from largest to smallest in color order along a single line on a white wall. Threads from each of the bones hang down to the floor creating a rainbow of colored thread. Here the bones are transformed into an aesthetic form. No less seductive is *More or Less the Same* (2011), a series of bones fused with hand tools such as pliers and spray guns wrapped in gray silk thread. There is something rather macabre about these works since they force us to think about human bones as instruments and remind us somehow of instances of mass exploitation.

In a number of ways Lin's work stands apart from many other artists in China born in the 1960s. For her generation, who began their professional careers in the 1980s and 1990s in the aftermath of the Cultural Revolution, it has been a journey of self-definition. For Lin this has meant an interest in gender differences at a time when great discrepancies between men and women in China remain. Through a practice centered on the body she has created lasting images and sculptures that are as much about her own life experiences as our own.

1. Liao, Wen. "Idea of Artists" in *Women's Approach to Contemporary Art*, 1995.

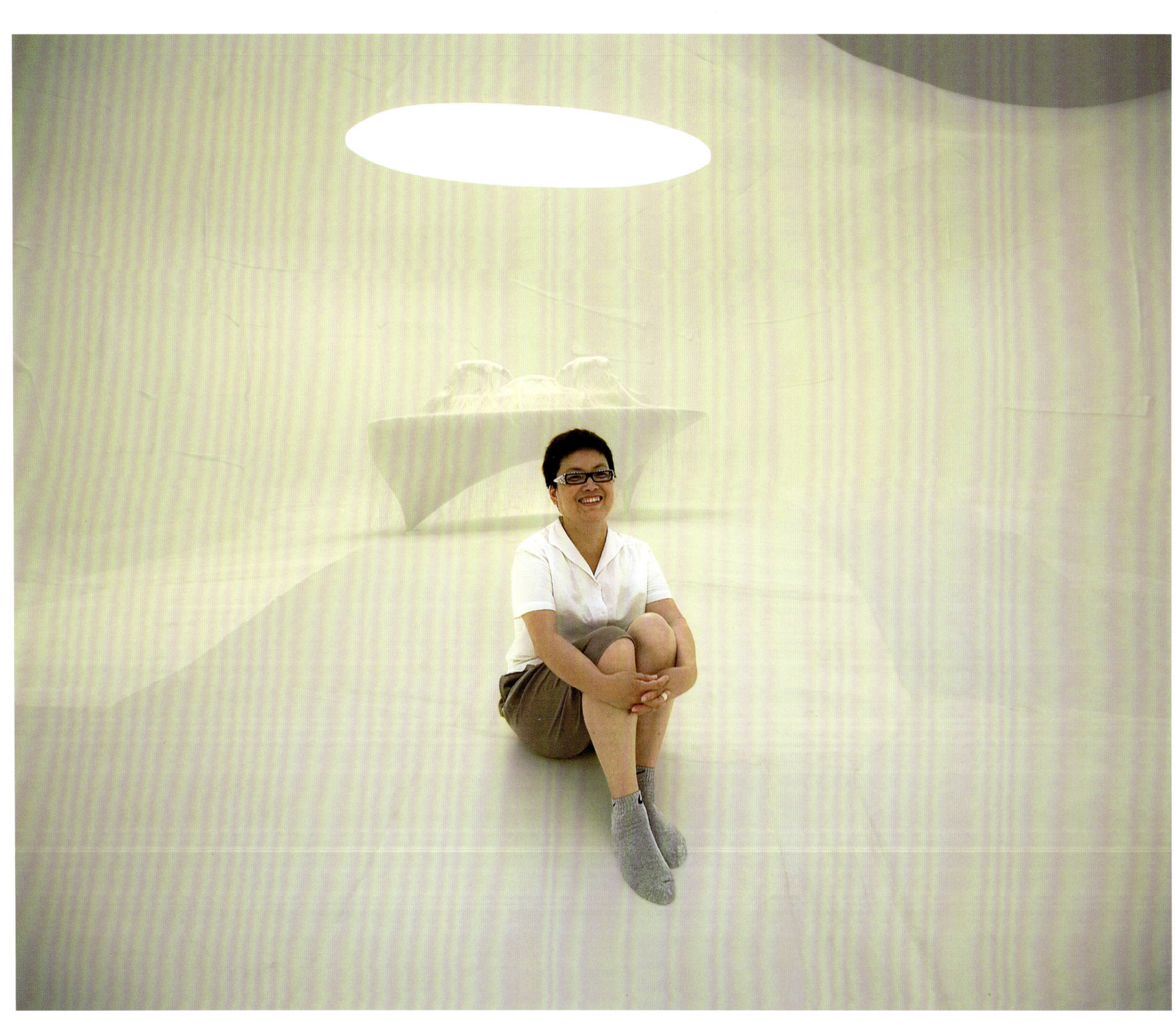

A Conversation with the Artist

Melissa Chiu and Lin Tianmiao

Melissa Chiu: Let's begin with your training in China. You've said that you did not really receive a formal art education, but I wonder if you can explain to me what your educational experience was. I understand, though, that you attended Capital Normal University in Beijing.
Lin Tianmiao: My father taught me traditional Chinese art. I practiced calligraphy and other traditional Chinese painting, such as *baimiao*. I had a number of influences from my family. Before the Cultural Revolution (1966–1976), my father was wealthy enough to buy art books from Russia and Europe. I also practiced working with color and preparation techniques such as stretching paper. It was really a traditional kind of training in this sense. At the Capital Normal University, I was a stand-by student for five months. I learned how to look at the human body and how to sketch. What I learned there was quite different from what I learned from my father. Traditional Chinese culture has a complete system that includes an inner, that is, a mental or spiritual, world as well as intellectual and aesthetic criteria; my father taught me the basics of China's traditional cultural aesthetics. The Capital Normal University in Beijing used the Soviet way of teaching; we studied some techniques, but we did not learn any constructive reasoning to apply to contemporary culture. I was confused by this, and I didn't like the environment very much.

MC: What about a formal training?
LT: I am quite rebellious. I have never been to art school in a formal way. It was my years in New York that taught me a lot. My life there completely changed my views on art. I learned how to look at and appreciate other people's art. I also learned how to be an artist. After I got over my initial culture shock, my inner, or spiritual, field of vision was completely opened.

MC: When did you come to New York and what brought you here?
LT: I went along with my husband Wang GongXin in 1988.

MC: What was your intention in coming? To be an artist?
LT: I went to New York because my husband wanted to be there. It only seems as if I went to New York searching for something else—a kind of free lifestyle way of thinking. I didn't study art. I actually don't believe that art can be taught in school. I spent three or four days a week visiting art galleries, studios, and art events—looking at other artists' work. After several years of "searching" and after experiencing different types of art, I quickly decided I wanted to become an artist.

MC: How did New York City affect you?
LT: I spent almost three years getting over the culture shock, and then I spent a few more years learning about contemporary art and the cultural context for contemporary art, as well as learning about the relationship between art and life.

MC: I haven't seen any work from this period. Were you making any while you were in New York?
LT: From my perspective, being in New York was a very important experience. It both destroyed and built my values equally; it led to a fierce change in my way of thinking. This impact continues today; it is as if the New York experience extended my life by ten years. I had no time and financial help to do art work at that time. It was already difficult for Wang GongXin to do his artwork. I started making art when I went back to China in 1995. I had more time and more inspiration in China. Every exhibition that I saw in New York influenced me deeply, first in terms of materials and second in terms of how to express myself. In the end, I began to think about the question of "Who am I?". I focused on the idea of individualism. It was painful.

MC: How do you think this idea of individualism was prompted by your experiences in New York?
LT: The biggest influence even today is that I learned how to respect individuals, respect all types of materials, and the power of even the smallest details. Rather than looking at everything from one perspective, I learned to look at things from different points of view.

MC: We first met in 1995 when I was writing an article about women artists in China, prompted by the dearth of women practicing art at that time. I remember that you had just finished *The Proliferation of Thread Winding* for the exhibition "Woman's Approach to Contemporary Art" to coincide with the International Women's Convention. What was the inspiration?
LT: Each individual has a unique set of experiences. In my childhood, my mother always let me help her with sewing and with making clothes. Even today I can remember it clearly, so it had a great impact on my work. I began helping my mother sew

Lin Tianmiao
Long March Space, 2008

and make clothes at the age of four or five. It was such physical labor, and I hated it. When I first came back to China after having lived in New York, I came across some cotton thread that had not been dyed or processed. It made me recall my childhood. I started using the material without hesitation. After I left New York to return to China, I was forced to intensely compare the differences between the governments, societies, and values of the two countries. I also had to compare the kind of Chinese life setting I had in 1988 with the one in 1995; this process was the most important source of inspiration and the origin of this group of art works.

MC: Was your mother sewing for the factory or for personal use for the family?
LT: My family has four children. We had to sew and make clothes for everyone in the family. It was for use in daily life.

MC: The idea of thread winding that began with these works—you have said on other occasions that they were inspired by helping your mother.
LT: I created the balls for my work, not based directly on my memory. I wanted to transform. I was thinking: May I make this little ball into something more powerful? Or may I transform something soft into something aggressive?

MC: Throughout your work, there is such a strong sense of gender. You often use human bodies in your work. I wouldn't necessarily call you a feminist artist, but what do you think about the issue of feminism in China?
LT: I have been asked this question several times, which has made me think about it. I don't know that feminism exists as a movement in China, as it did in the West. You can only think about this question when the society is developed enough to discuss rights. A feminist movement is when women begin to understand themselves well enough to know what they want. Right now in China, women have not reached that stage. This is a particularly low point of Chinese culture; it's a most uncivilized and unhealthy aspect. Today the government and society do not extend women their due rights, which is the opposite of the environment that they need, and does not take into account their real care.

MC: What are your thoughts on being a woman artist in China? What are the main challenges?
LT: Today we can go abroad easily and see the situation of Western women. Here in China people were given more rights after the Cultural Revolution. But a lot of Chinese female artists haven't yet reached the point where they are confident and comfortable. We must assume the most important thing for women artists is a self-awakening and the establishment of self-worth. With an emphasis on respect, collaboration, and awareness of regeneration, a unique outlook and understanding of survival techniques should emerge that perhaps will result in no marginalization.

MC: What are the main challenges for younger women to be an artist?
LT: I think that the biggest challenge women face is themselves. Chinese women artists first need to resolve the problem of being "women." They cannot reach a certain level of art without reaching a certain level of self-discovery or self-confidence. There were some recent exhibitions that focused on the female figure, and I am against this. We need to better discover ourselves rather than allow ourselves to be marginalized.

MC: What about your own works that have used your face as in *Focus* or even the female body?
LT: First of all, I grew up in a political environment. Portraits of Mao were everywhere. The portraits were the symbols of power. I began to do the *Focus* works in the early 1990s. At that time, it was shocking. I got rid of any personal effects: glasses, hair, even the facial expressions of the people. In the end, it is how a human being should look.

MC: There is an image where you appear without any hair! Did you really shave all your hair off for the artwork?
LT: Yes, it is true that I shaved my hair when I was in Germany, but it was for fun, not for the exhibition. I shaved my hair after the show. The picture that was used in the work was actually made by Photoshop.

MC: For women, hair is such a sign of femininity. To shave a woman's head is a real statement.
LT: Before I cropped my hair, I was not thinking of making any kind of statement, but after cropping my hair this seems to be the implication in my heart. I feel stronger with short hair.

MC: Your works do include women's bodies but they are rarely the conventional idea of physical perfection, such as those in *Chatting*, for example.
LT: First of all, I wanted to remove sexual desire. Secondly, middle-aged women bear more, such as the impact of love, the impact of children, and the impact of marriage. Your children have grown up, and they don't need you anymore. Your body also displays whether or not you have confidence. Even your attitude towards sex may change. Within the tradition of sculpture, women's bodies have always been depicted as beautiful and sexual. Sculpture adopted the male standard of beauty, but in life the female form takes on different shapes and sizes. You can see why I think that the restoration of self-worth is so important.

MC: What is the relationship between the figures?
LT: The relationship between the women is quite different from that between the men. The relationship between the men is more superficial; however the relationship between the women is more primal, instinctual, and sensitive.

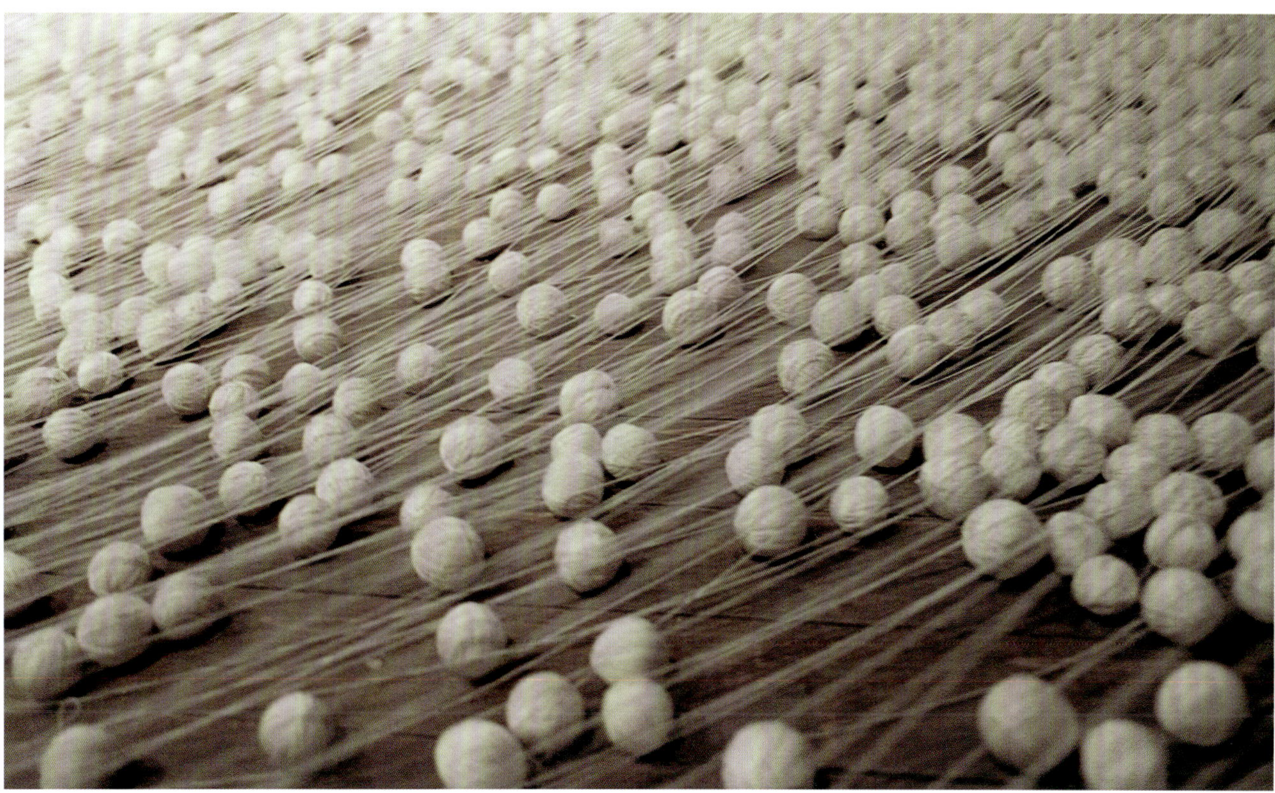

The Proliferation of Thread Winding (detail), 1995

MC: What about the work, *Mother's!!!*?

LT: There is a big difference in the treatment of the body in *Mother's!!!* from my other works. I focus more on inner expression in a deep, careful, delicate, and struggling way, and I combine that with strong self-consciousness. I also discovered the existence of the powerful and subtle expressions of the body and materials, which fascinates me. This artwork is an important phase in restoring my own self-awareness as a woman reaching middle age.

MC: With more recent works, there is a transition from the use of the body to the use bones. Why did you decide to use bones?

LT: As an artist, I am not unfamiliar with using bones, they are mysterious and therefore a natural choice for me. Bones of birds, dogs, cows, pigs, and human beings are all products of the earth and are very similar, although I did not know this before working with them. For me, bones are just like any other material; they are similar to the thread, silk, and fabric that I have used in the past and still use today. I believe that the bone is the only perfect object left in the world. Bones do not have the difference of hierarchy, culture, classes, politics, and social property between them. I use them casually to transform, continue, or reconnect with my artistic imagination. They are also another way that I incorporate my body into my art. The most interesting thing about bones is they lead us to face our mortality. When I use bones as a material for creating art, I find that it is even easier to bring in the reality of society along with a bigger discussion about values. Skeletons inspire me with a passion for creation even more so than other materials; skeletons have an even deeper meaning.

MC: Your works for the past decade have been almost entirely devoid of color, yet in your recent works over the past year, color has become an important part of your paintings and sculpture.

LT: I am very careful in employing color because it is an element that you cannot use without careful consideration, otherwise it will interrupt the purity and order of the artwork. In many of my recent works I have used color purposely, which I also think is necessary. I have the choice to go in the direction of the stereotypical understanding of one color, or not. For instance the use of the color pink produces different psychological reactions from different gender groups and the exclusivity associated with the color gold has a similar effect on different social classes. I find this very interesting.

MC: What is it like to live in China today as a contemporary artist?

LT: Currently in China I have a strong feeling that there is no respect among people or between people and animals, men and women, different races, or culture and politics. The only relationship they all share is that of robbing and being robbed. This feeling is becoming stronger and stronger in every corner of society from the upper class to the lower class. Standards can be casually determined and changed as one wishes. People are wasting resources without thought and bottom-line morals and endless extravagance have become fashionable. People never consider the future. I had these deep feelings when I made the series, *The Same*.

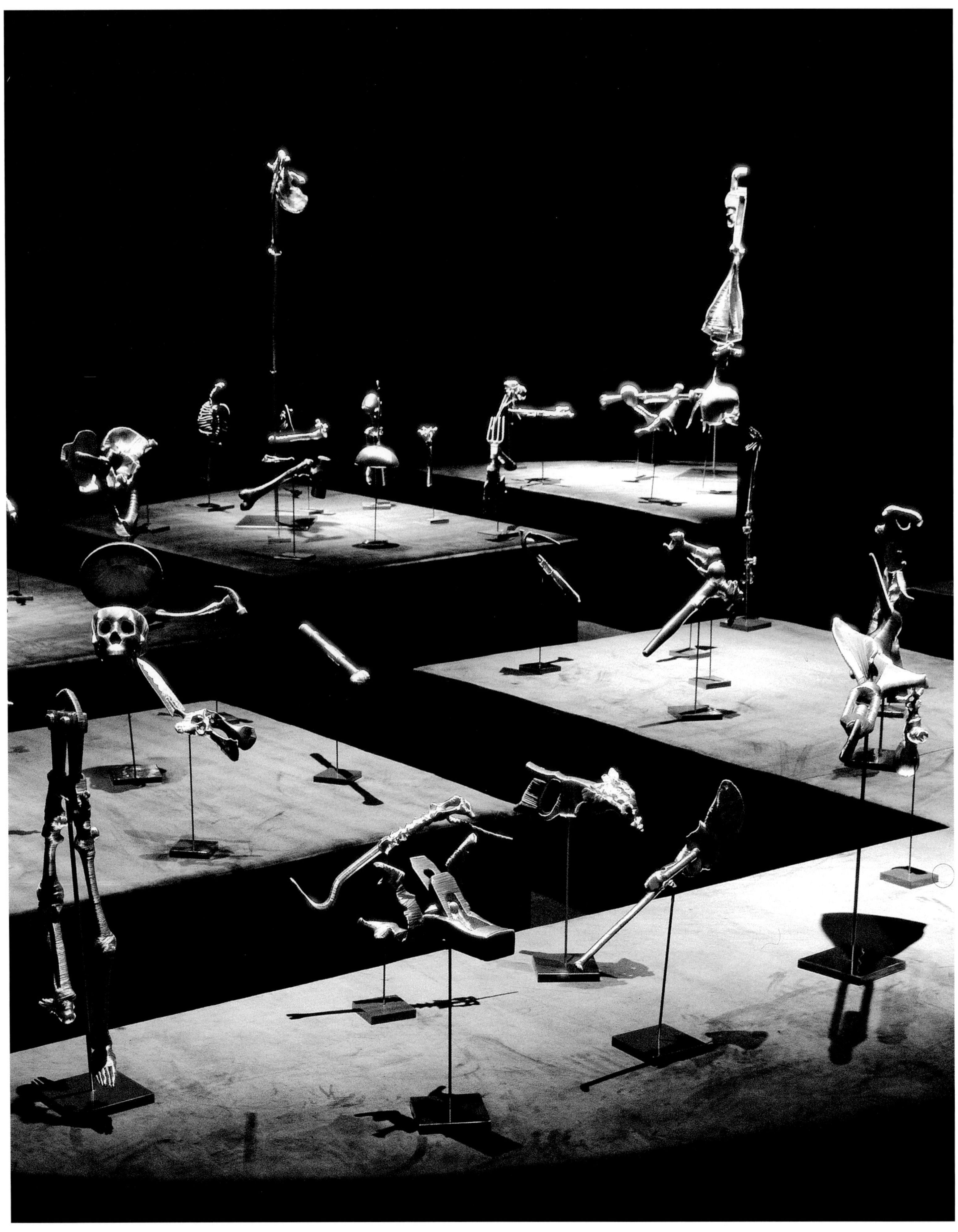

The Defiant Narratives of Lin Tianmiao

Guo Xiaoyan

Lin Tianmiao's solo exhibition, "The Same," mounted by the Beijing Center for the Arts in December 2011, encompassed a wide range of practices the artist has been developing in recent years and also reinforced her distinct position in the art world. At the entrance, in an unexpected theatrical gesture, 206 replicas of bones of the human skeleton, from the smallest auditory ossicle to the largest hipbone, were classified, wound with colored silk thread, and deliberately positioned according to the color spectrum: purple, blue, cyan, green, yellow, orange, and red. This rainbow-like overture created the illusion of a historical timeline. The first floor exhibition gallery became a dark theatre of pillars and beams wrapped in textured black velvet and skeletons of animals—from human to bird to fish—were wrapped in gold thread and dispersed throughout the intricate space. Works on both a massive and modest scale were presented in the dimly lit gallery that included large-scale works such as *The Same for N Times* and *The Gold Sameness*. Colorful silk threads bind finely constructed bird skeleton as well as rough tools like axes, saws, and gear wheels; everything here is stilled. The artist has woven a poem of time suggesting both longing and zeal. Tiny bird bones perch on the pall made of black or golden silk thread. They are woven in this poem like a sigh from the remote wilderness of the distant past, not ashes, as much as a kind of apocalyptic relic of the terrible time that destroyed everything. The human experience also lingers here, and that is what is fascinating about the female narrative: it describes the limbo of desire, the position of arrogation, accident, spark, metaphor, ambiguity, and ambivalence.

In 1996, after eight years spent traveling in America, Lin Tianmiao and Wang GongXin returned to China where she made and presented her installation, *The Proliferation of Thread Winding* and *Sewing*. This was the first time she showed her own art. Her work explored the problems of cultural understanding in the contexts of migration; female identity and awareness; self-identity; and historical and cultural memory, as well as issues regarding political reality and cultural circumstances by means of personal observation and judgment of other cultures. This was a very significant exhibition with regards to Lin Tianmiao's career as an artist. The installation seemed like a metaphor of the male and female body: the implied tension of that metaphor was represented by intertwined white balls of yarn and cotton threads that flowed from the rice paper mattress down to the floor, and the suspended men's trousers made of rice paper stuck with steel needles. The works introduced antagonistic topics in a contemporaneous political context by using metaphorical, ironical, and constructive images. Meanwhile, the choice of her medium was also noteworthy. From the beginning of her practice, her choice of materials seemed to propose contradiction: needle versus thread, intertwined as opposed to cut-off, complicated weaving contrasted with straightforward expression. The way she used materials and the relevant lexicon of her practice could be easily interpreted in the context of a female narrative style focused on self, body, history, and memory. Nevertheless, under close and careful examination, it becomes apparent that Lin Tianmiao is attempting a radical point of departure to avoid this kind of referential knowledge rather than indulge in it. She pulls that language out of the current predetermined popular context. This is a choice drawn from her instinct and talent, and it is also a very good starting point for consideration of Lin Tianmiao's practice.

In 1997 the solo exhibition "Bound and Unbound" in the gallery of the Central Academy of Fine Art, and the 2002 Shanghai Biennale for which she collaborated with artist Wang Gongxin on *Here? Or There?*, provided the perfect opportunity for Lin to begin to sort out her thoughts and ideas. The following years, from 2002 to 2007, were crucial for the artist's development. During that period, Lin's work was inspired by very personal concerns and psychological conflicts. In a series of exhibitions such as "Non Zero," "Focus," and "Seeing Shadow," she addressed different issues such as how power, women's consciousness, and the body construct identity. The idiosyncratic signature use of thread, balls of yarn, and weaving which are integral to her thinking paved the way to a highpoint of Lin's career and established her reputation in both the Chinese and international contemporary art scene.

As an influential and respected Chinese female artist who is celebrated in the global art community, Lin has focused on a self-constructed world which that utilizes condensed but complicated forms and rich, incisive, and direct language. The works are usually large in scale and range from sculptures and installation to video and multimedia. In both the theater and beings she crafts, the resulting objects come from a subtle and emotional experience to produce a poetic aesthetic experience in the viewer. Lin is very good at using details to make a maze: her acute observation and meticulous representation weave a labyrinth which is full of metaphors, puns, and ambiguity of time and space. The audience is invited into the maze and urged to find the answer through consideration of the details. As a female artist, she uses a unique instinct to cast doubt on the existing power system by contrasting inner and outer worlds; female and male; and good and evil. In her writings, readers find curiosity, as well as acute observation and rebellion. She exposes a personal inner conflict in her repeated use of forms intertwined and cut-off; her attitude toward the uselessness of the things and nihilism; and the difference in value systems between men and women. Her works maintain an ongoing dialogue of contradictory materials and underscore the impact that both the body and apparently insignificant life can have on art. In recent years, she has continued her discussion about the female body in relationships of power, along with the relationship of the body and time, woman as author, and antagonism toward

More or Less the Same (detail), 2011

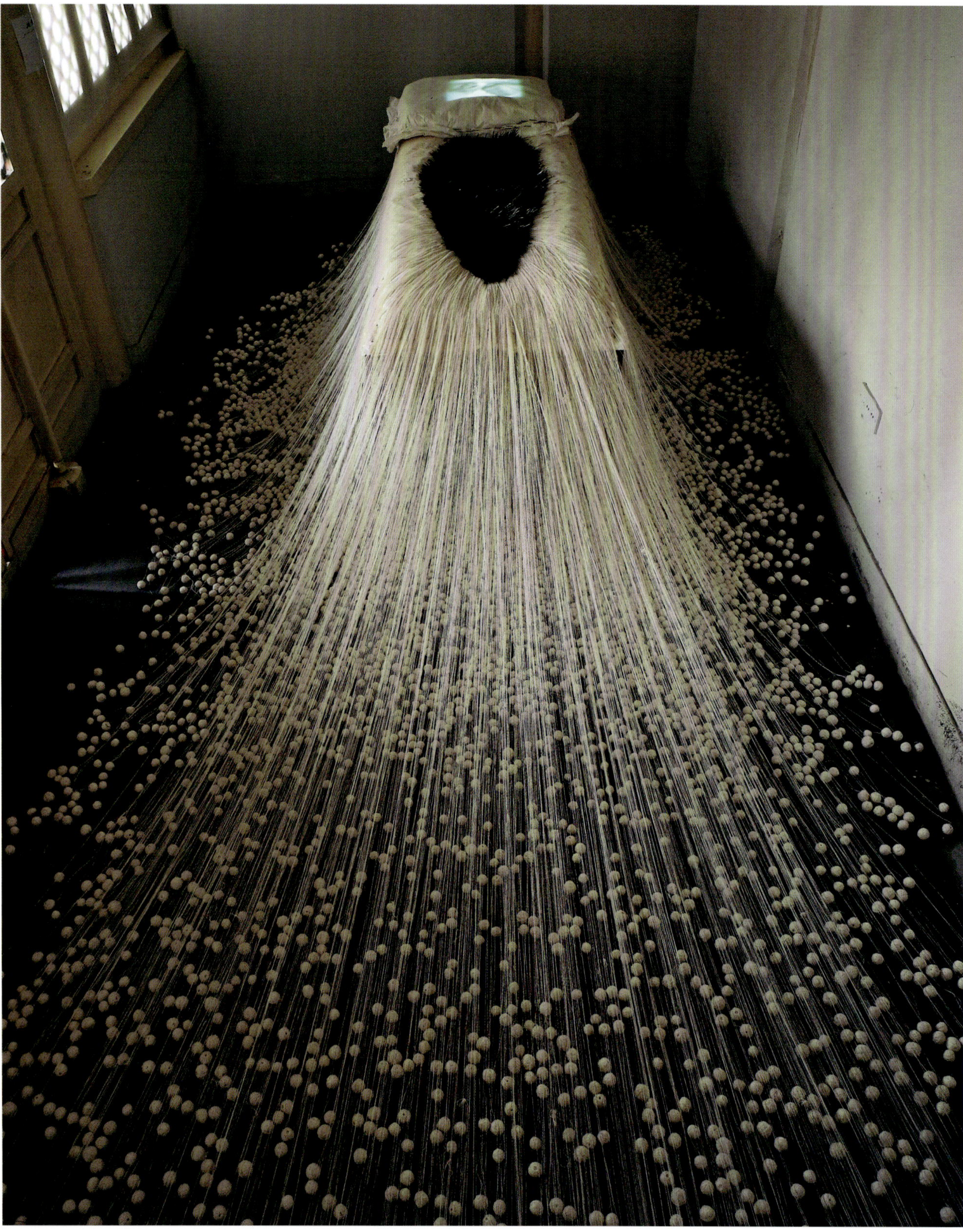

The Proliferation of Thread Winding, 1995

The Golden Mean (detail), 2012

the body in her works while at the same time being aware of hermeneutic misunderstanding: that is, she doubts the knowledge constructed by a so-called woman's perspective and the pitfalls of female narrative language. In the active repetition of the narrative at which she excels, she alters the customary method of narration and raises questions of her own in a more complicated contemporary context. Her personal energy is apparent through her unique expression.

How to become an artist is a frequent theme in the arts. For many, it is to understand the artist as a contemporary observer and interpreter of politics and reality. In short, all of our practice and discussions regarding art are associated with our thinking on life and politics.

The solo exhibition in New York will provide the opportunity to observe the idiosyncratic, psychological, and thoughtful connections among the works by the same artist, from the connections to the transformation. It is a careful examination of Lin Tianmiao's works so far, and more important, it is also a mobilization of her future actions.

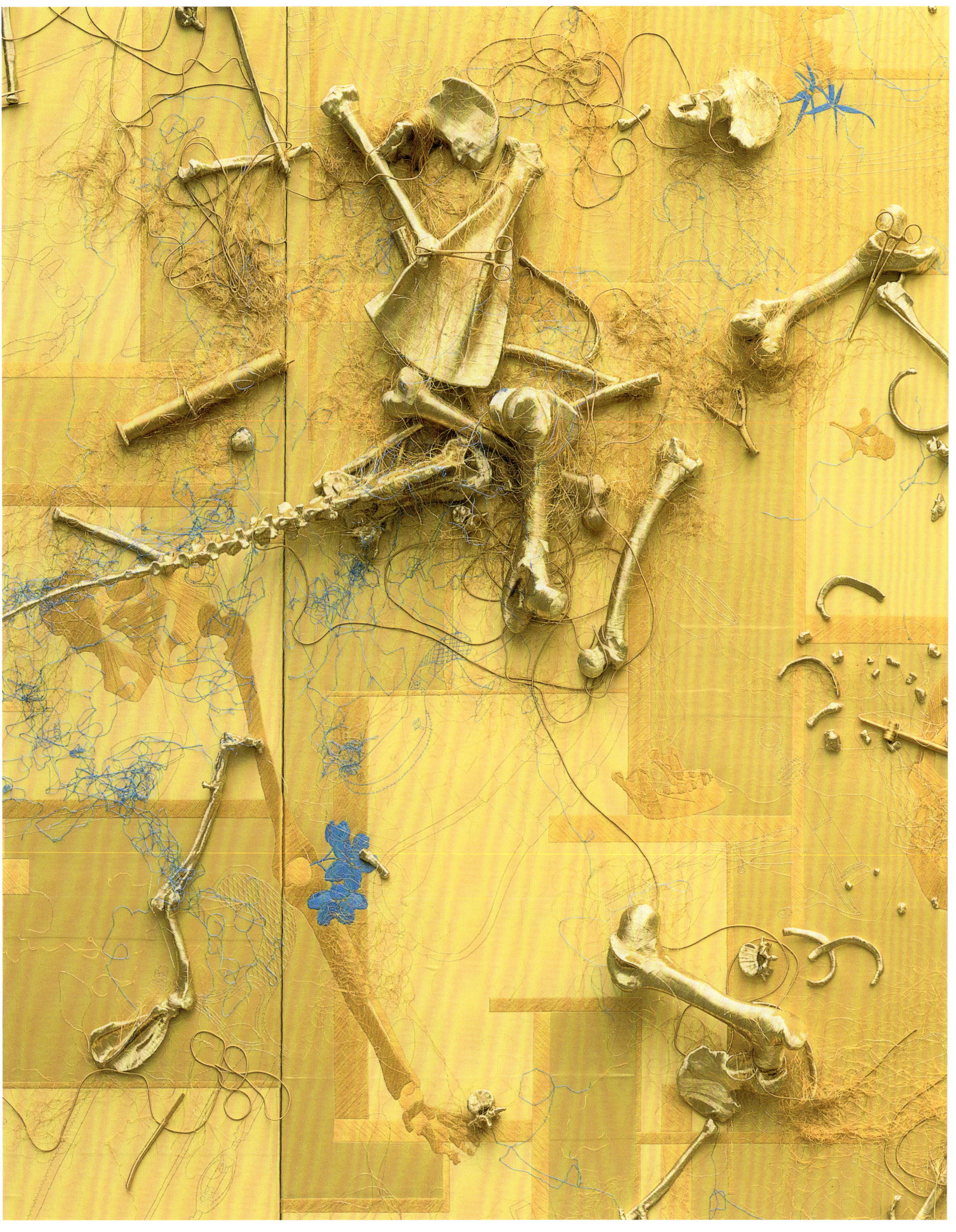

Works

Unless otherwise stated, all artworks are in the collection of the artist.

The Proliferation of Thread Winding, 1995
White cotton thread, rice paper, 20,000 needles
(12–15 cm in length), a bed, a video player,
a television monitor
Dimensions variable
Open Studio, Baofang Hutong 12#, Beijing, 1995

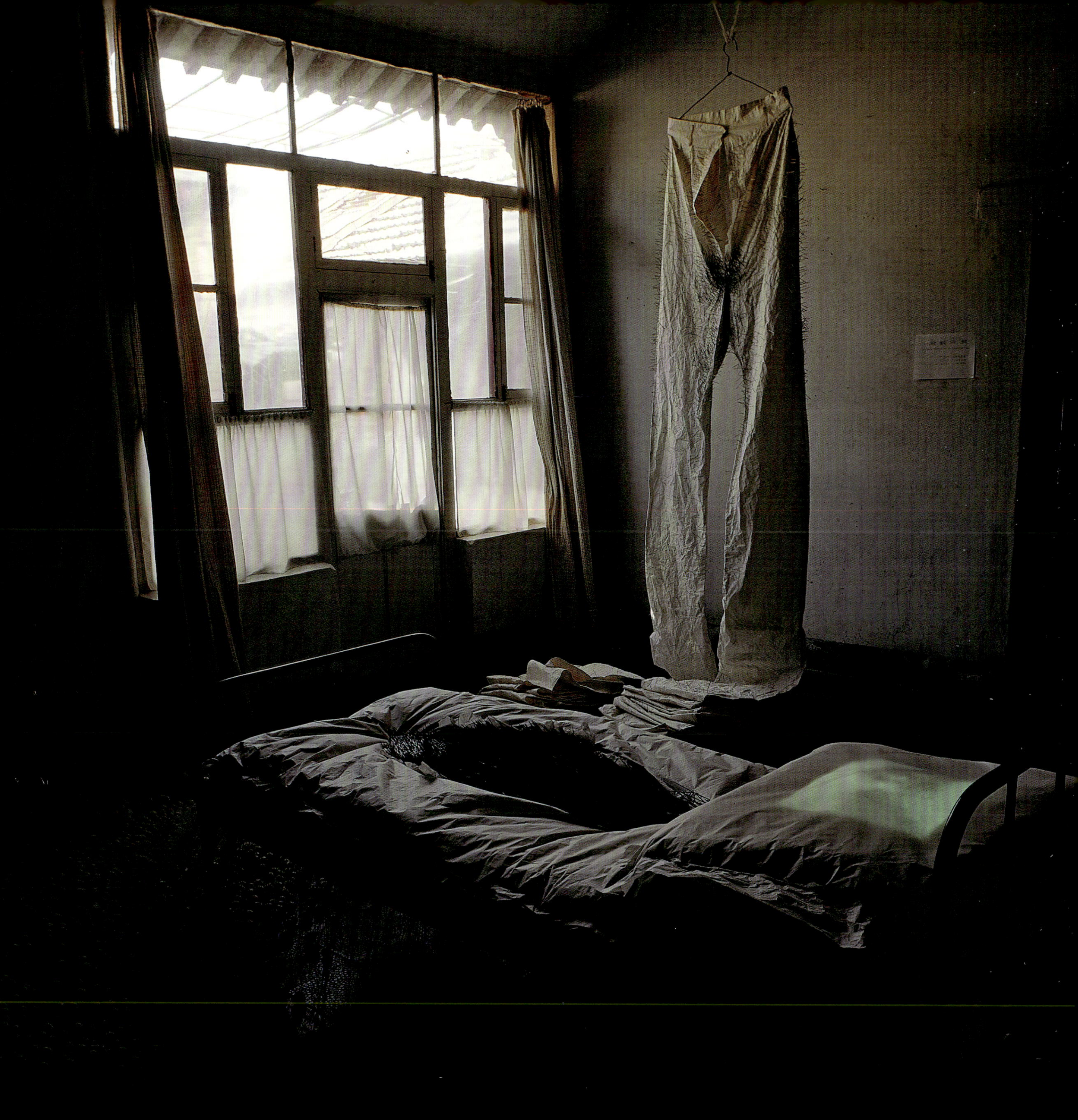

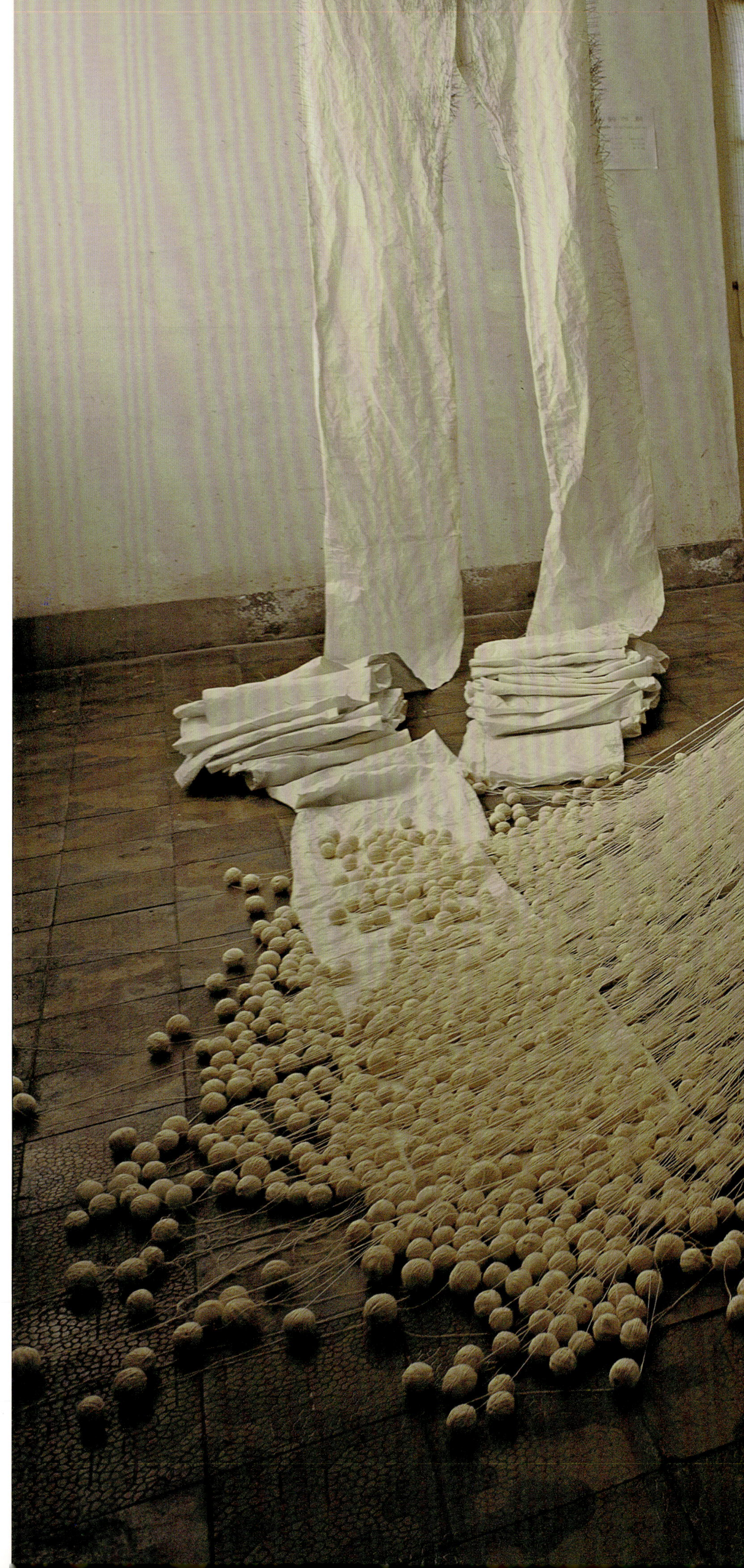

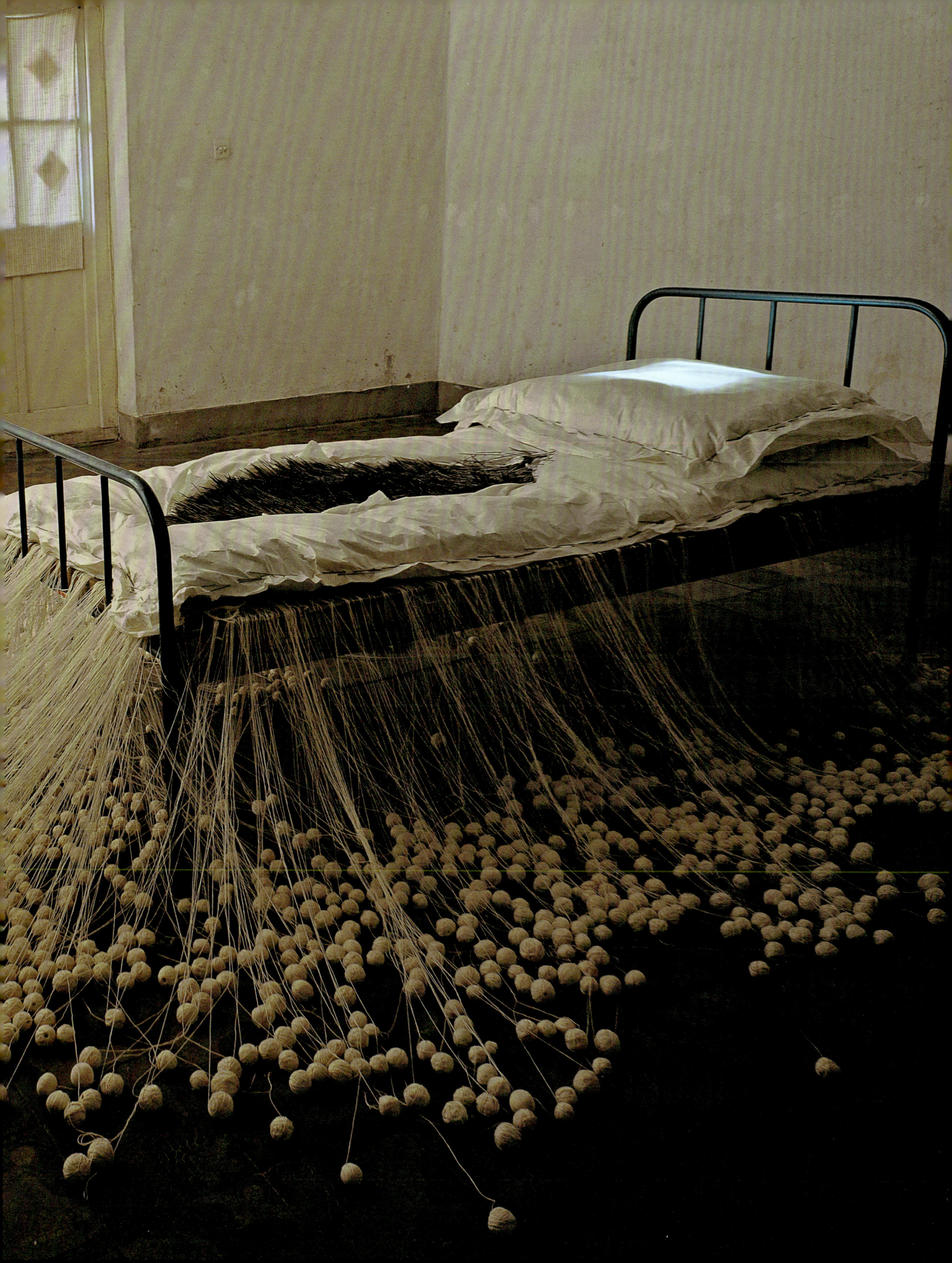

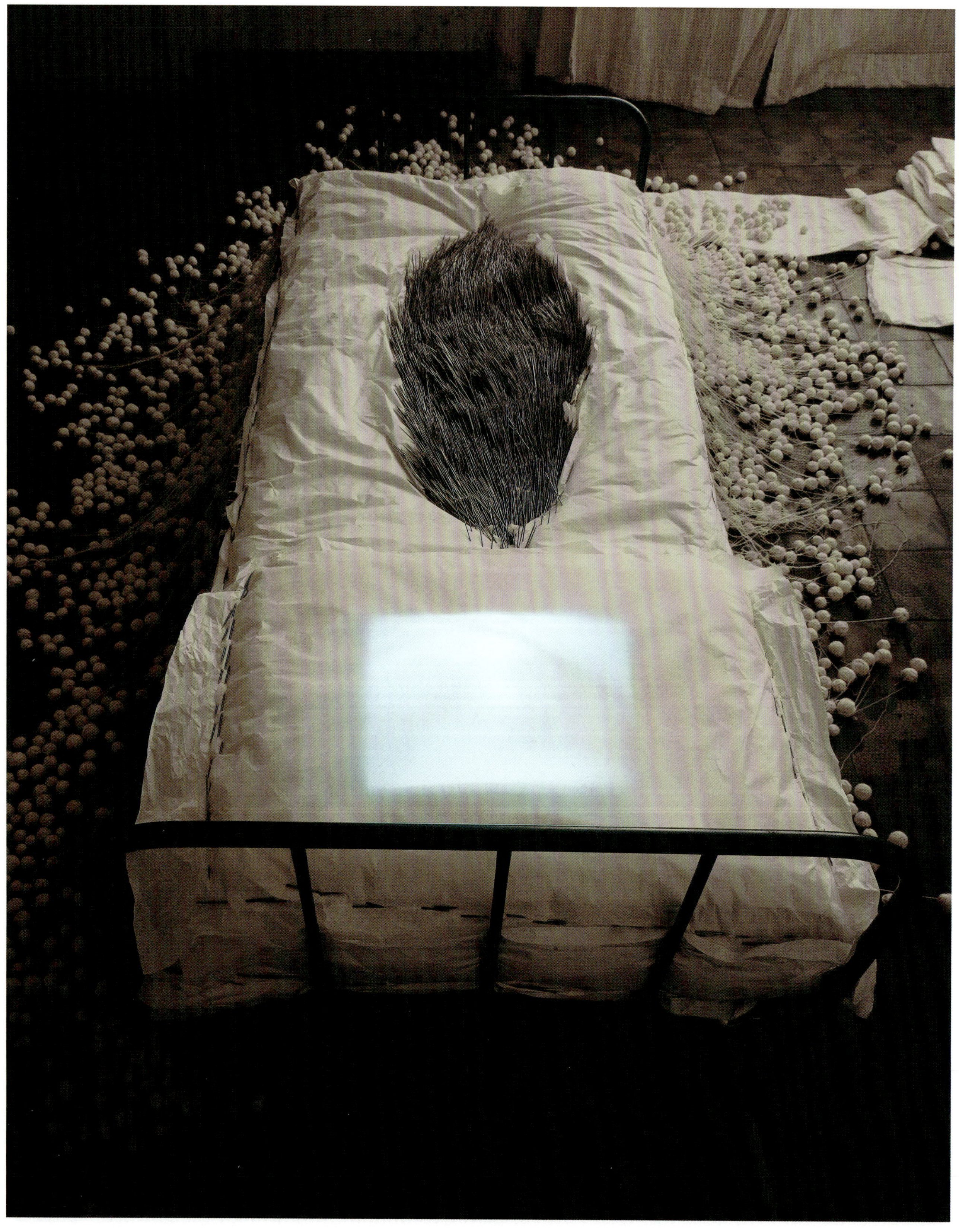

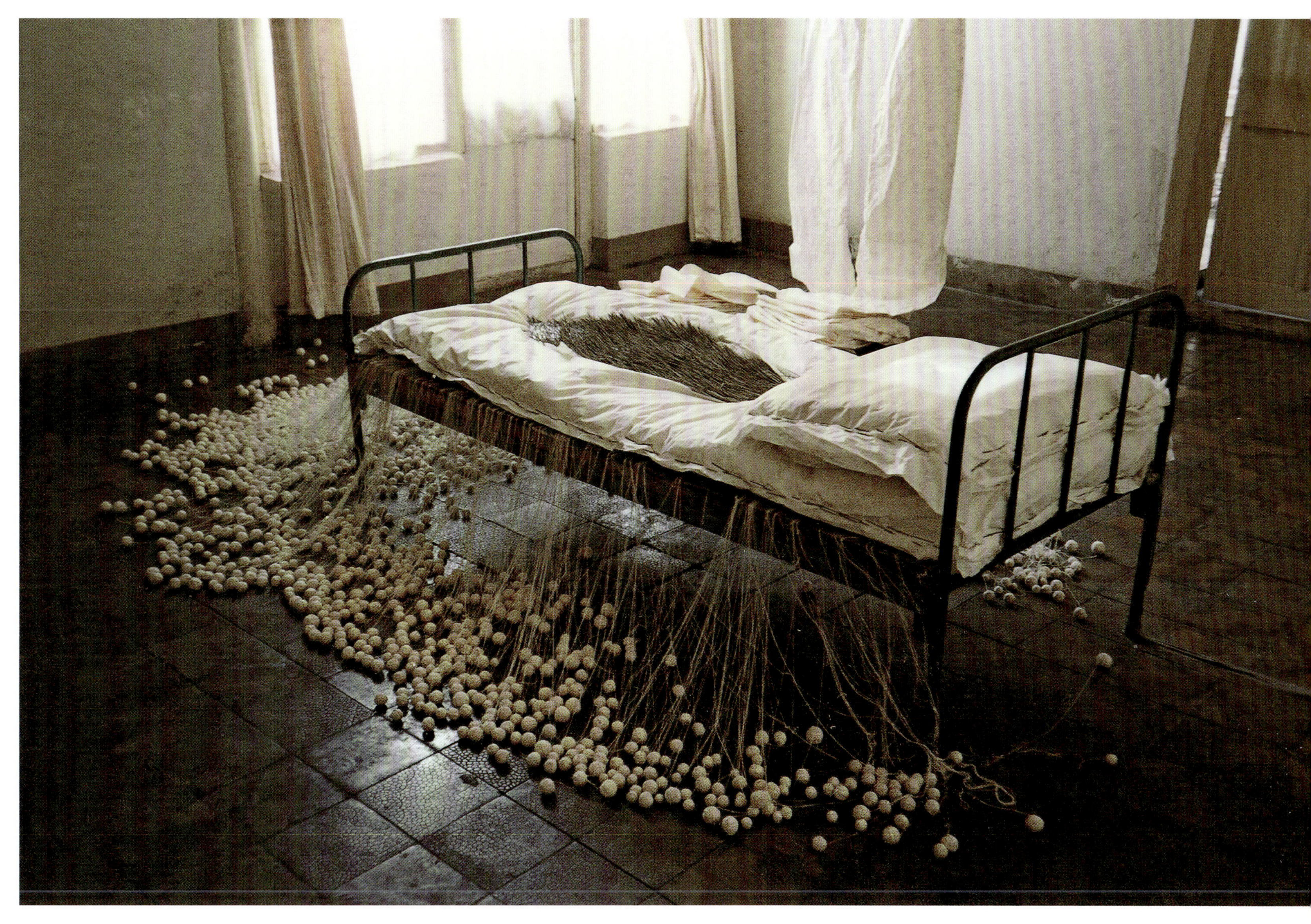

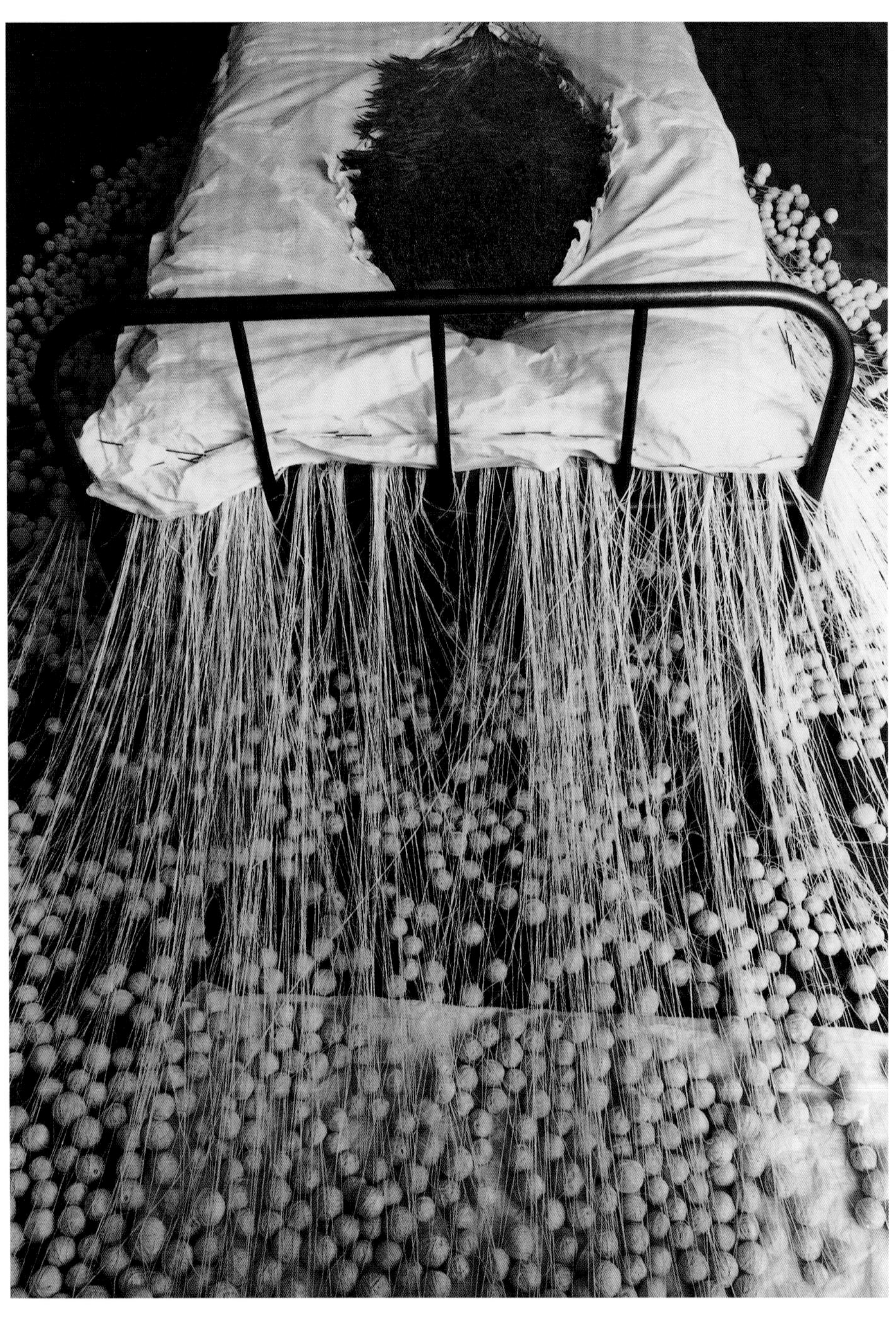

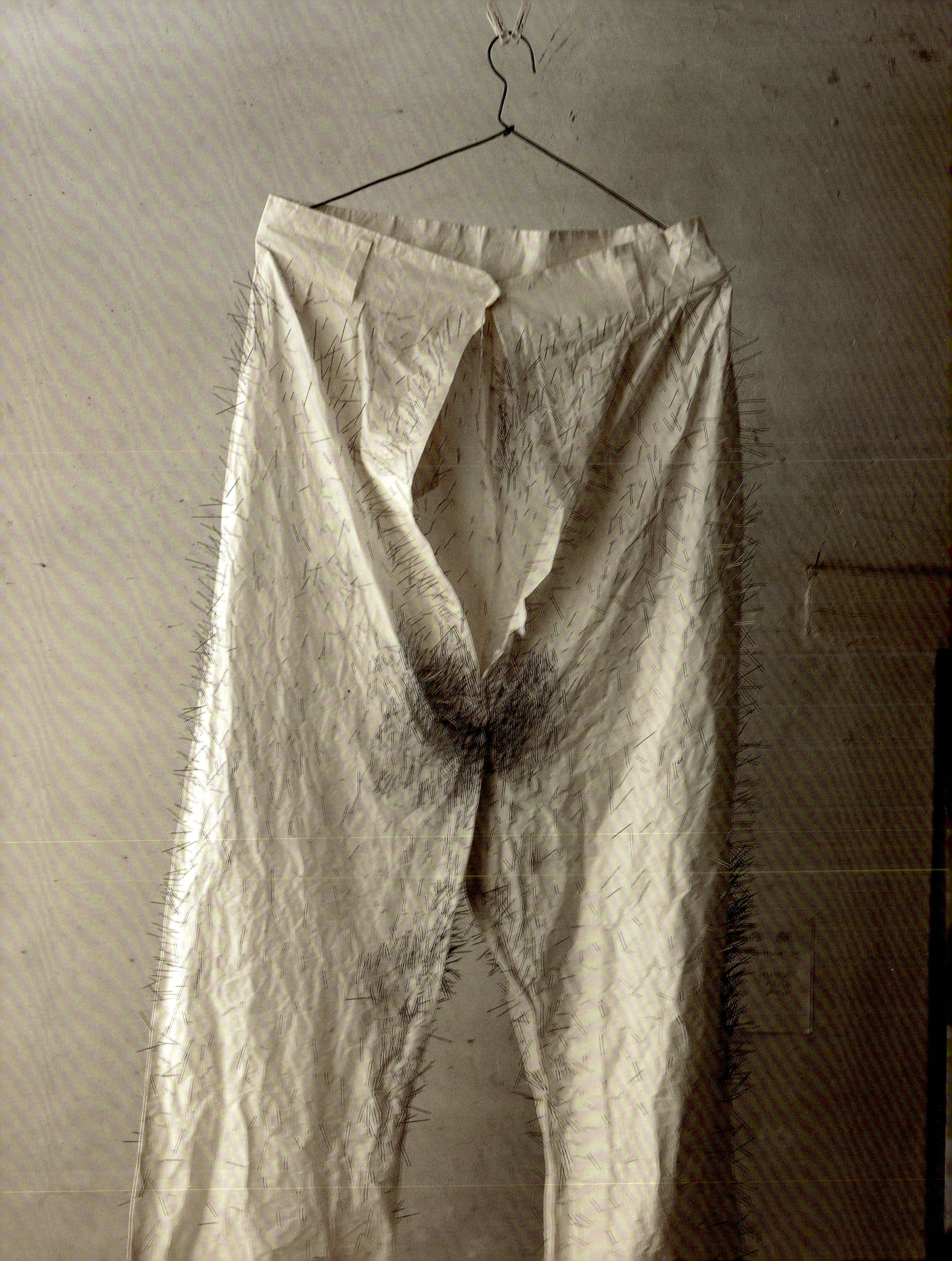

Sewing, 1997
Sewing machine, white cotton thread, video projector, and speakers
35 ½ x 15 ¾ x 39 ¼ in. (90 x 40 x 100 cm)
Take a Step Back Collection

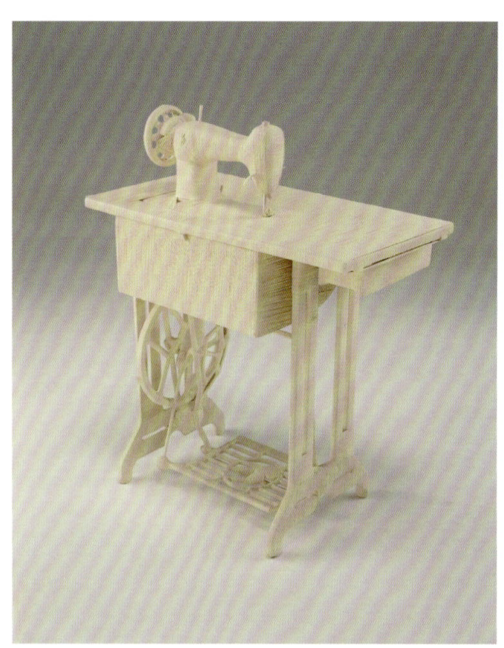

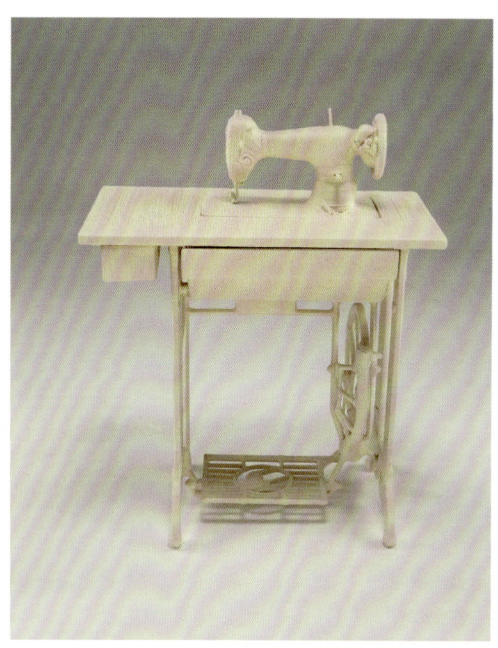

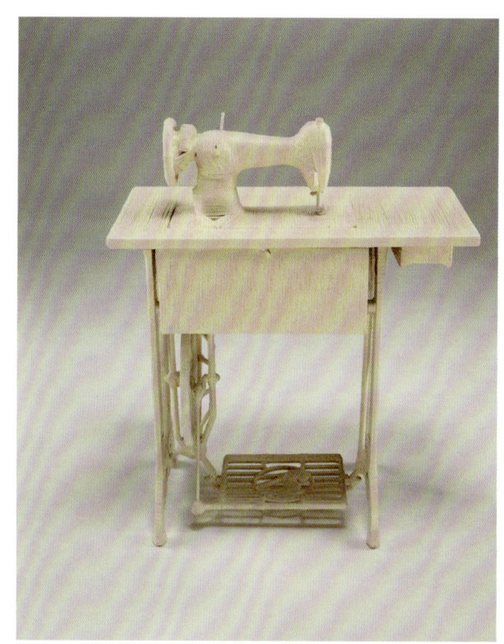

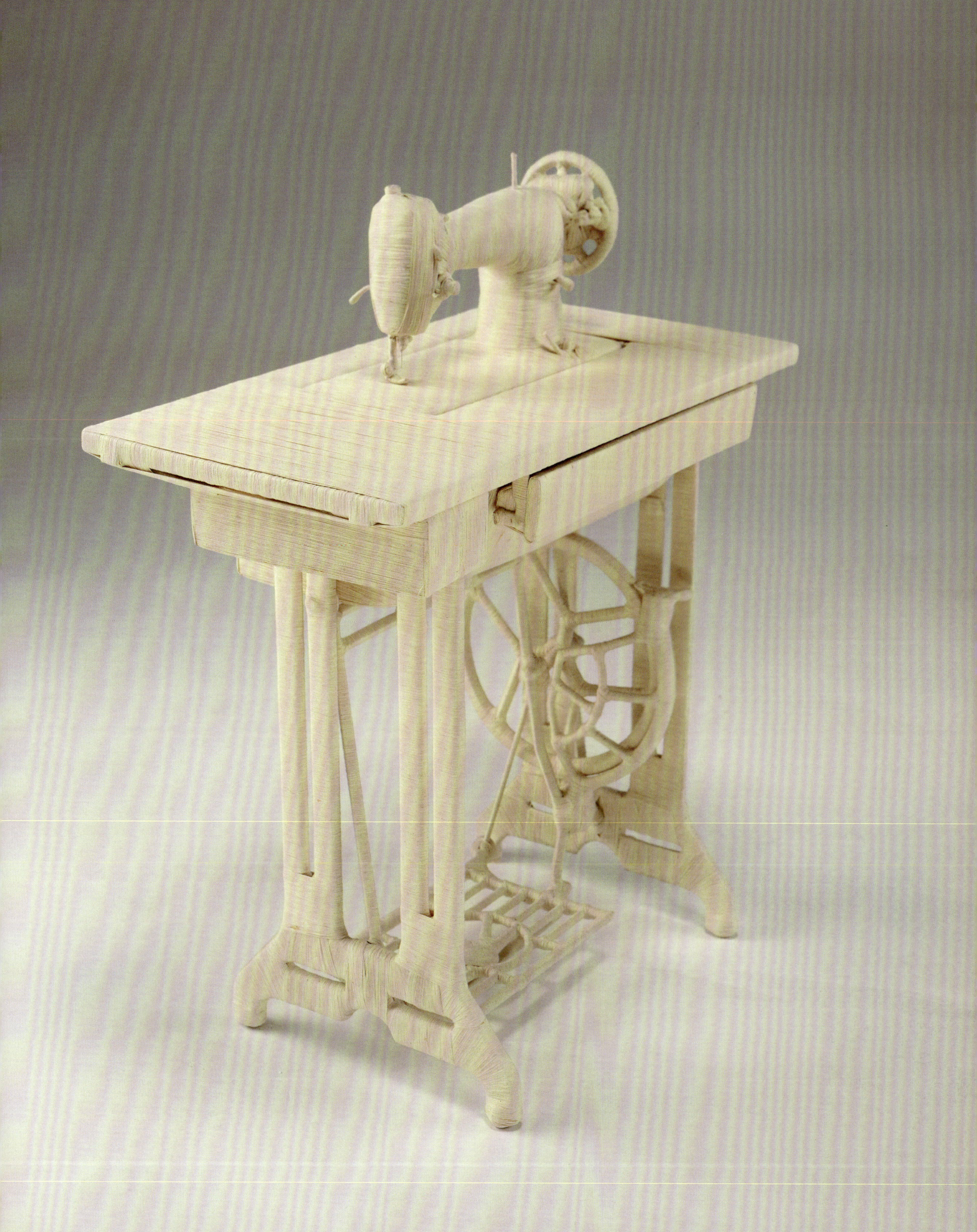

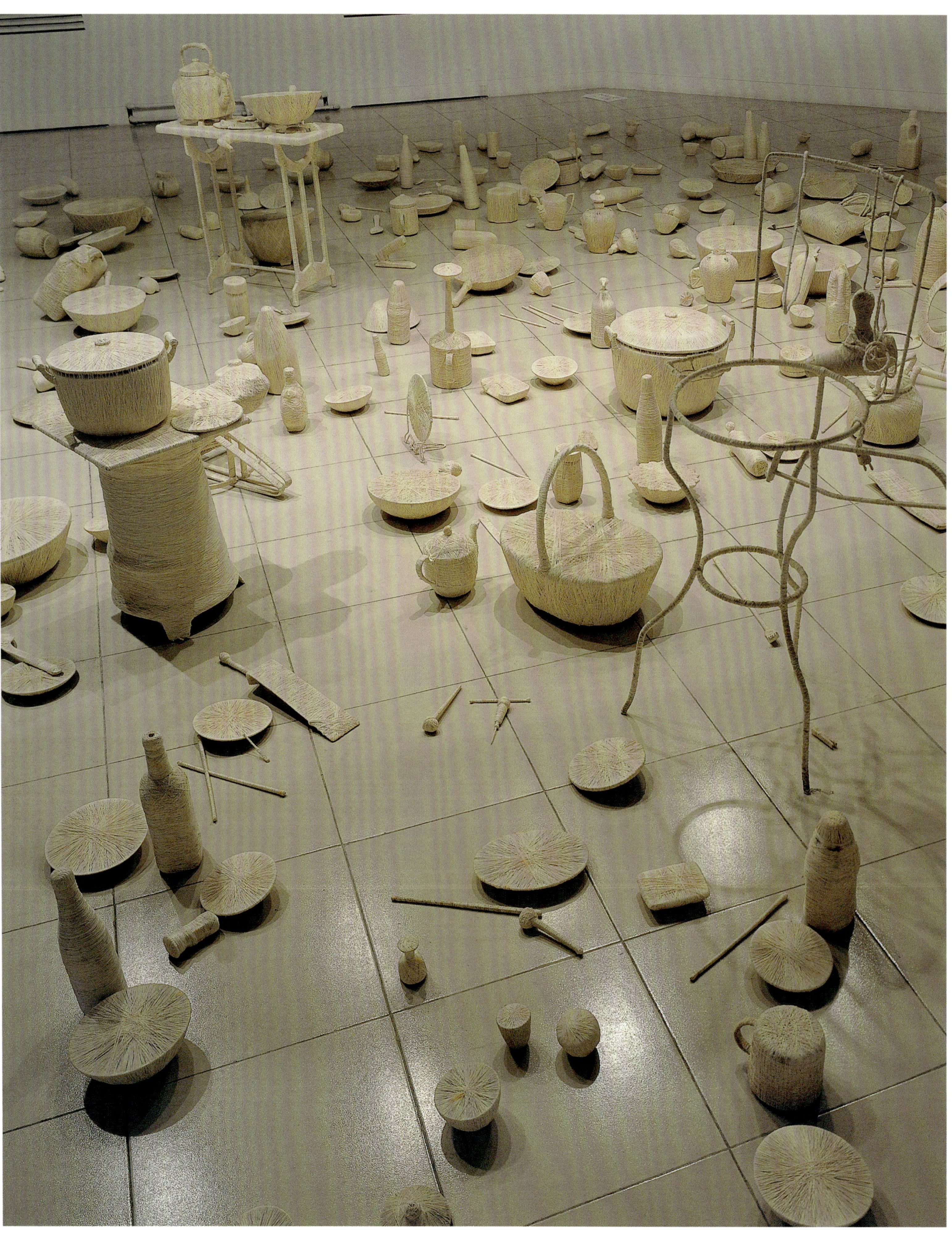

Bound and Unbound, 1997
White cotton thread, 800 pieces of household objects, video projection, sound
Dimensions variable
"Bound and Unbound," China Central Academy of Fine Arts, Beijing, 1997
Collection of Hong Kong Museum of Art

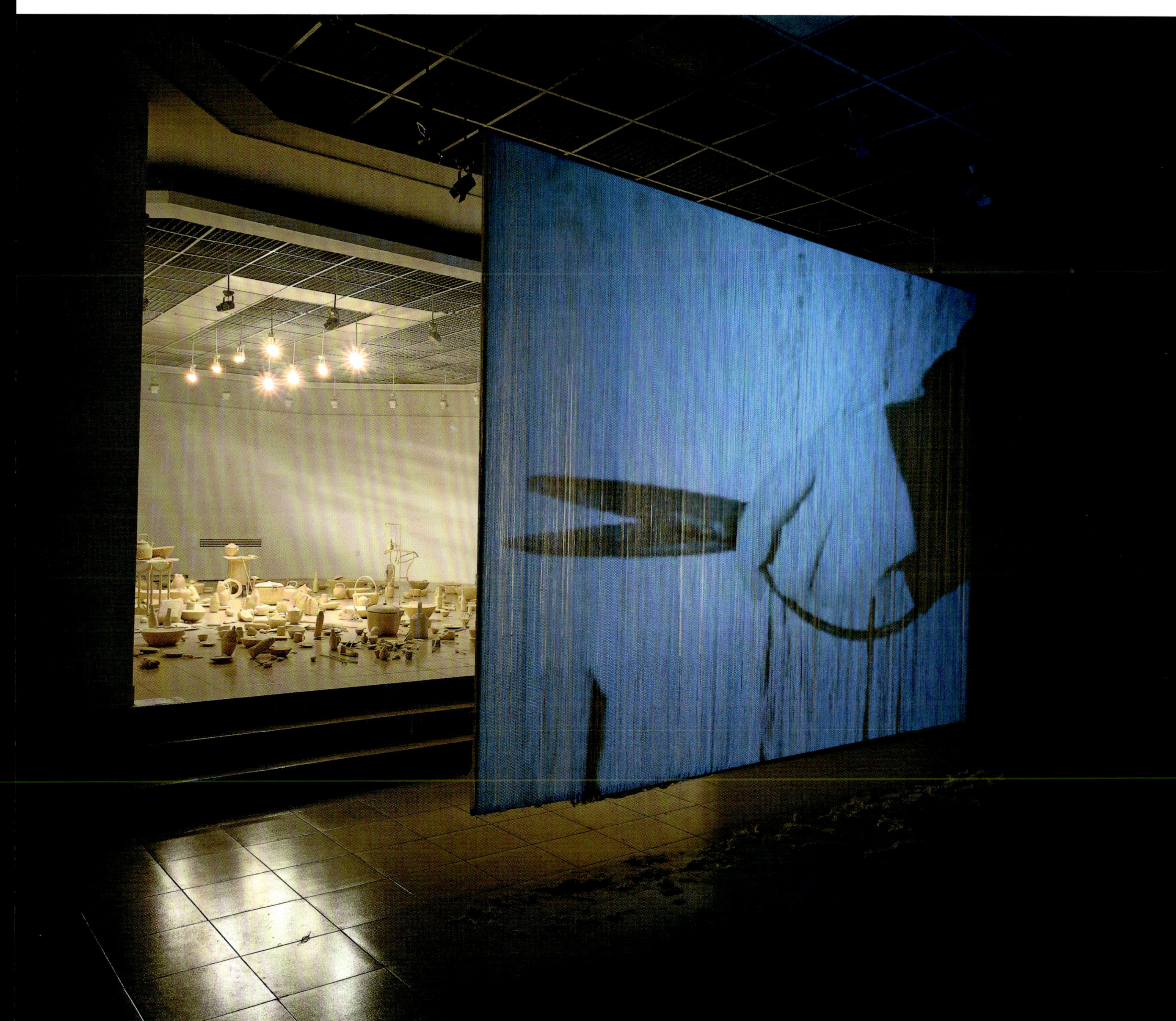

Day-Dreamer, 2000
White cotton threads, white fabric, digital photograph
59 x 86 ½ x 196 ¾ in. (150 x 220 x 500 cm)
IT Park Gallery and Photo Studio, Taiwan

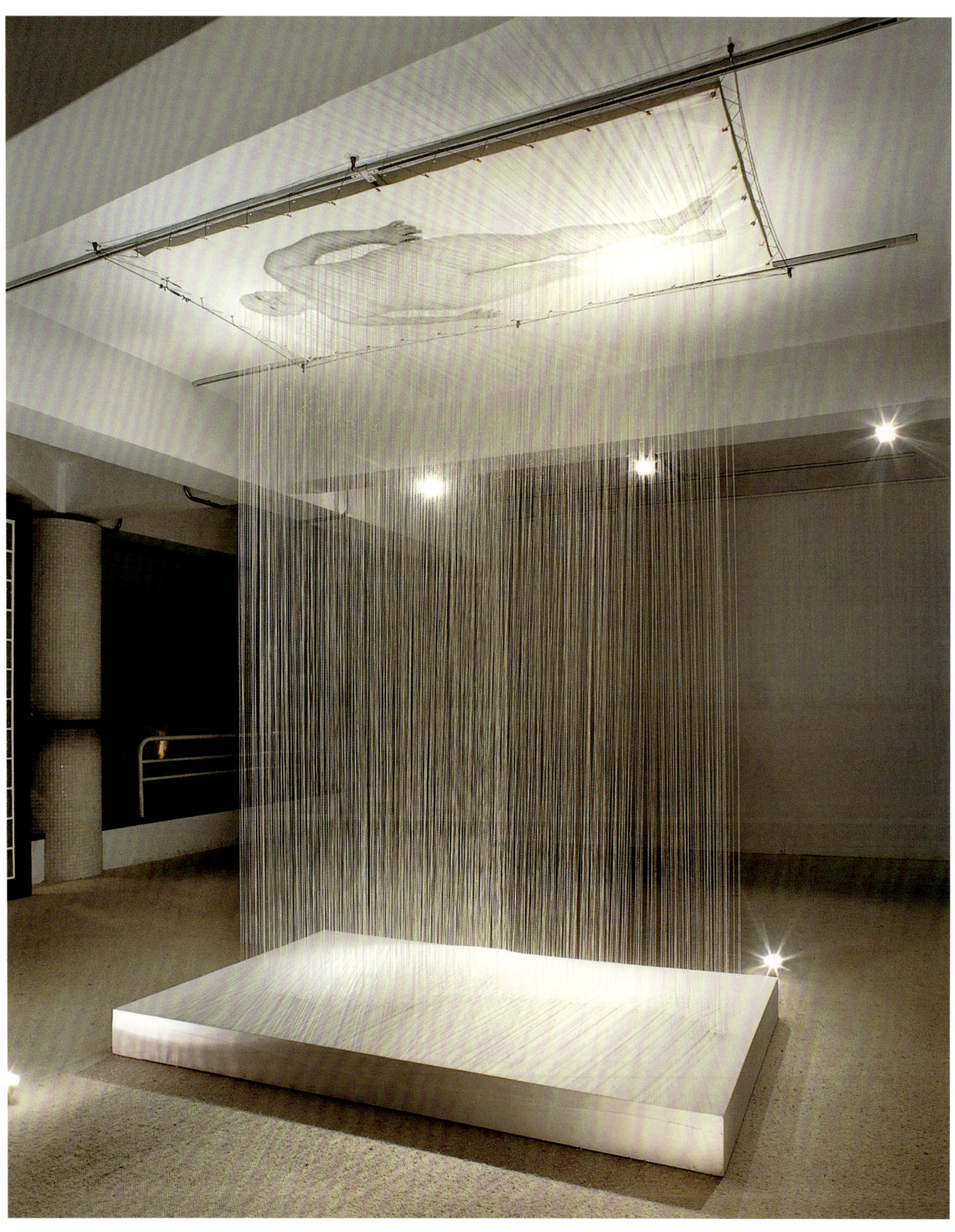

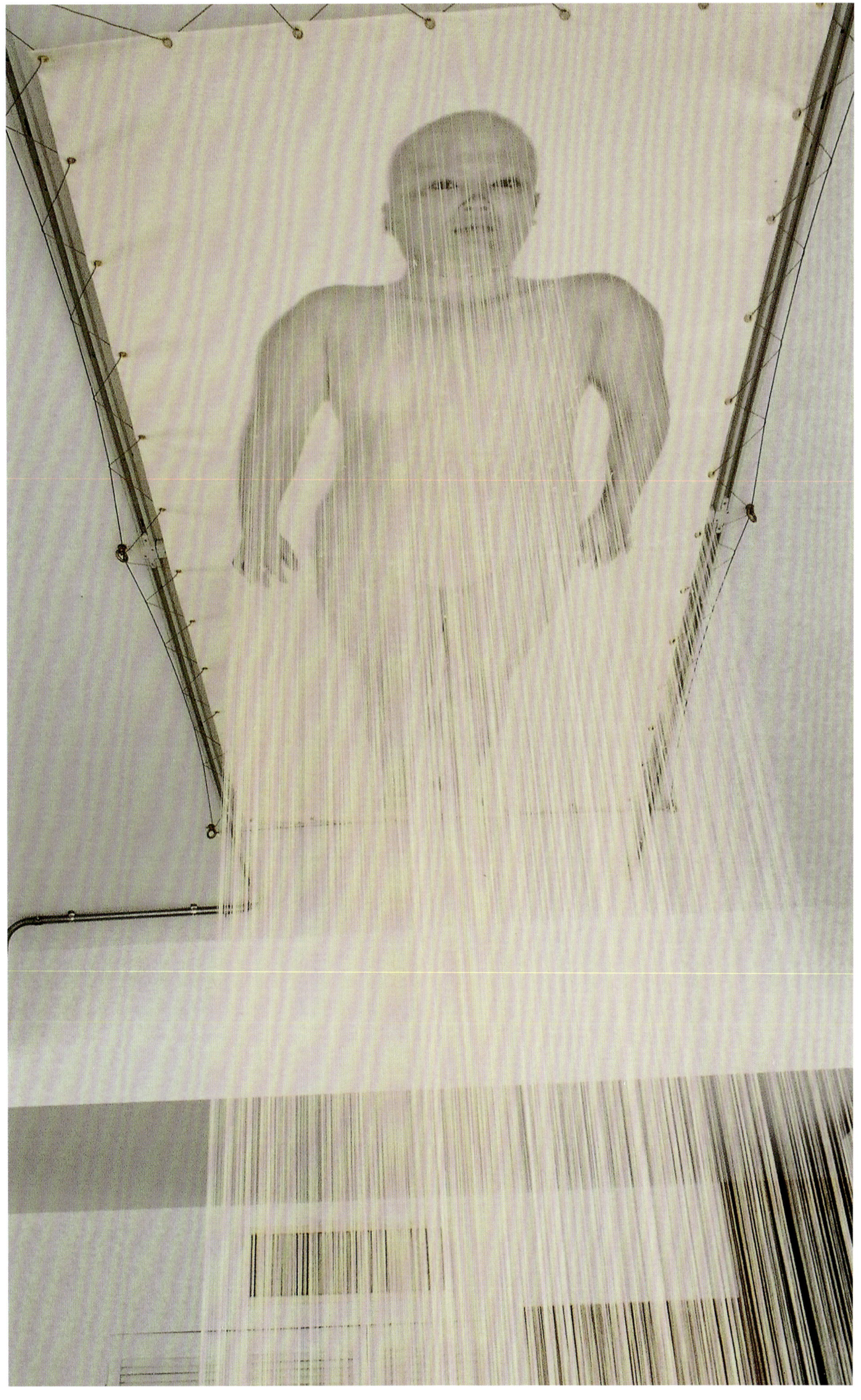

Spawn, 2001
Threaded and digital print on canvas
157 1/2 x 51 in. (400 x 129.5 cm)
"Imagined Workshop: The Second Fukuoka
Asian Art Triennial," Fukuoka Asian Art
Museum, March 21, 2002–June 23, 2002

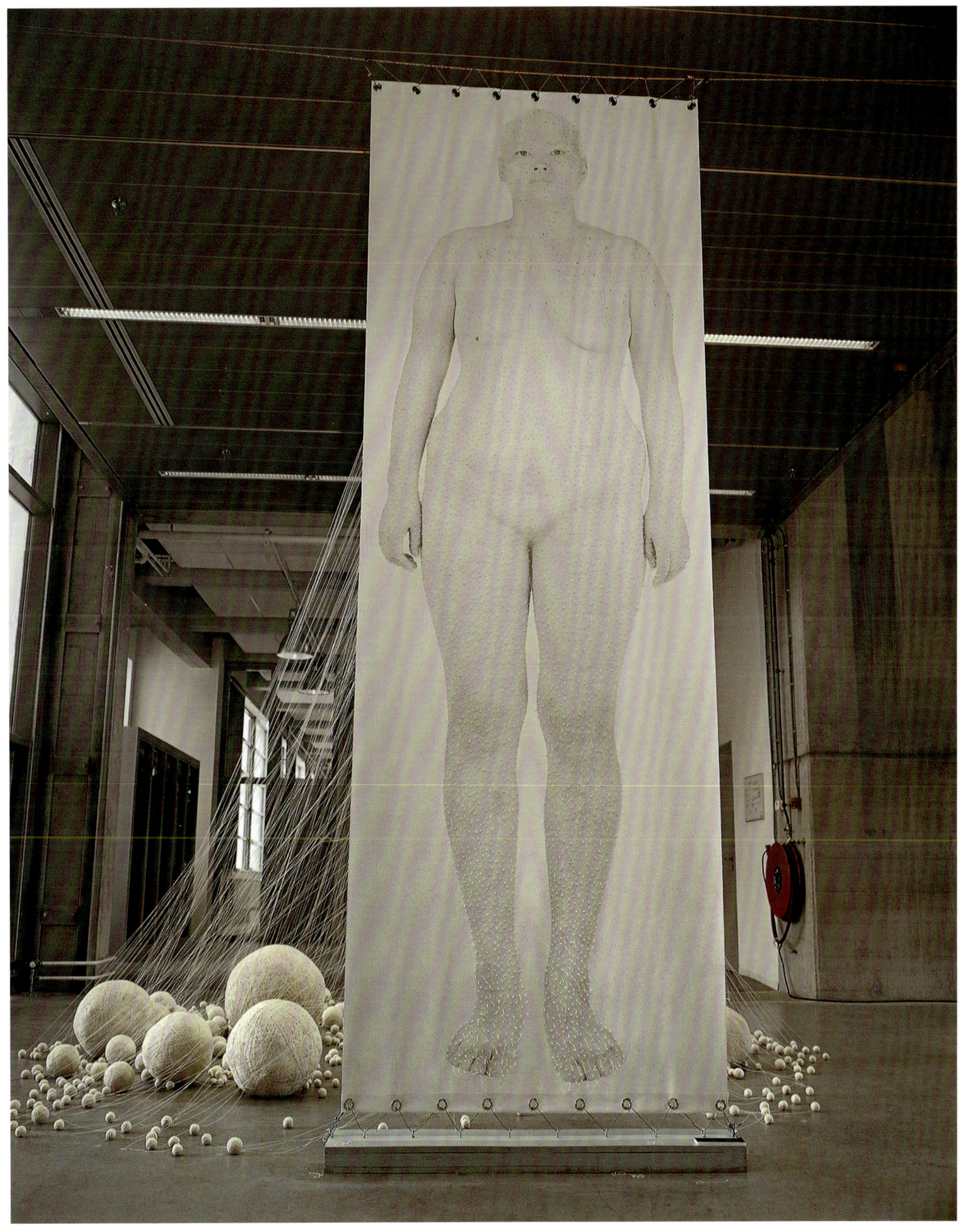

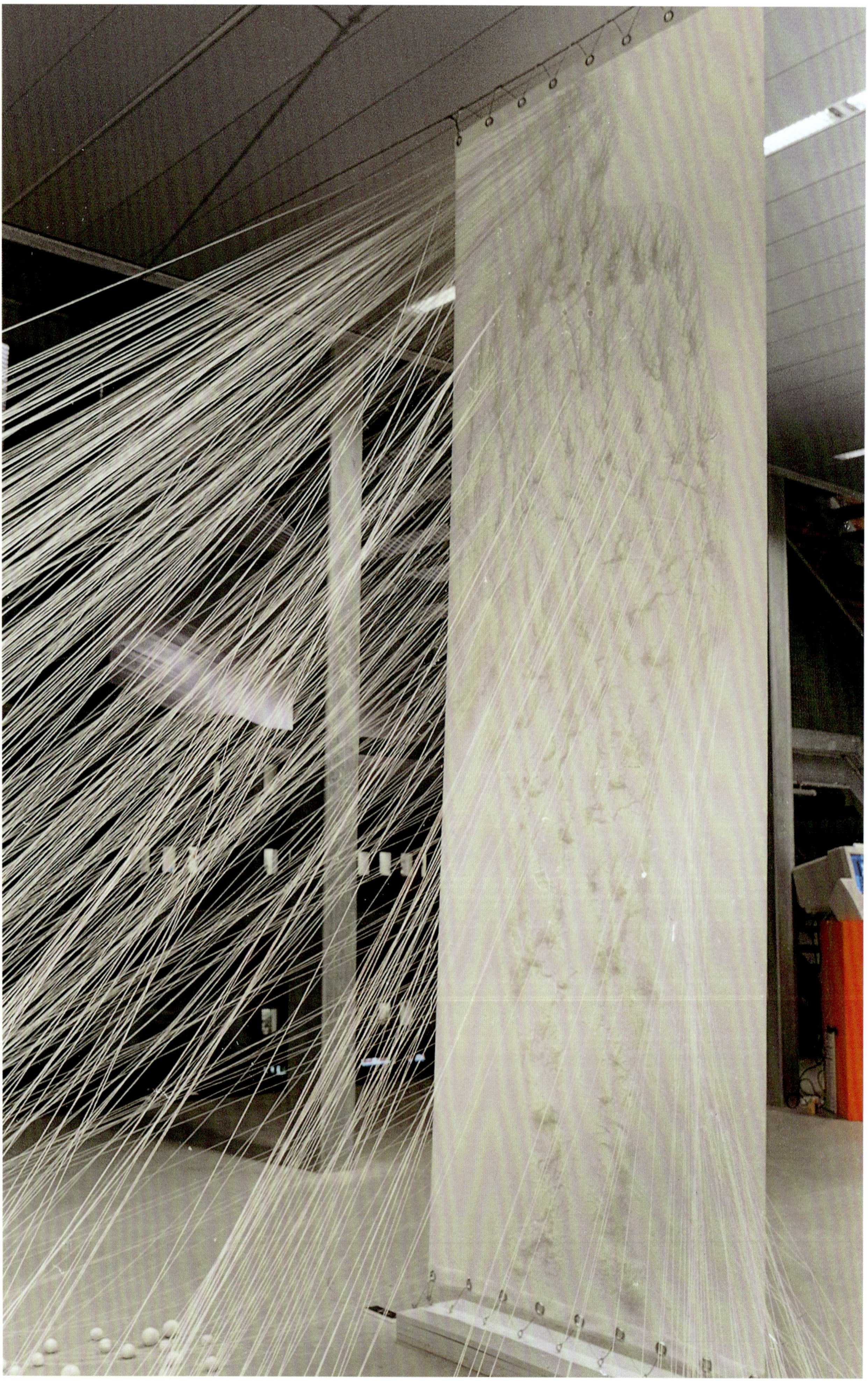

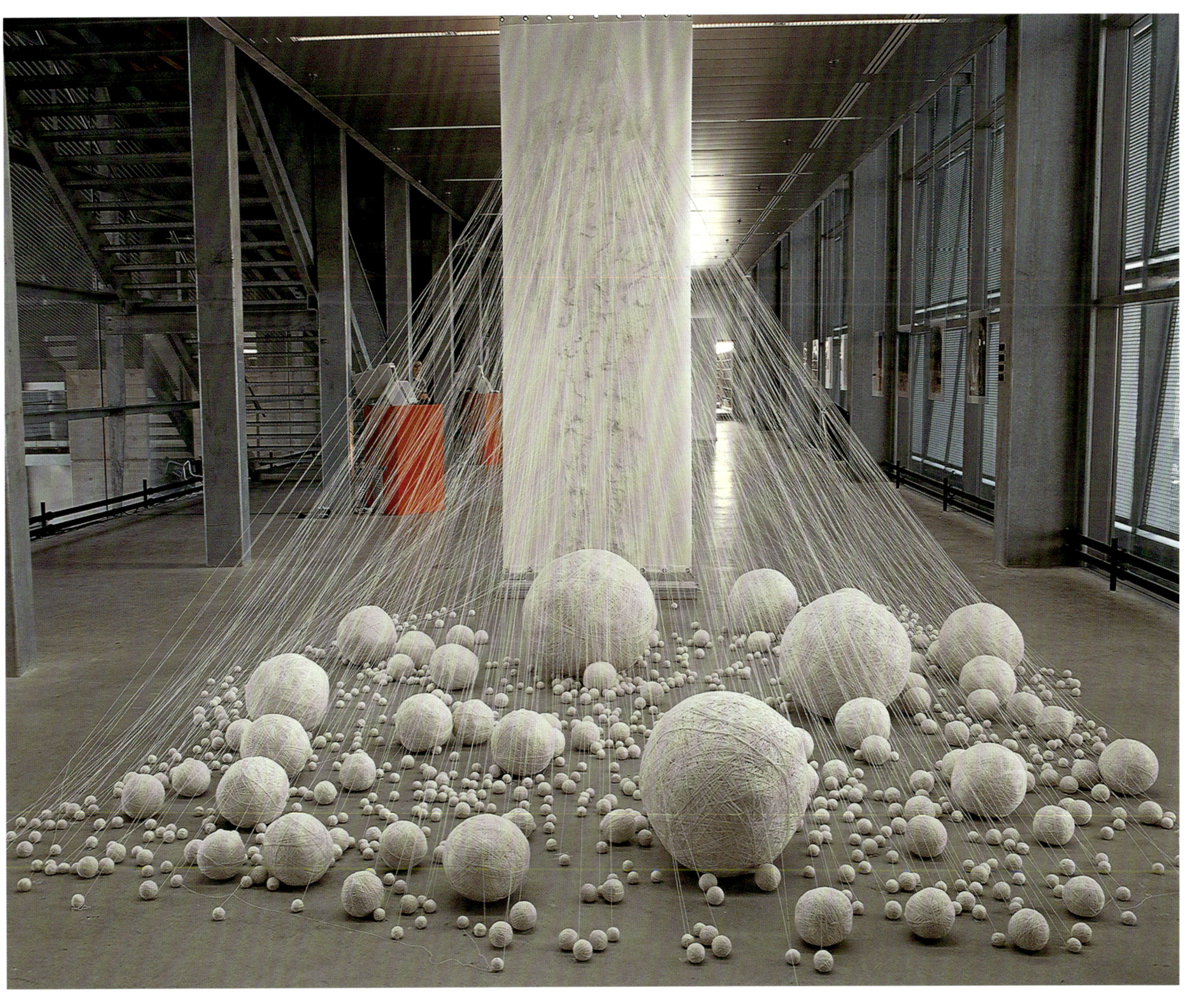

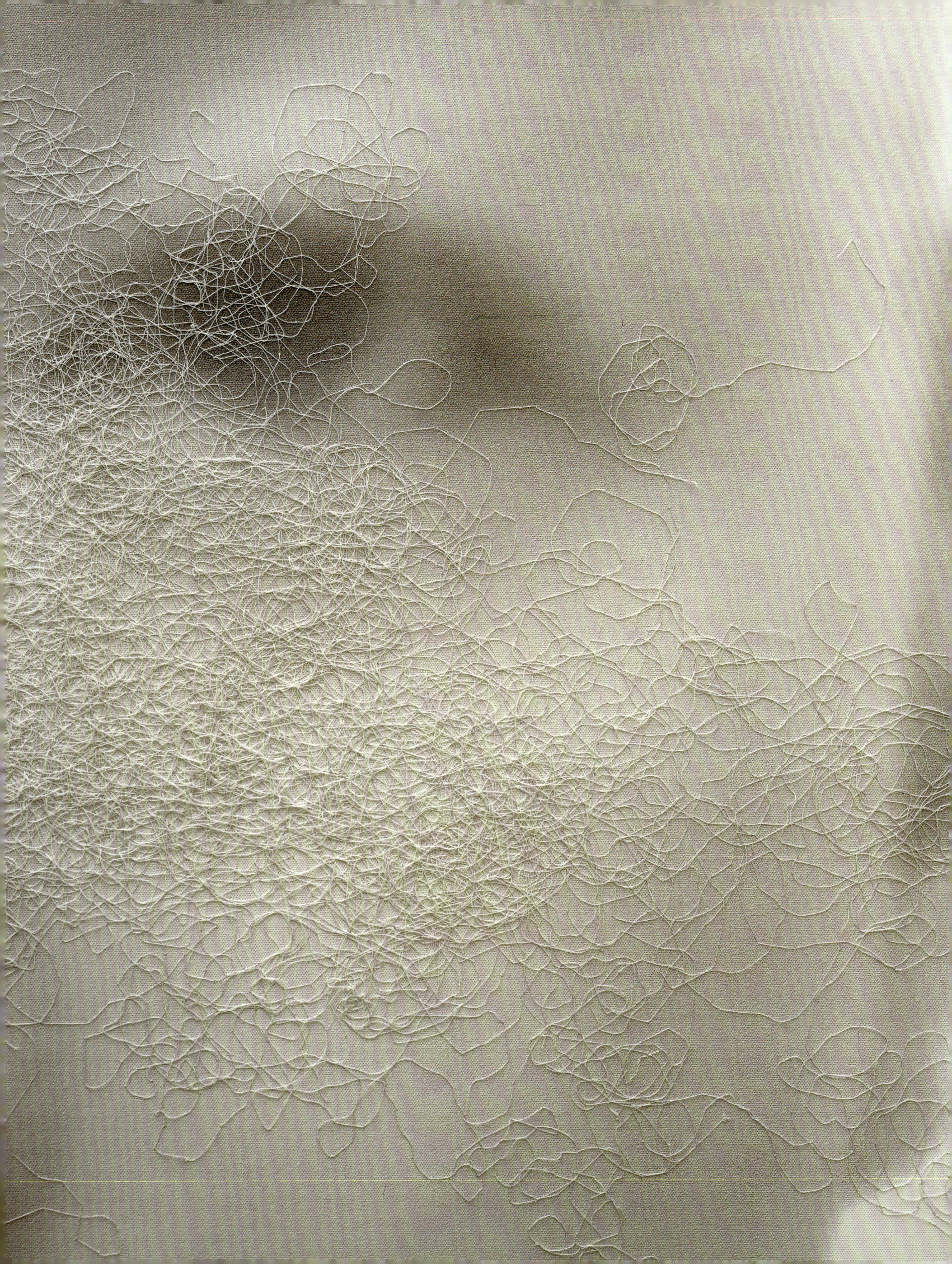

Focus, 2001
Digital C-Type print on canvas, hair, silk threads, and cotton threads
95 ¼ x 5 x 69 ¾ in. (242 x 13 x 177 cm)

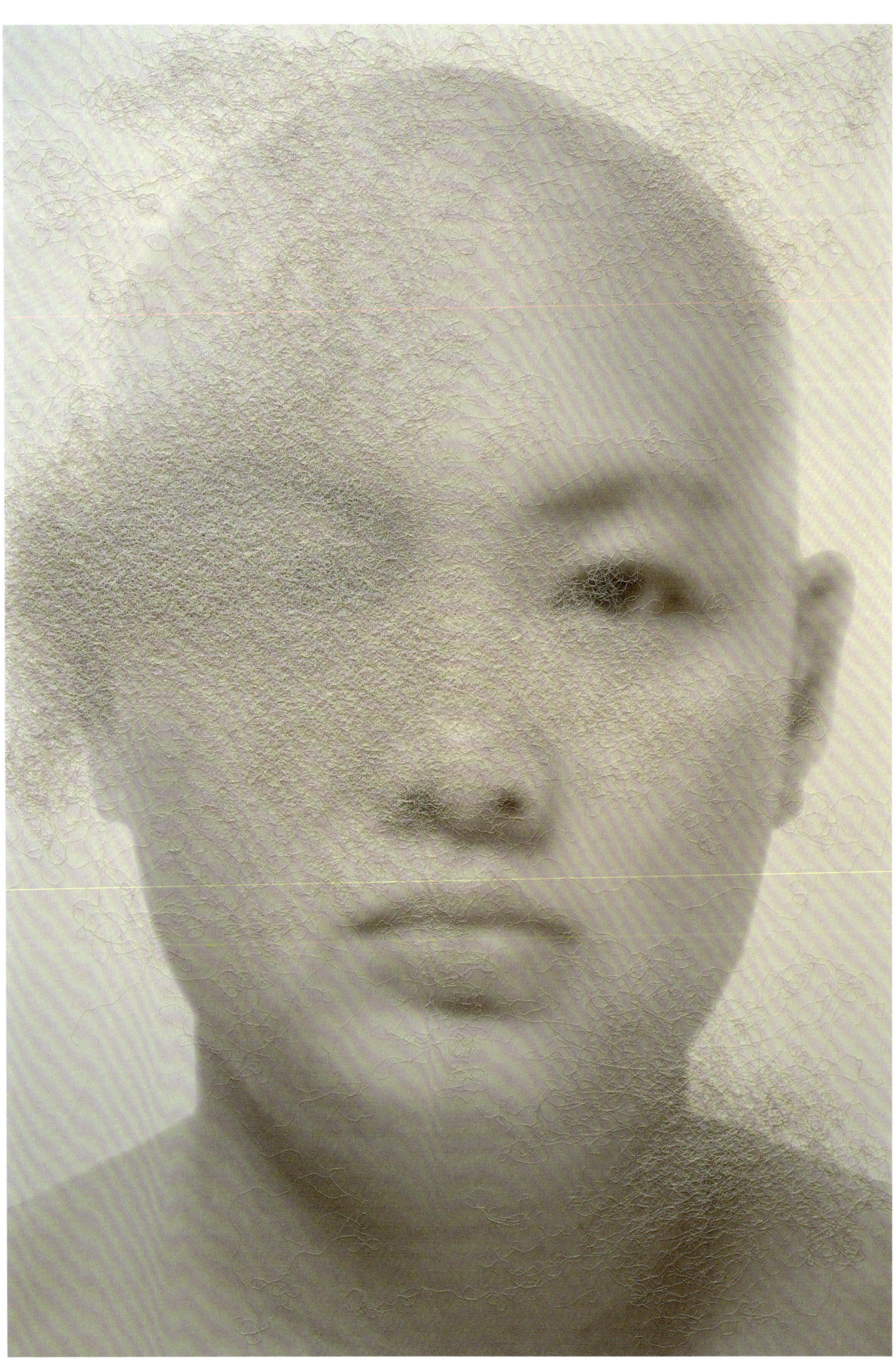

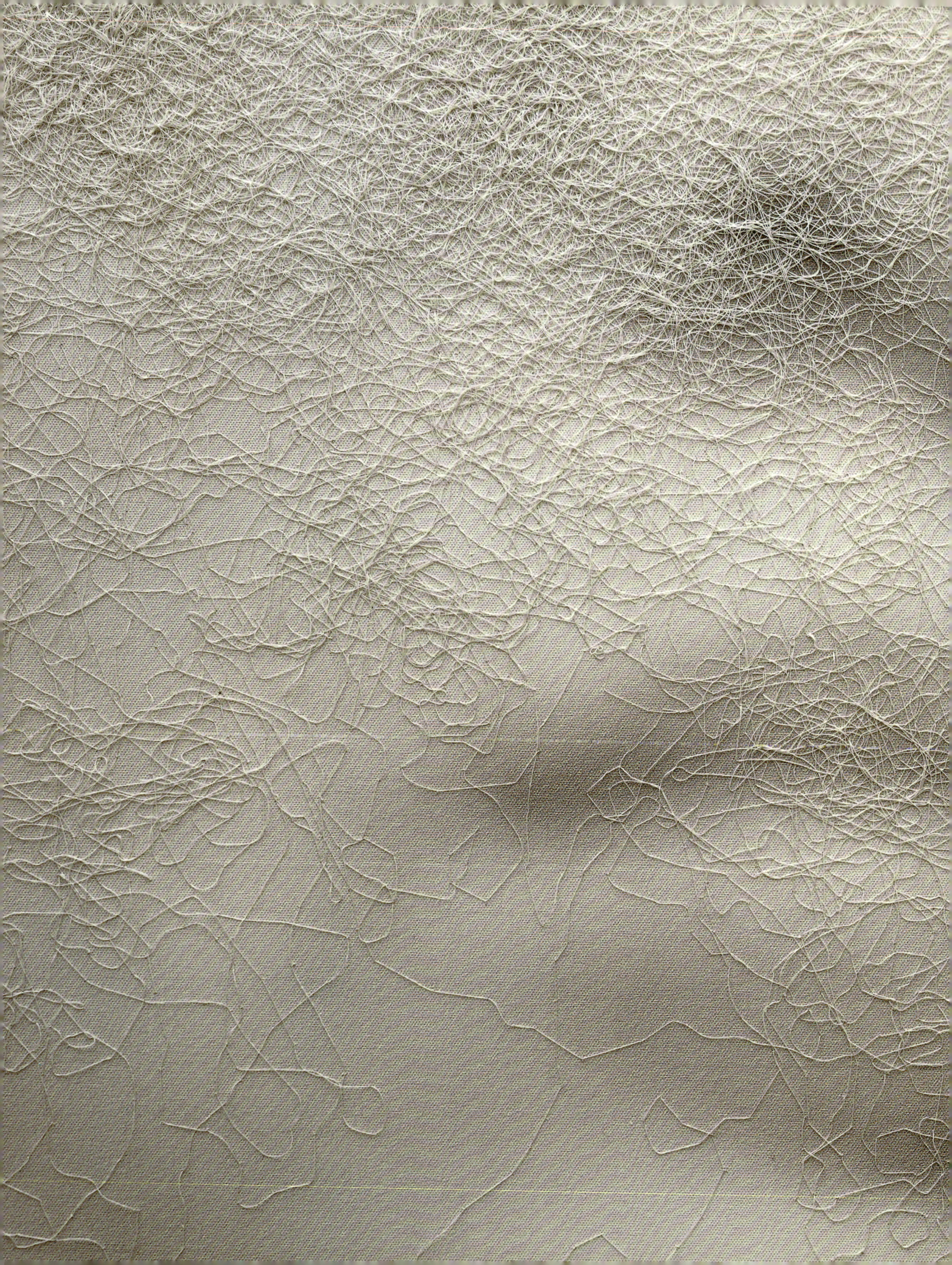

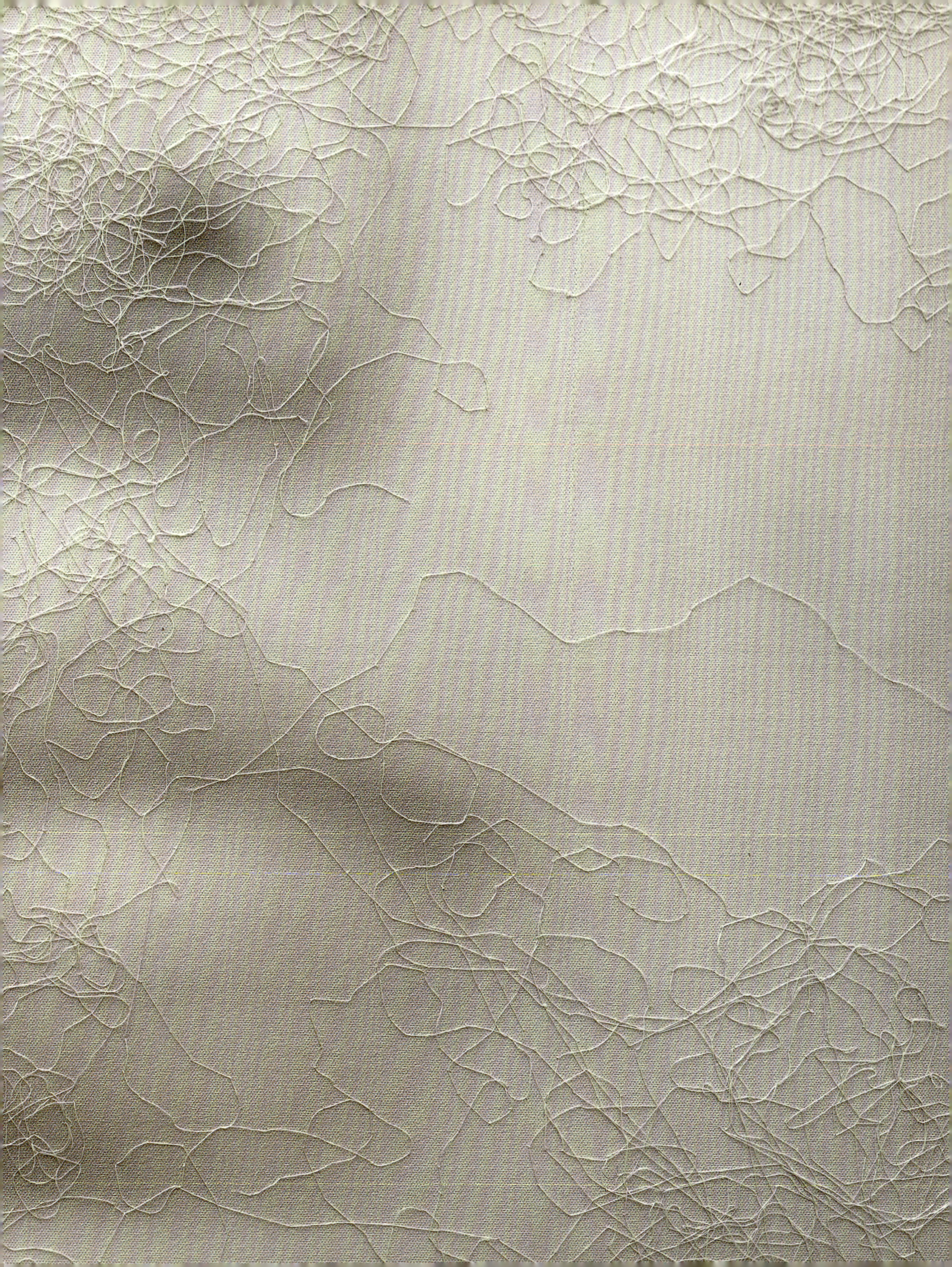

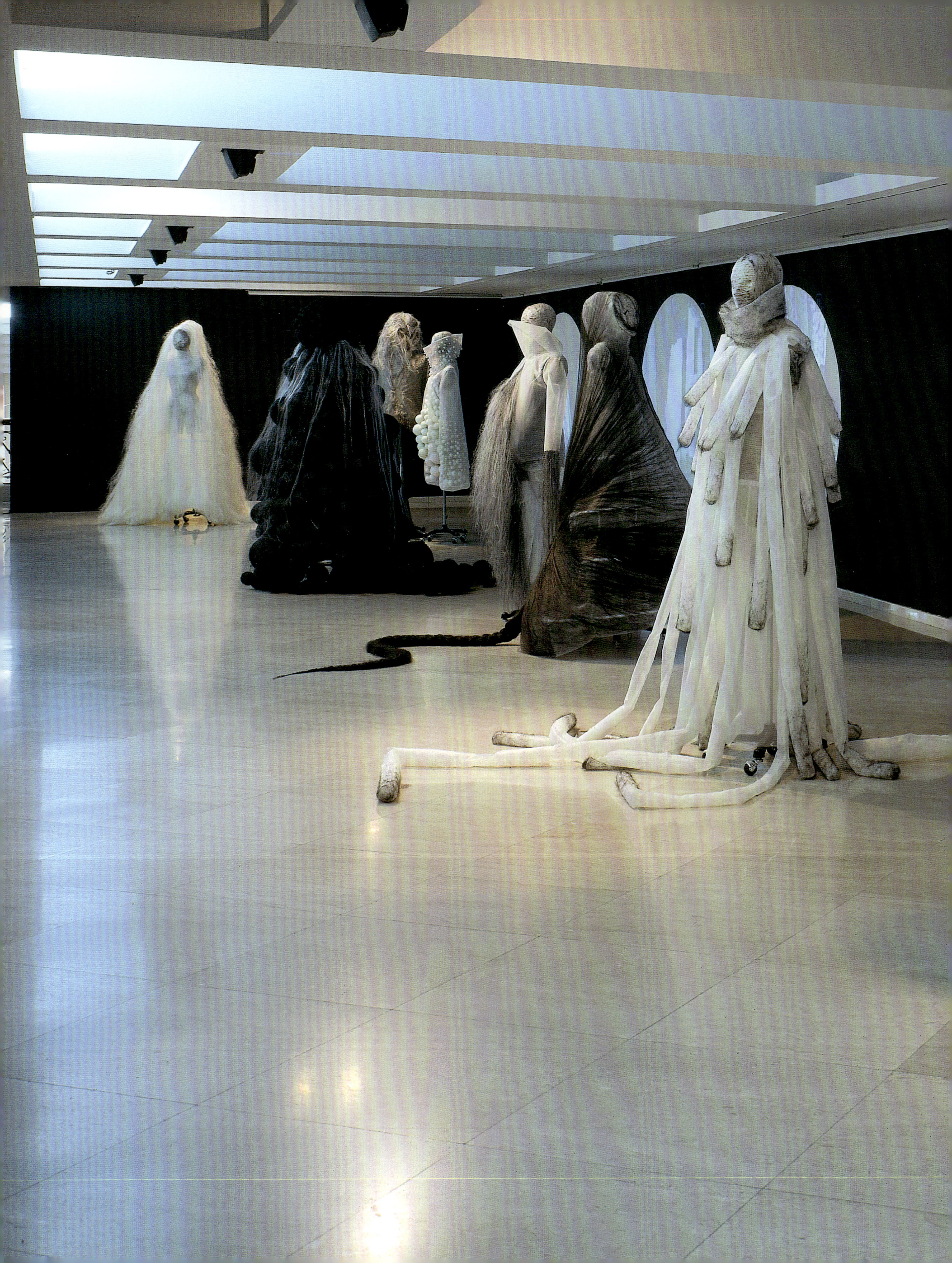

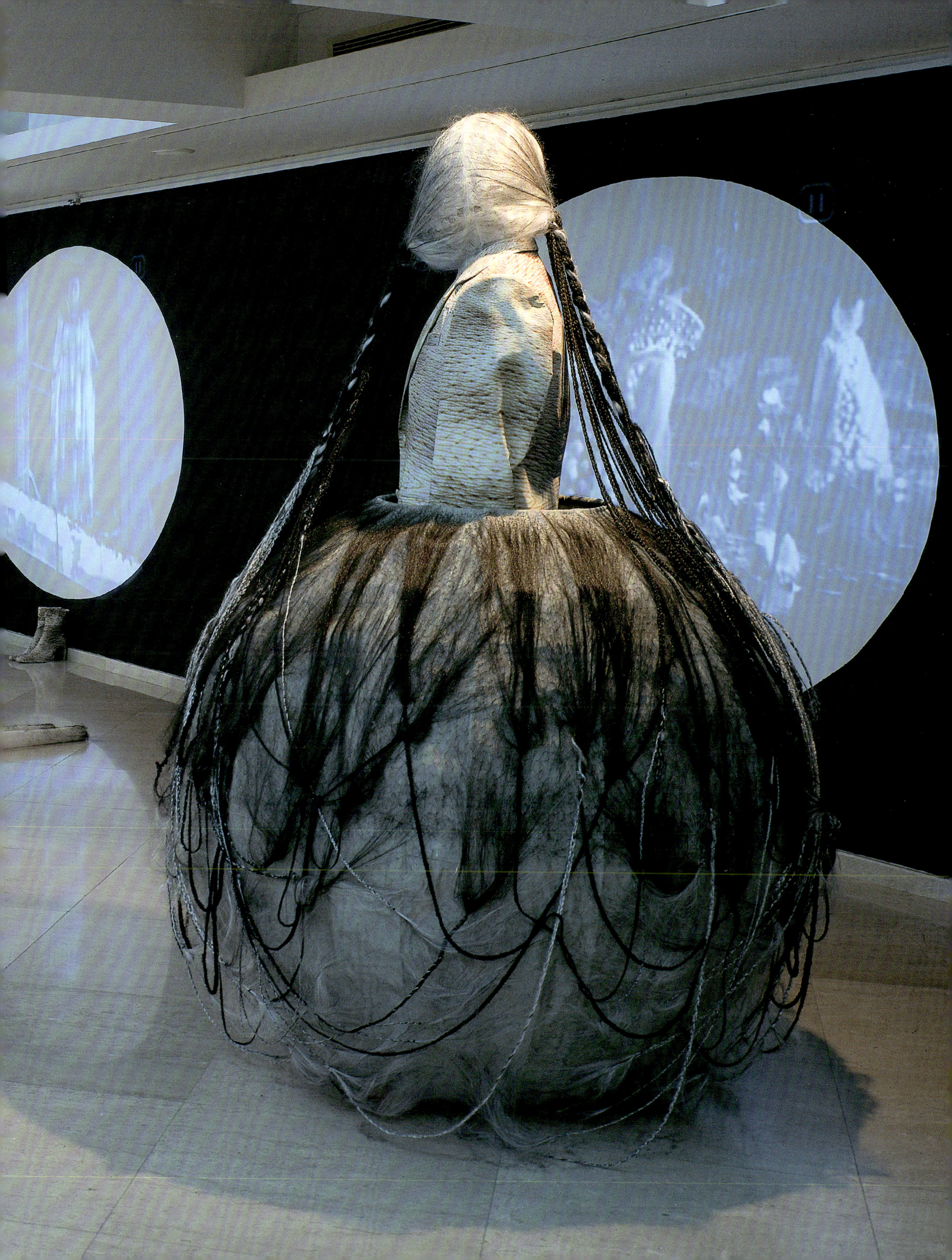

Here? Or There?, 2002
Fiberglass, fabric, thread, mixed media
Dimensions variable
Fourth Shanghai Biennale, Shanghai Art Museum, November 22, 2002–January 20, 2003
(from page 48)

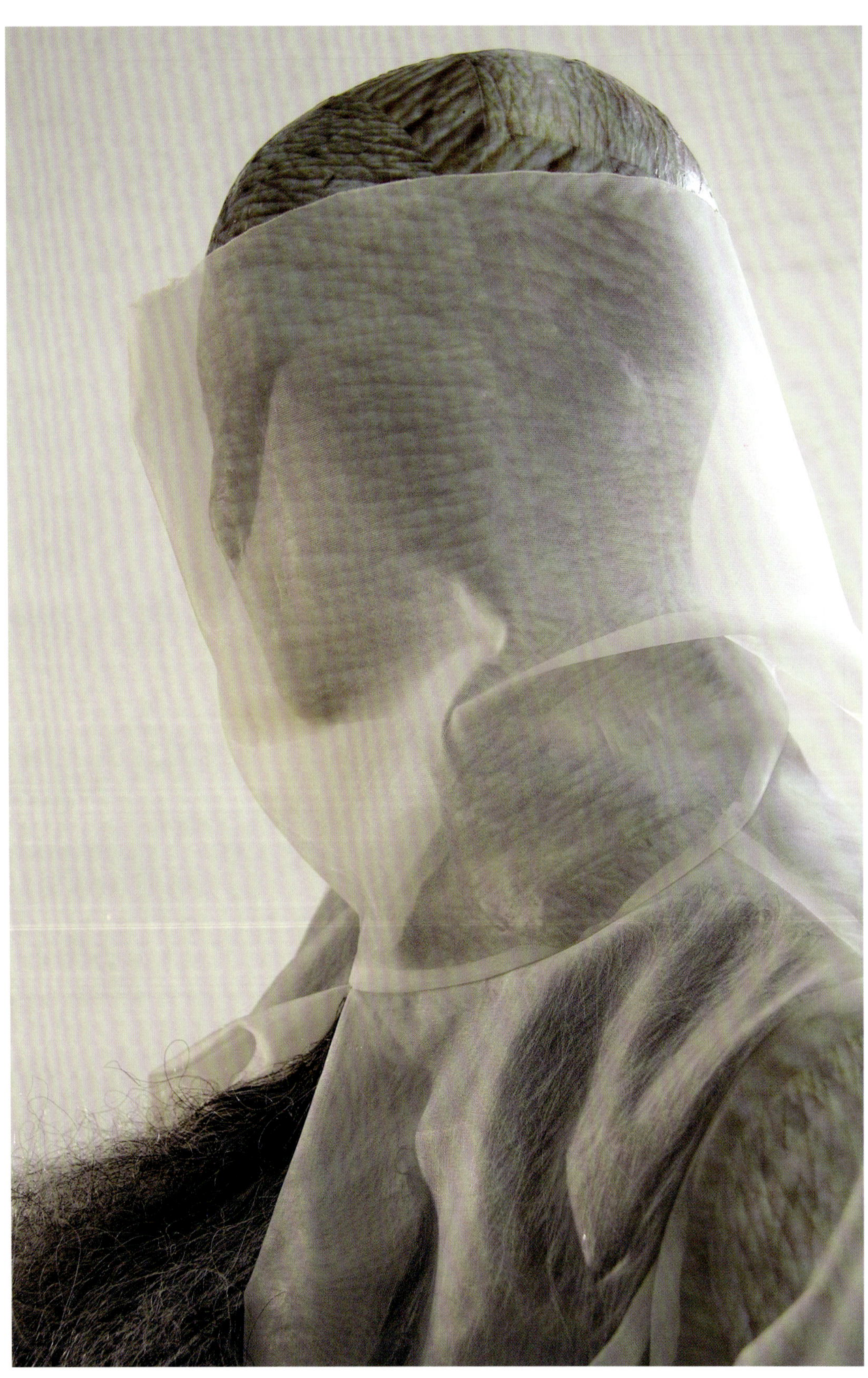

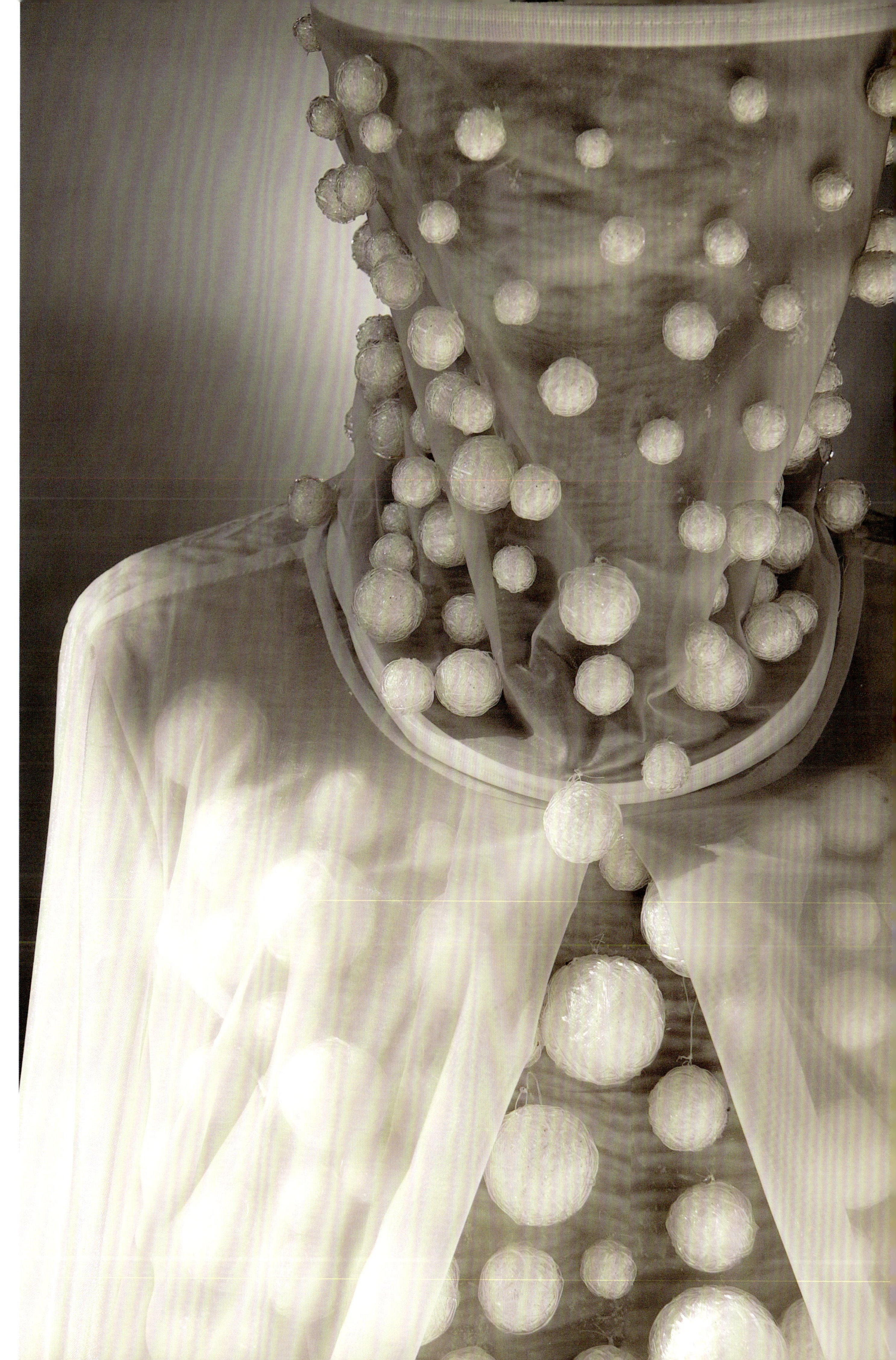

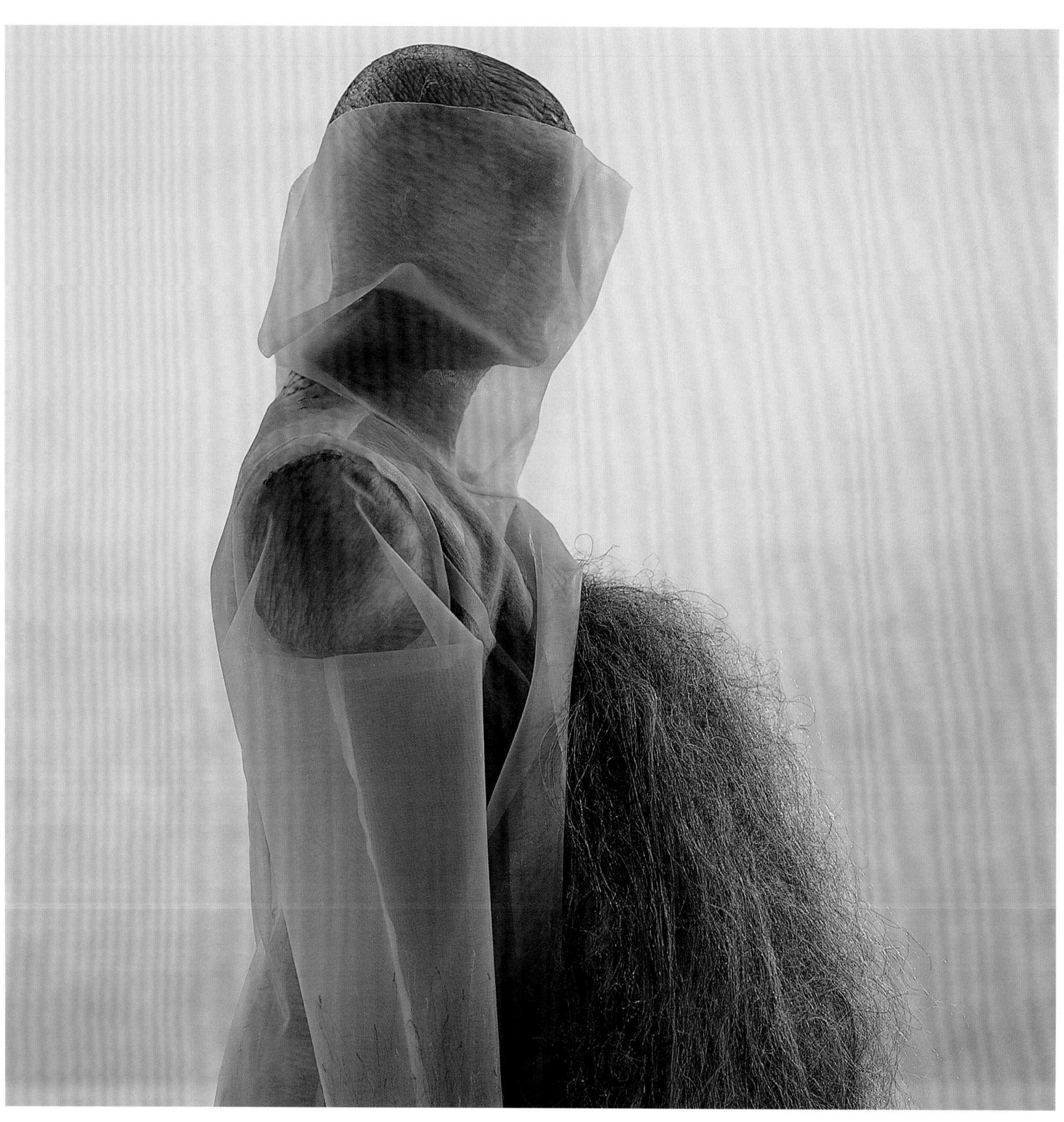

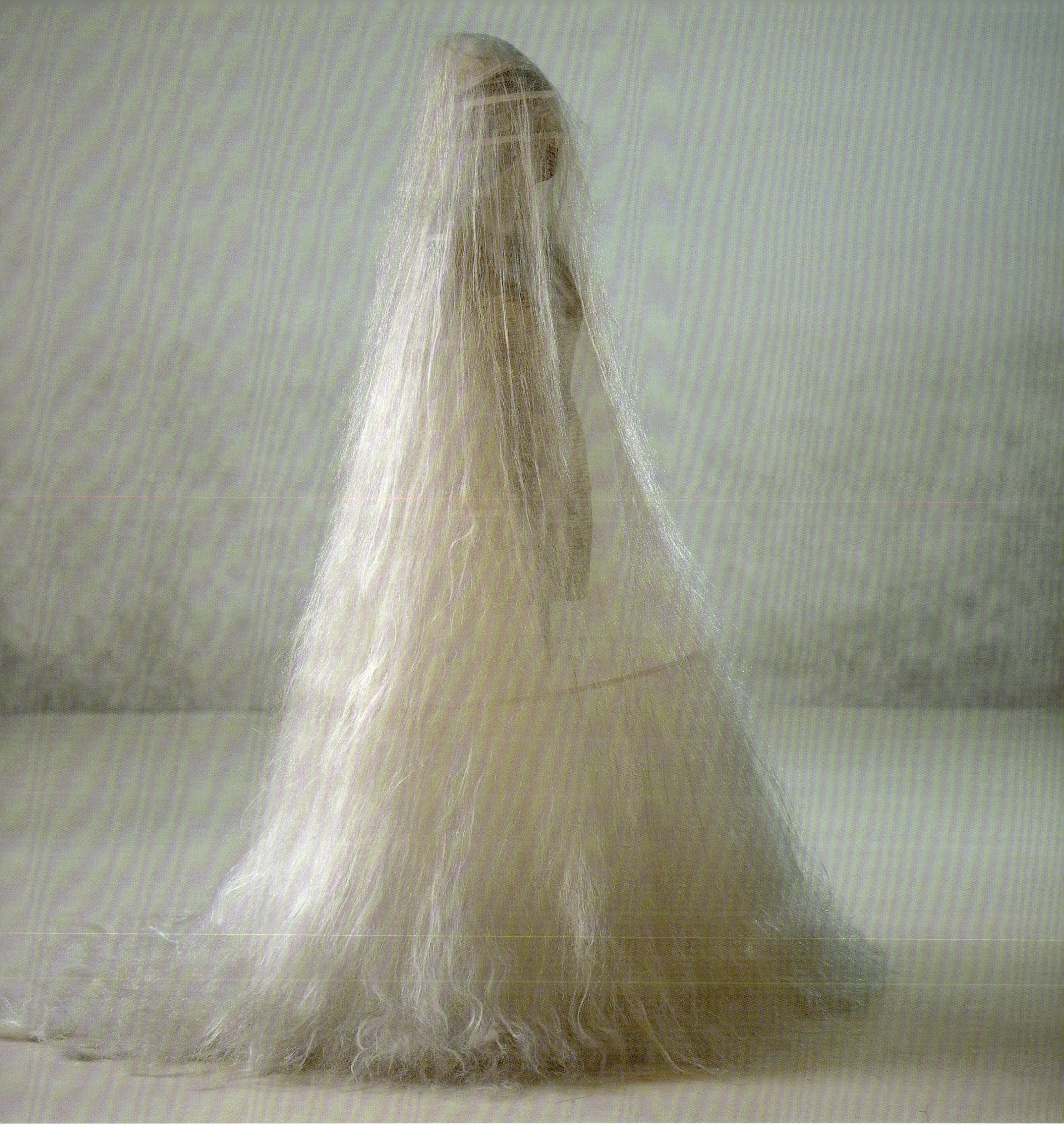

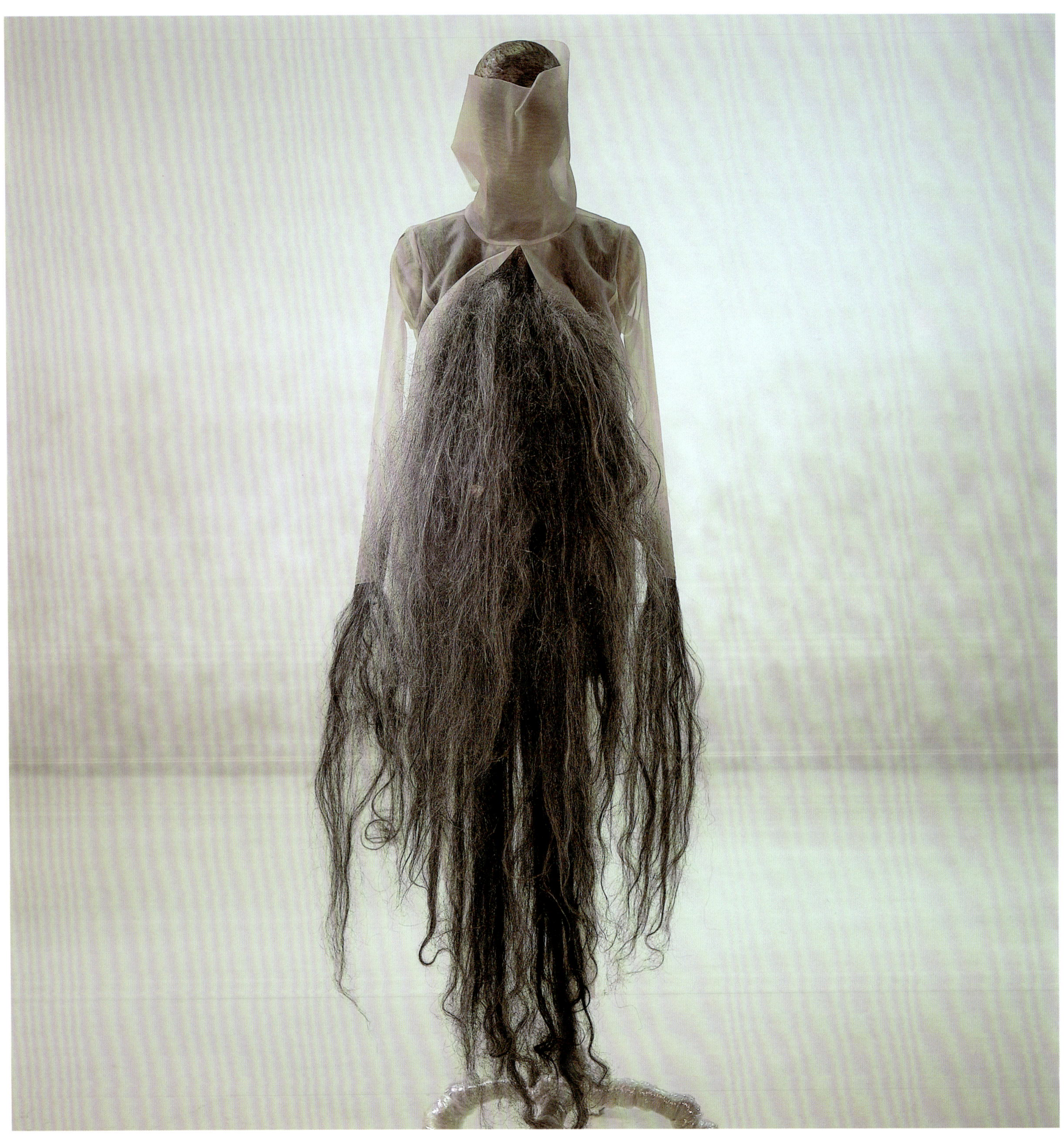

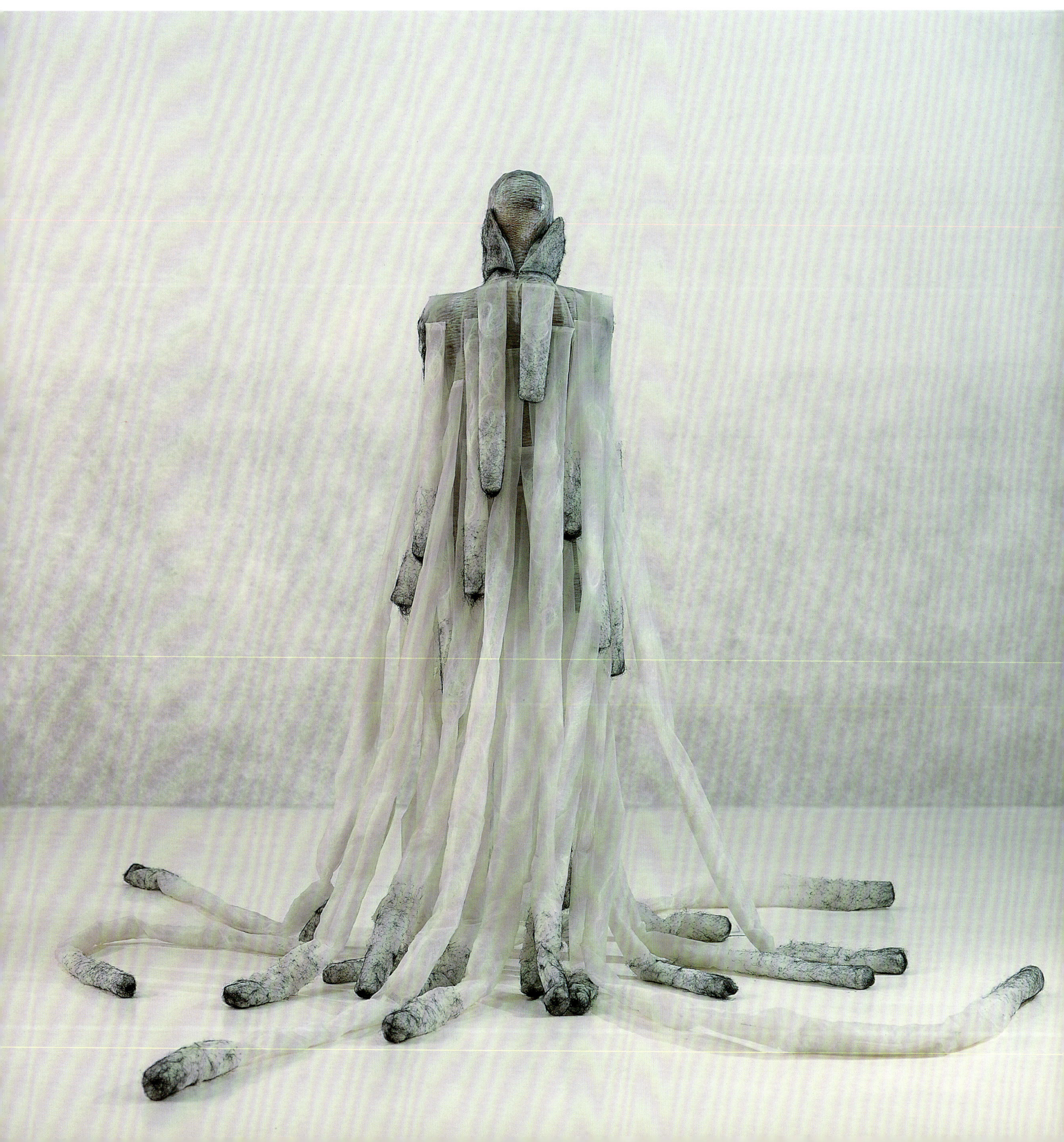

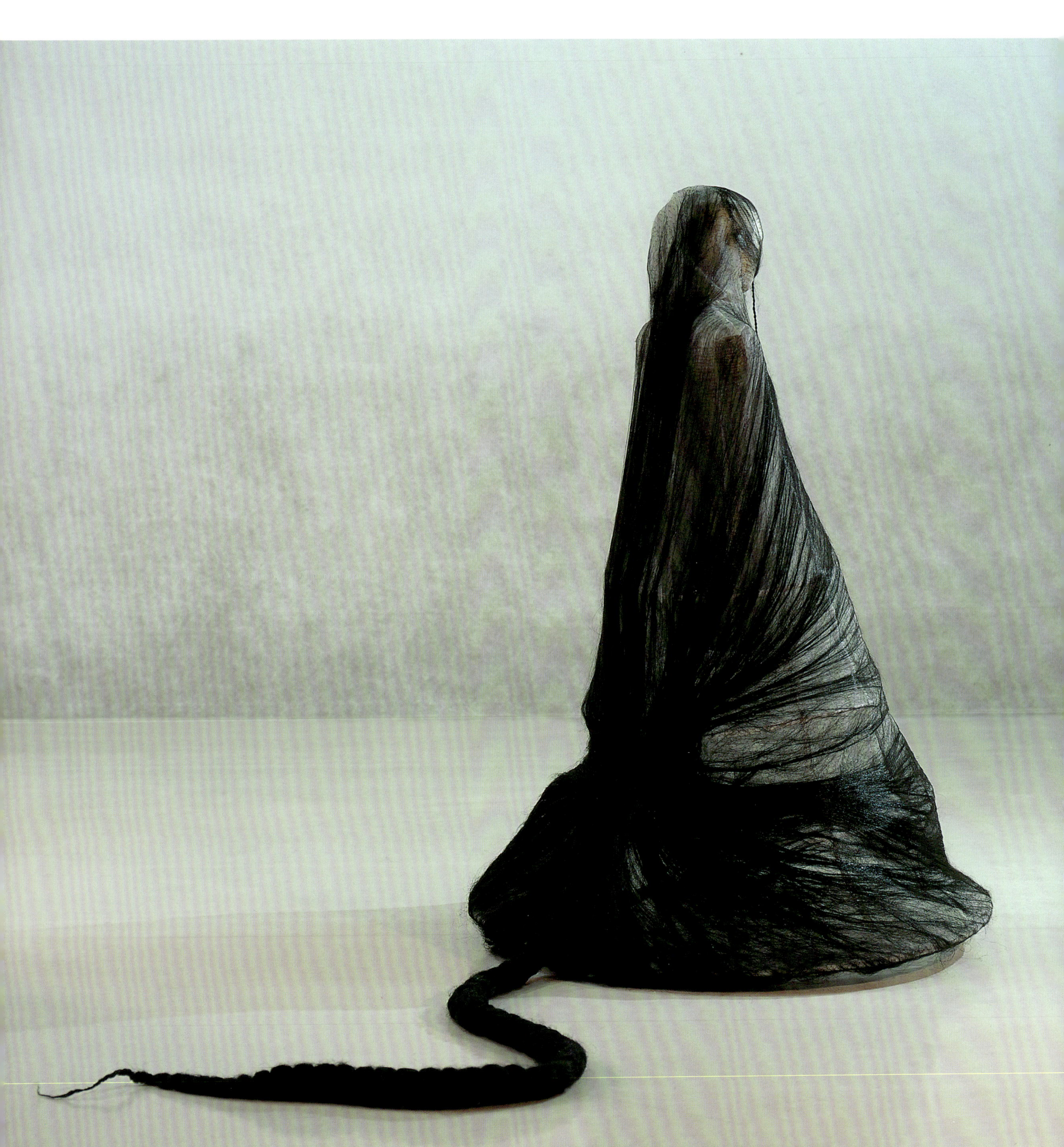

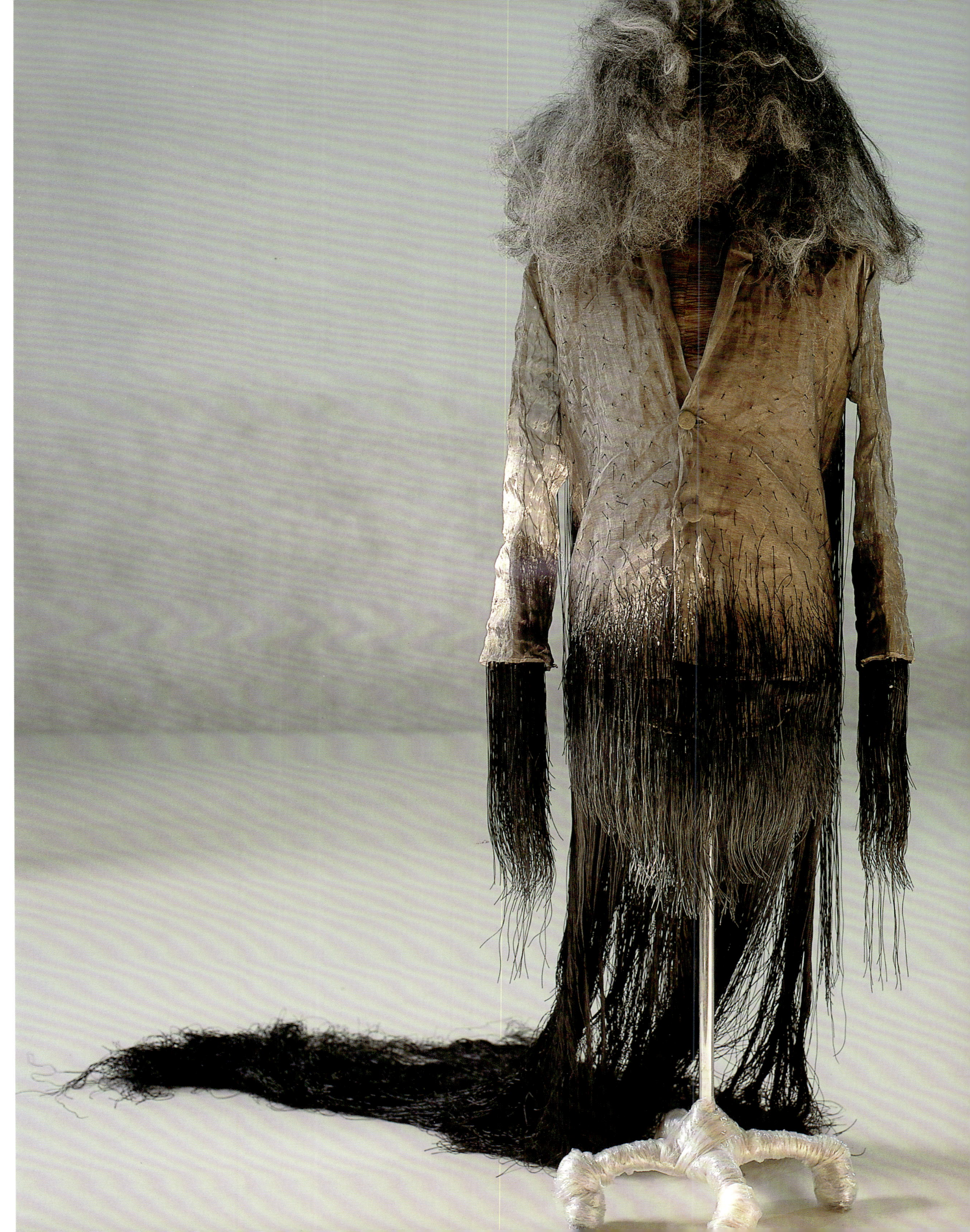

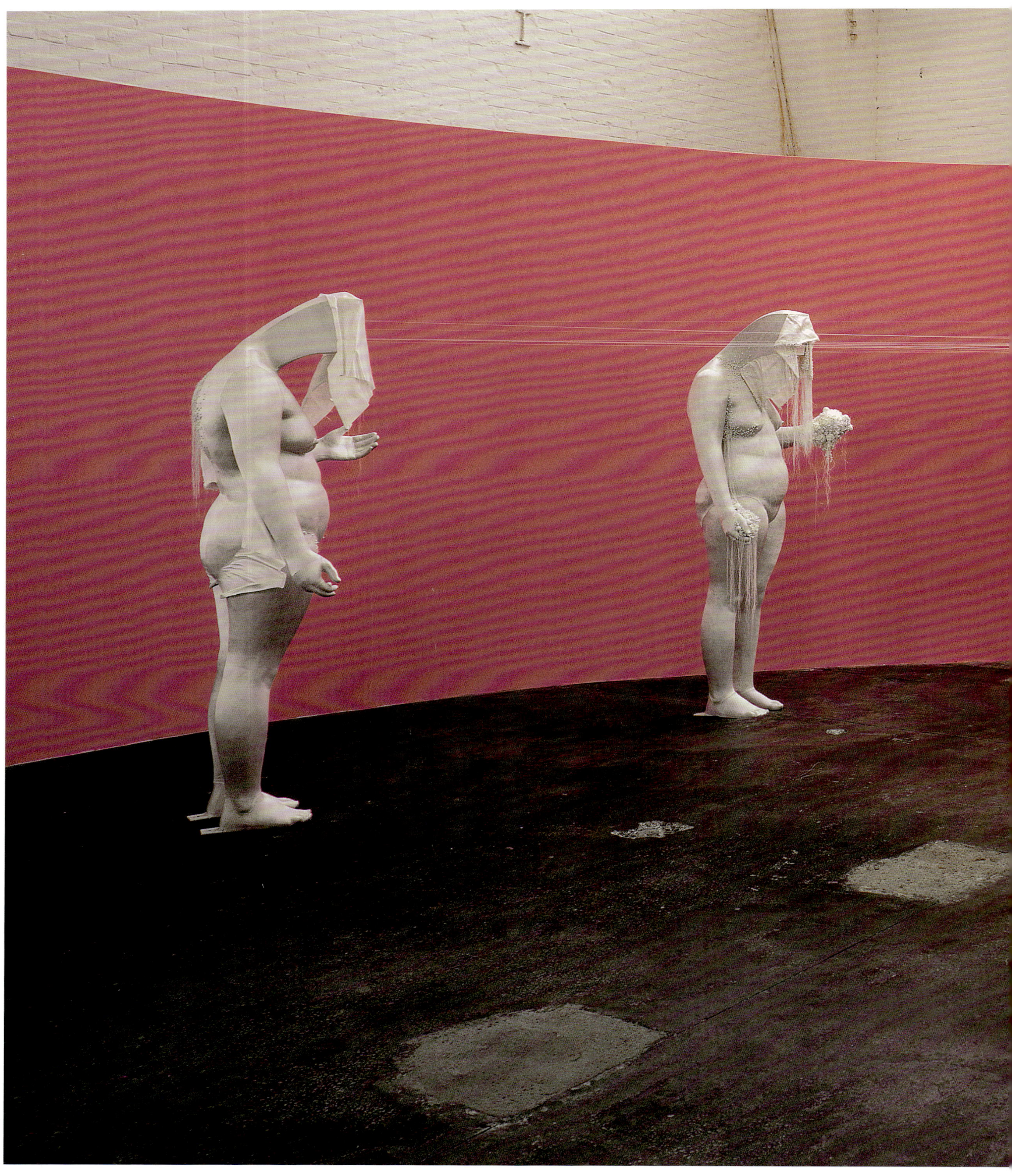

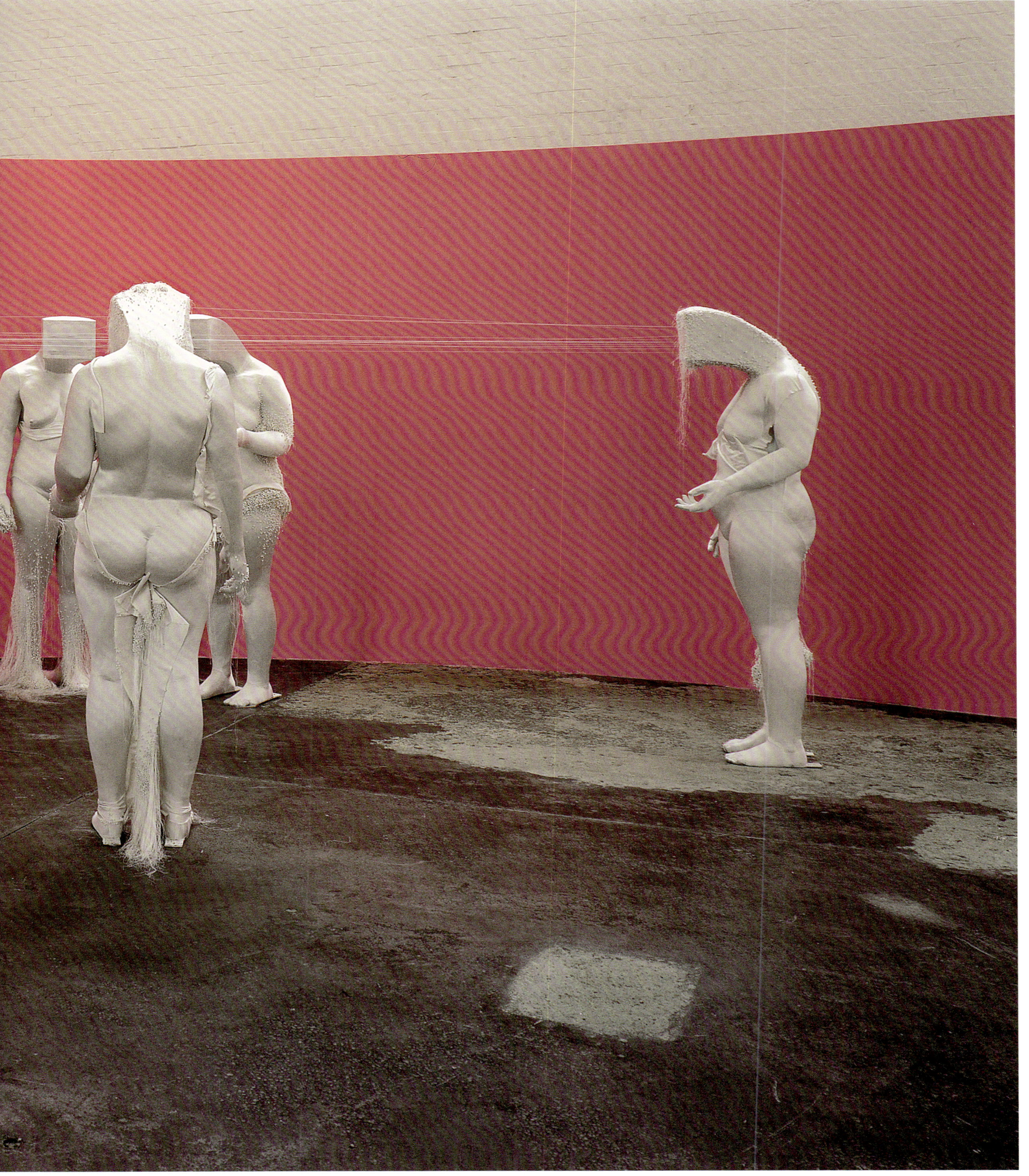

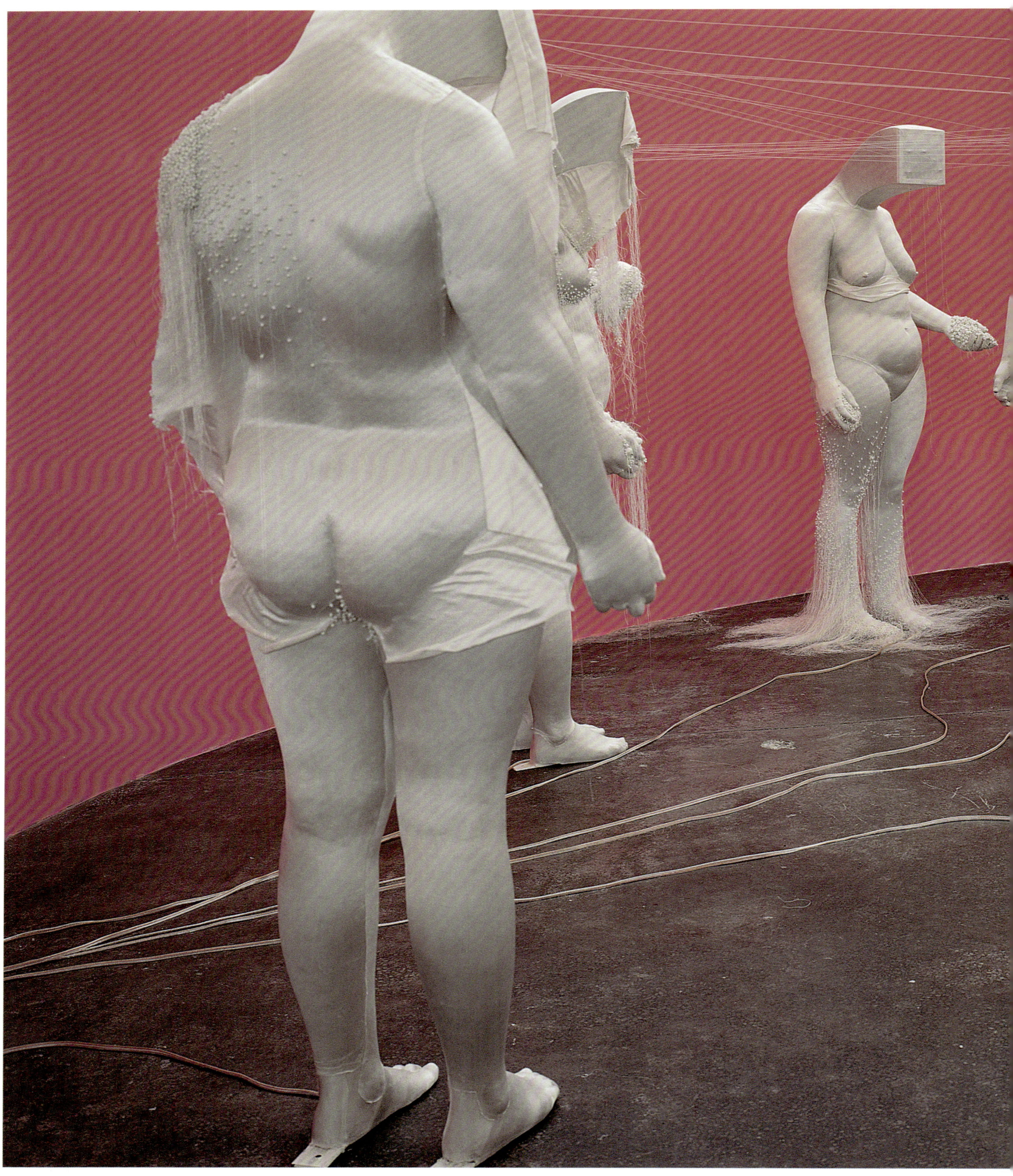

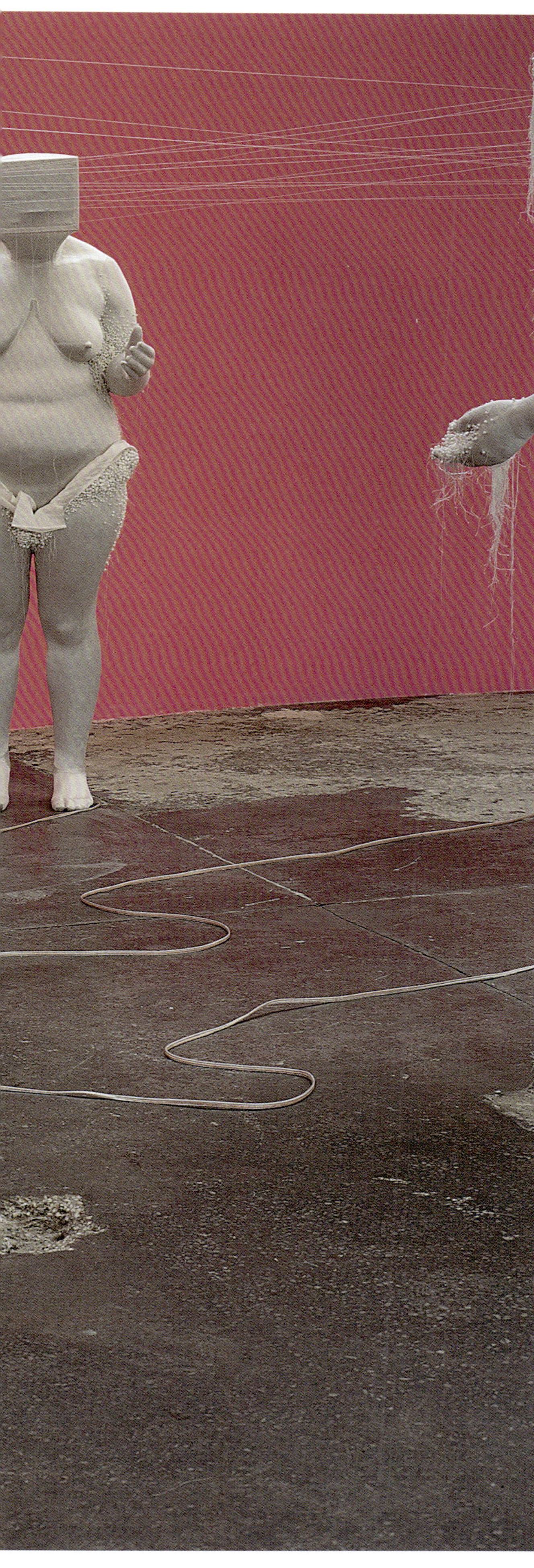

Chatting, 2004
Fiberglass, silk threads, mixed media, sound
Dimensions variable
"Non Zero," Beijing Tokyo Art Project,
September 18–October 3, 2004
(from page 58)

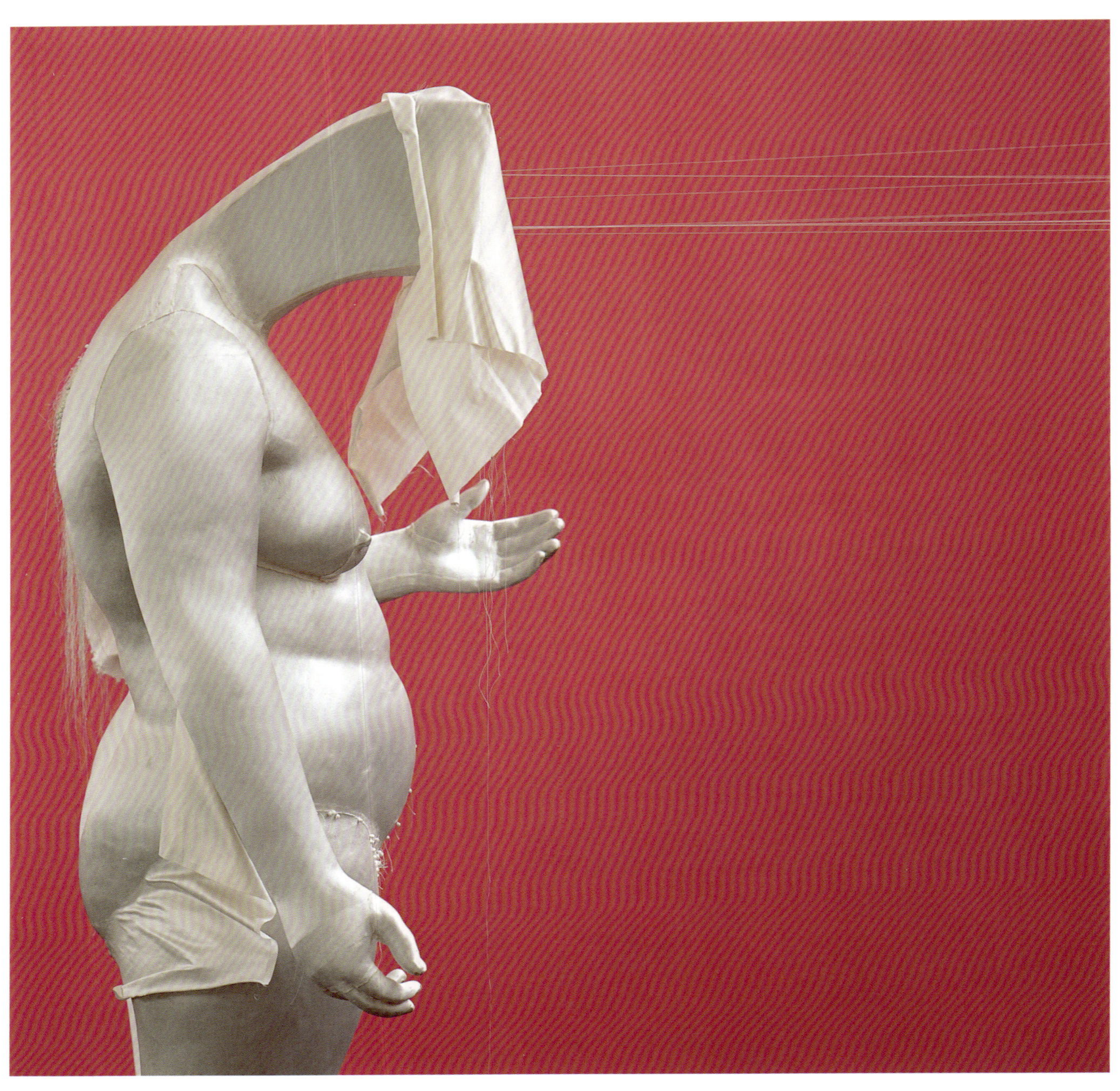

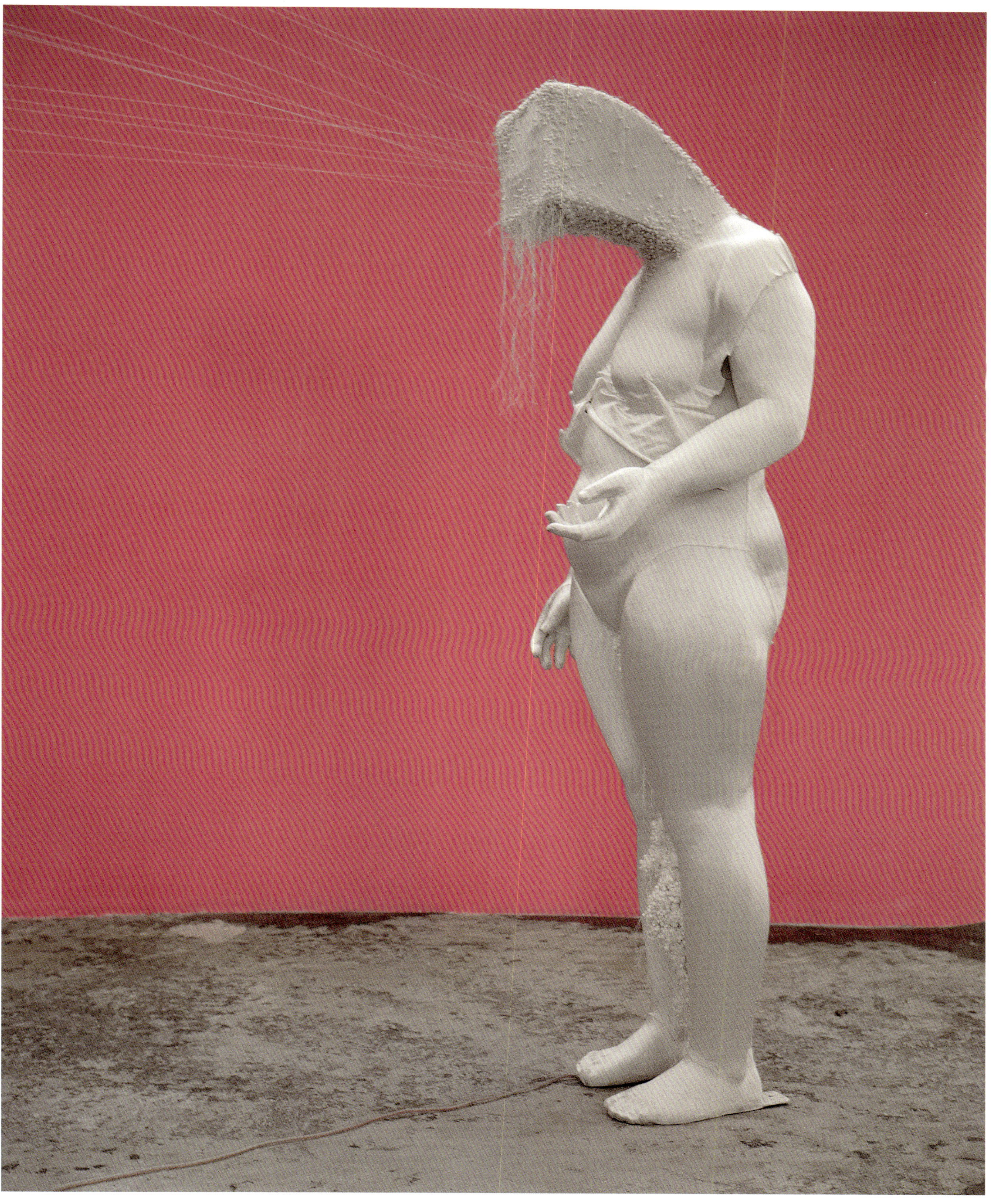

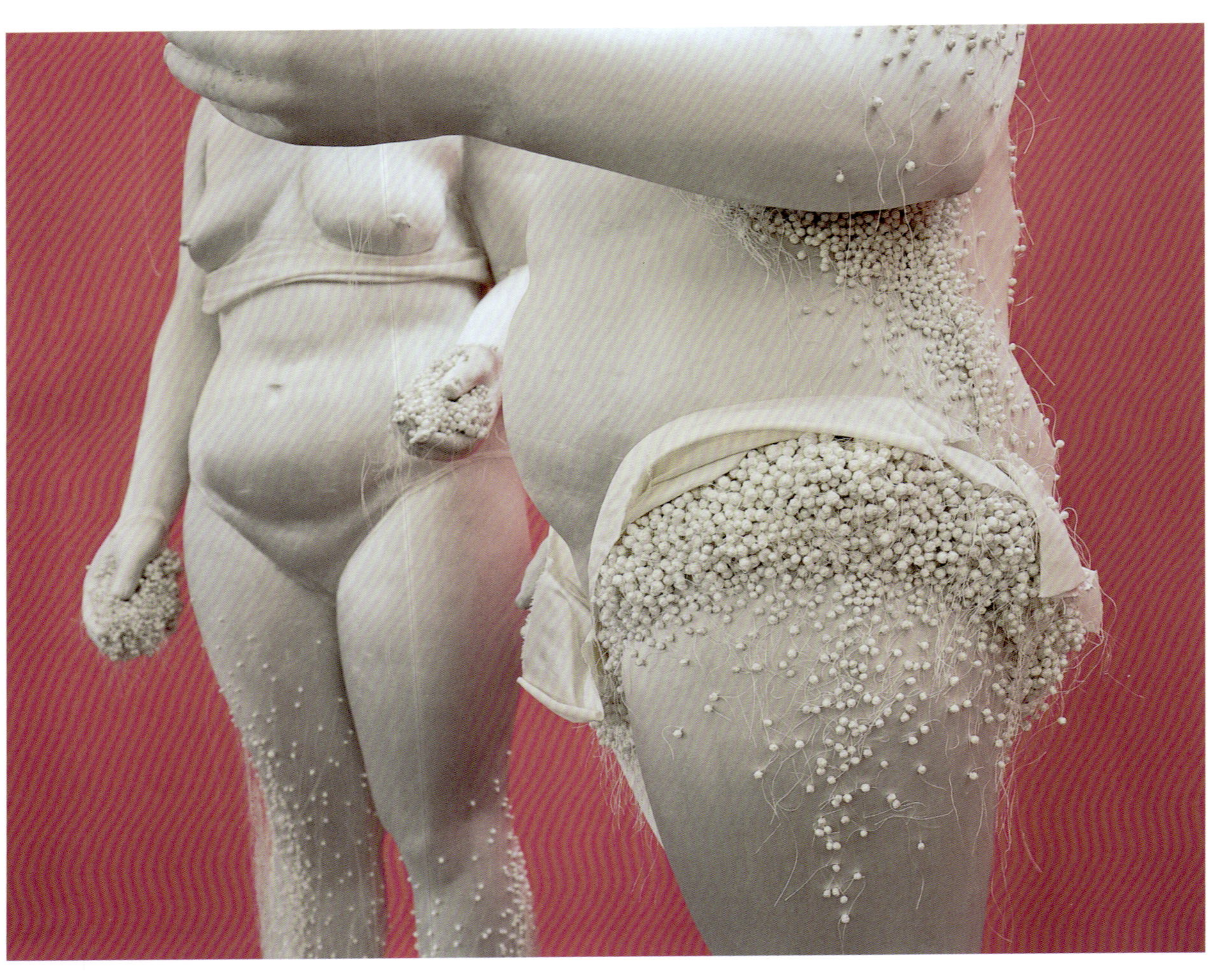

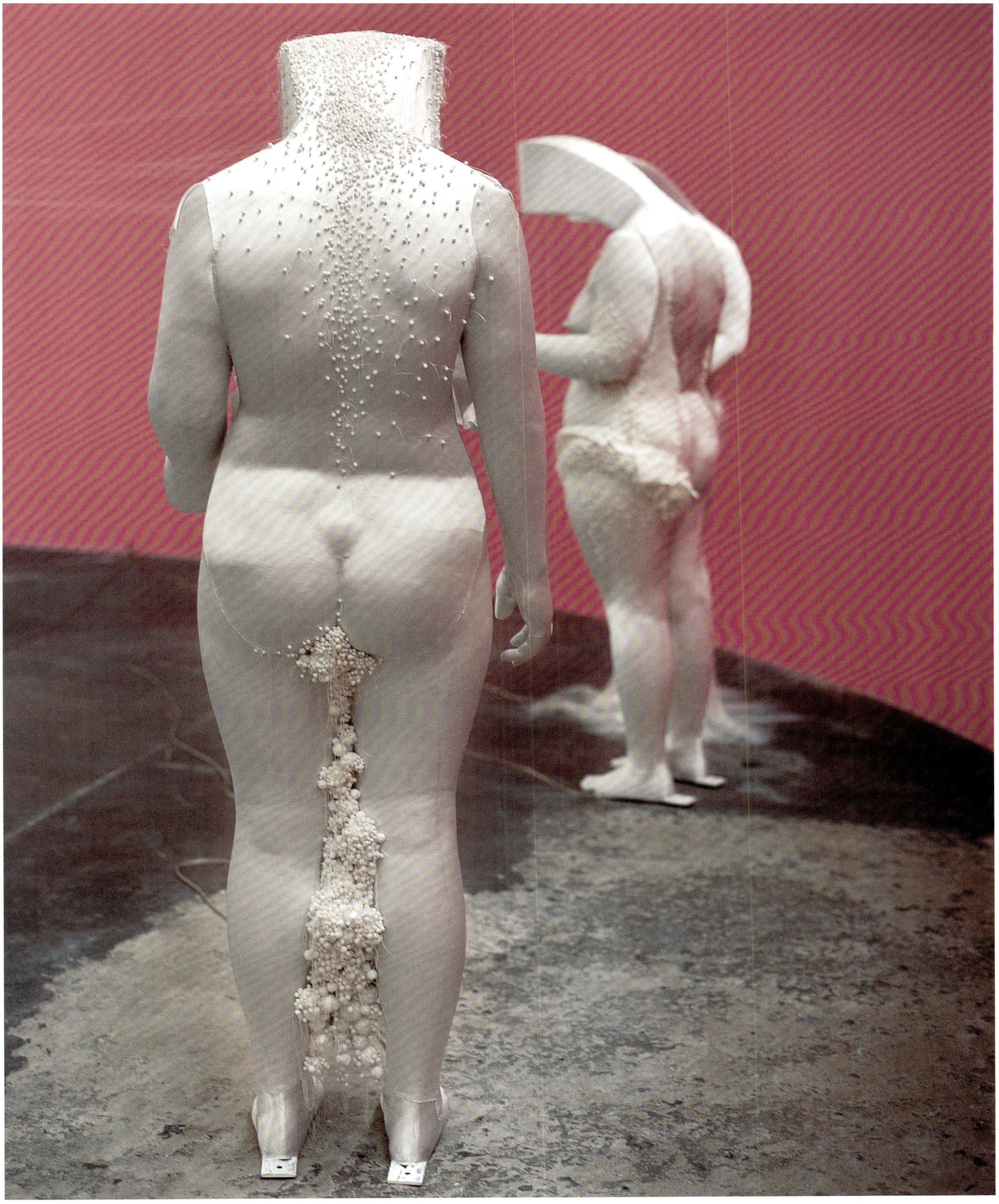

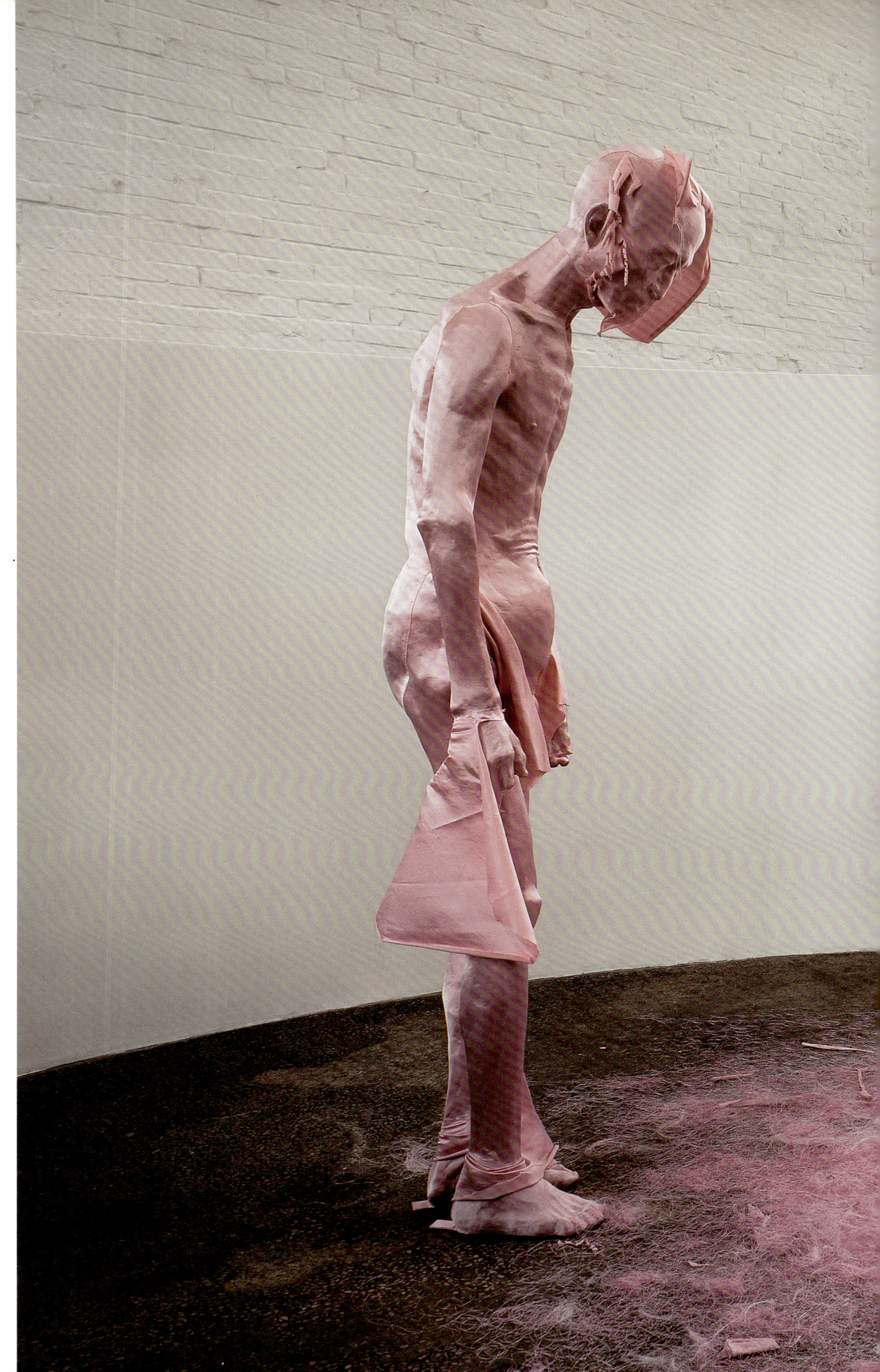

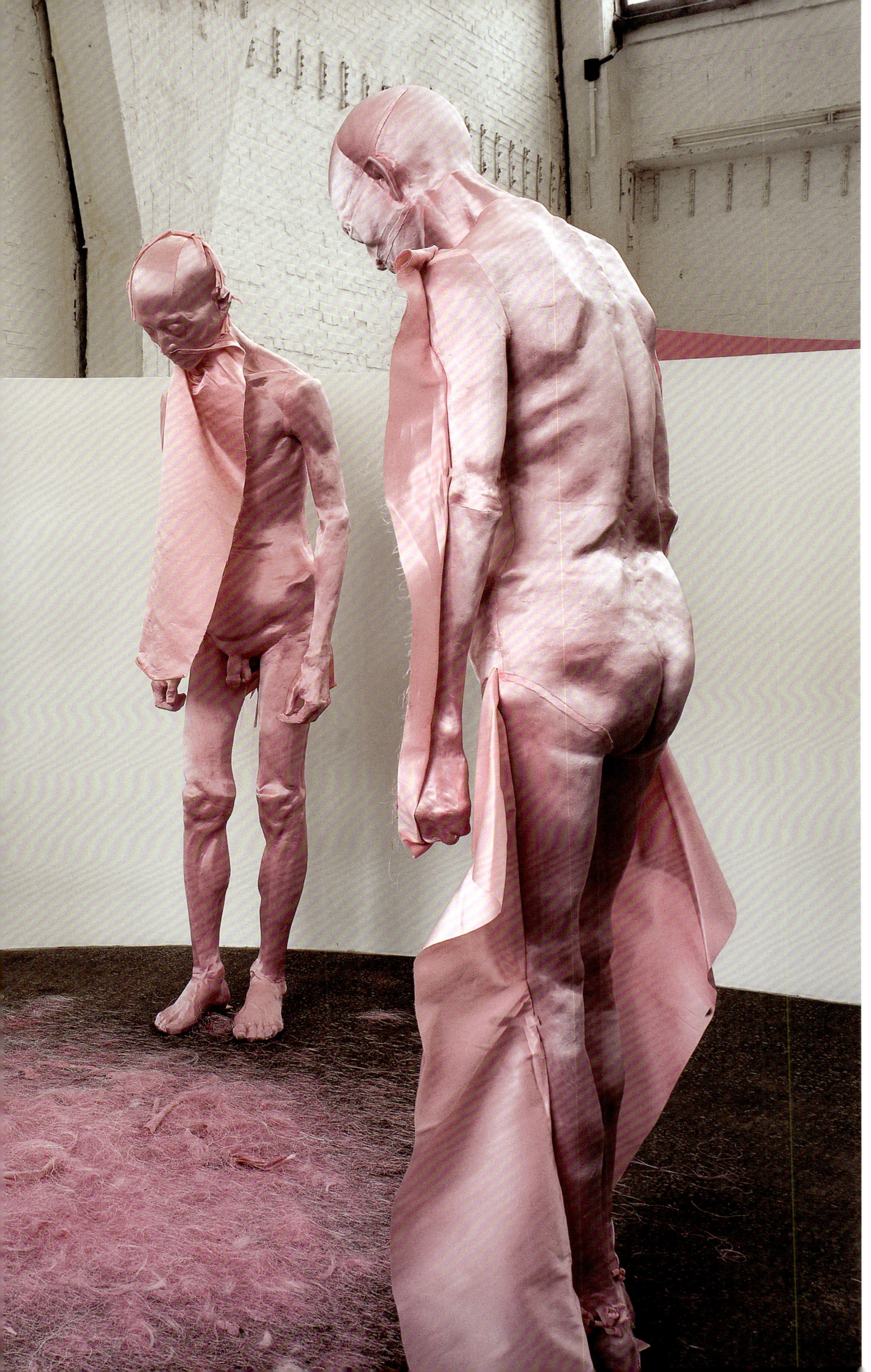

Endless, 2004
Fiberglass, silk, mixed media
Background wall: 55 1/8 x 196 3/4 in. (140 x 500 cm);
set area: Dimensions variable
"Non Zero," Beijing Tokyo Art Project,
September 18–October 3, 2004
(from page 66)

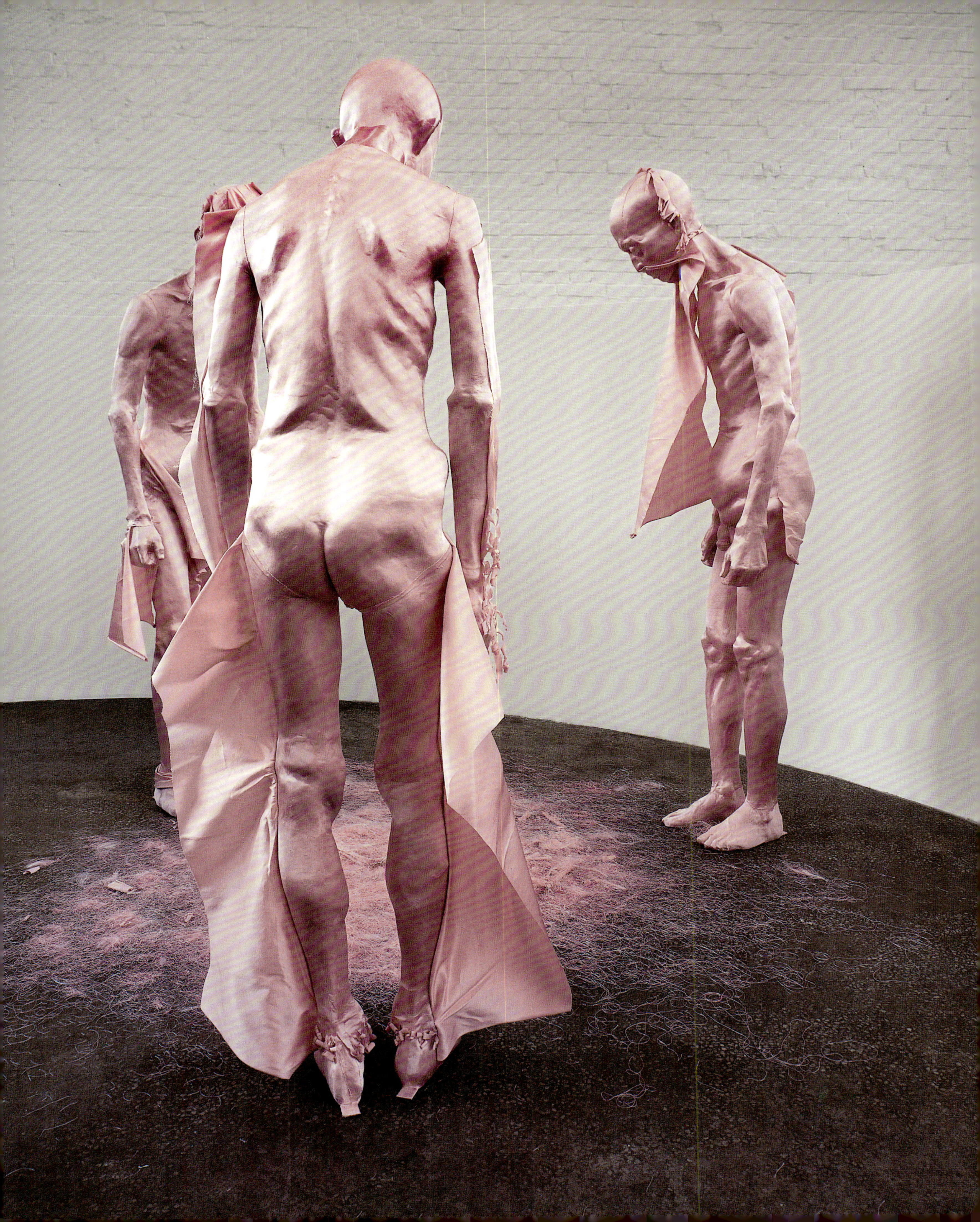

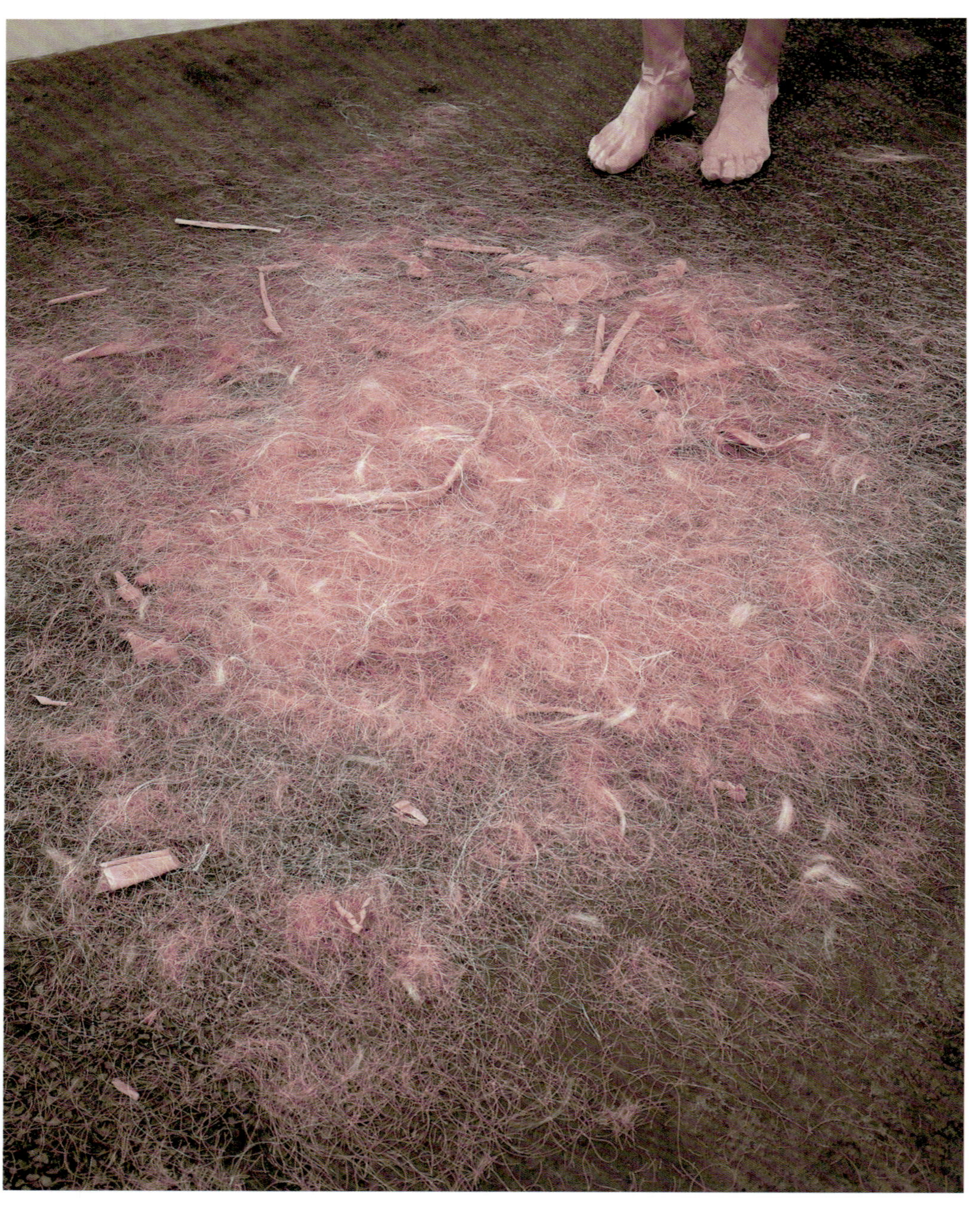

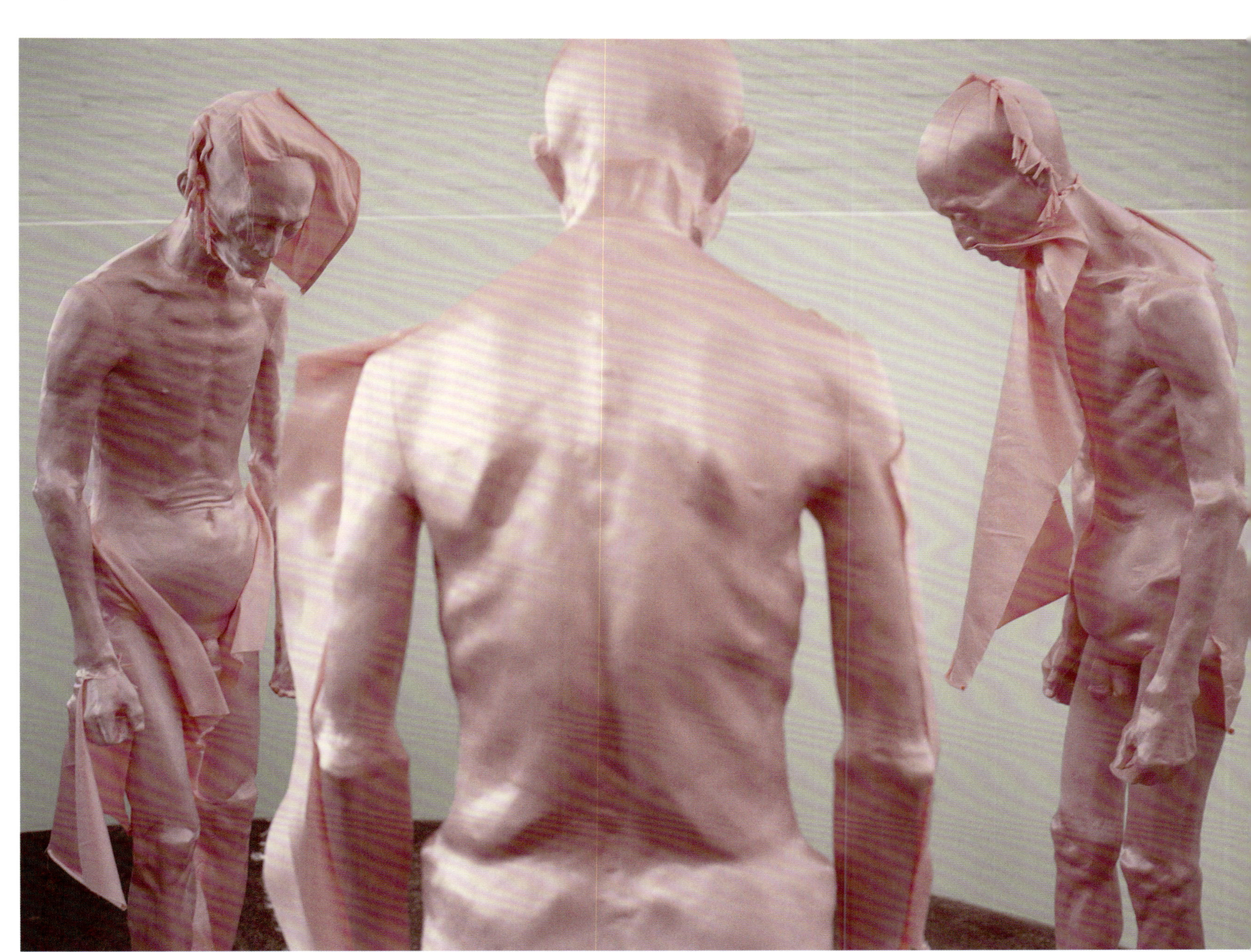

Untitled No. 2, 2006
Felt, wig hair piece
Approximately 78 ¾ x 96 ½ in. (200 x 245 cm)

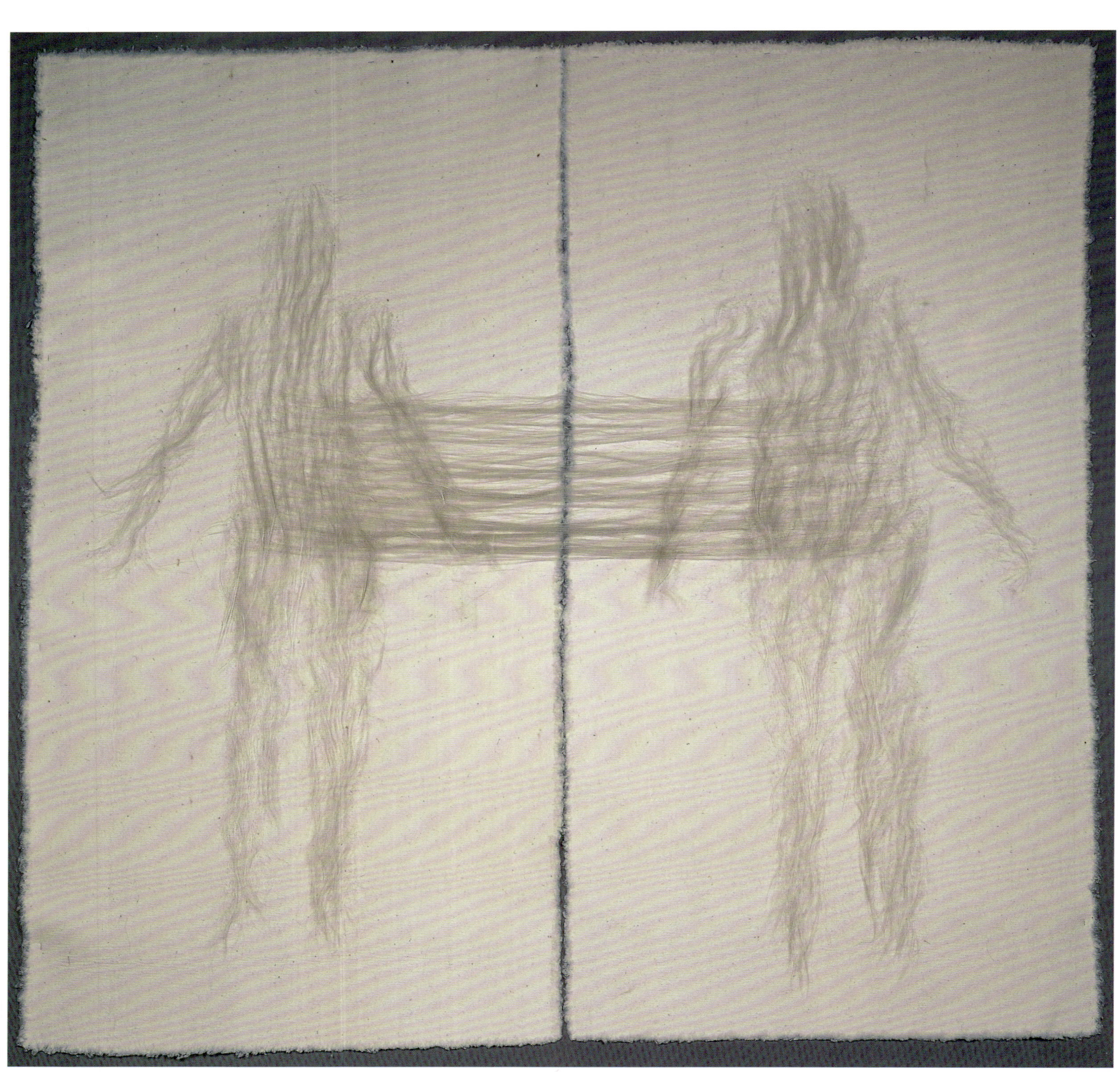

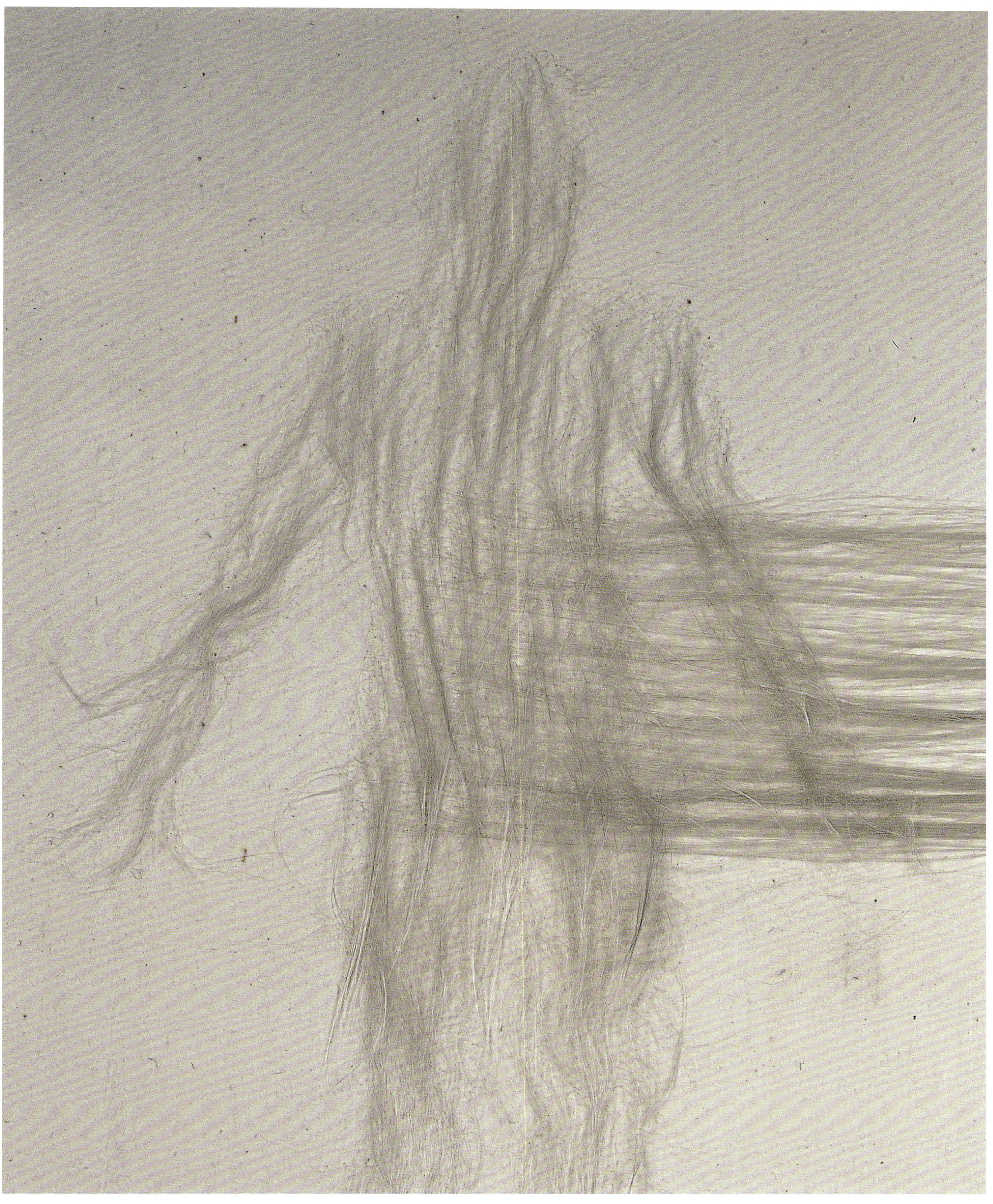

Mother's!!!, 2008
Polyurea, silk, cotton threads, etc.
Dimensions variable
"Mother's!!!," Long March Space,
July 26–August 24, 2008

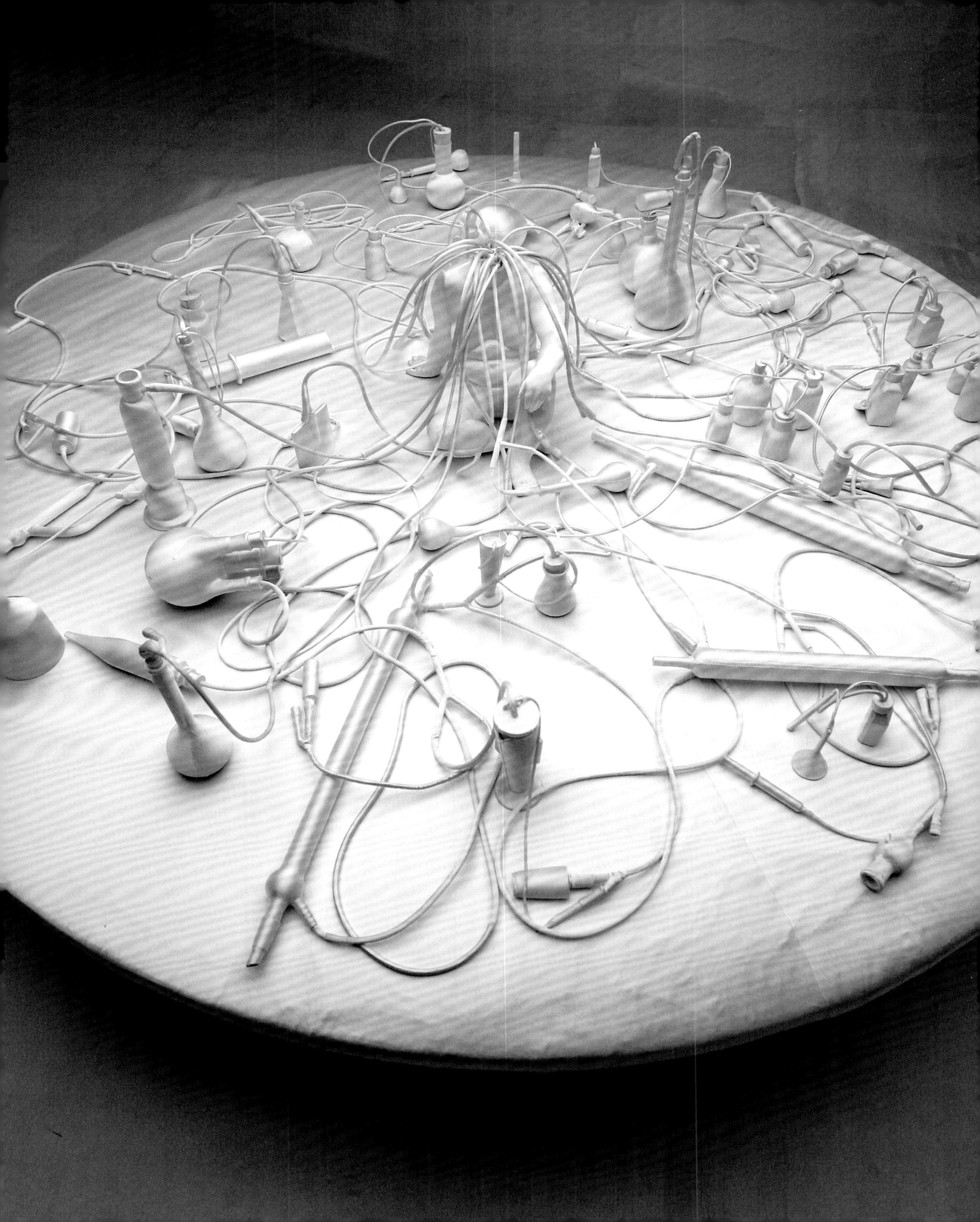

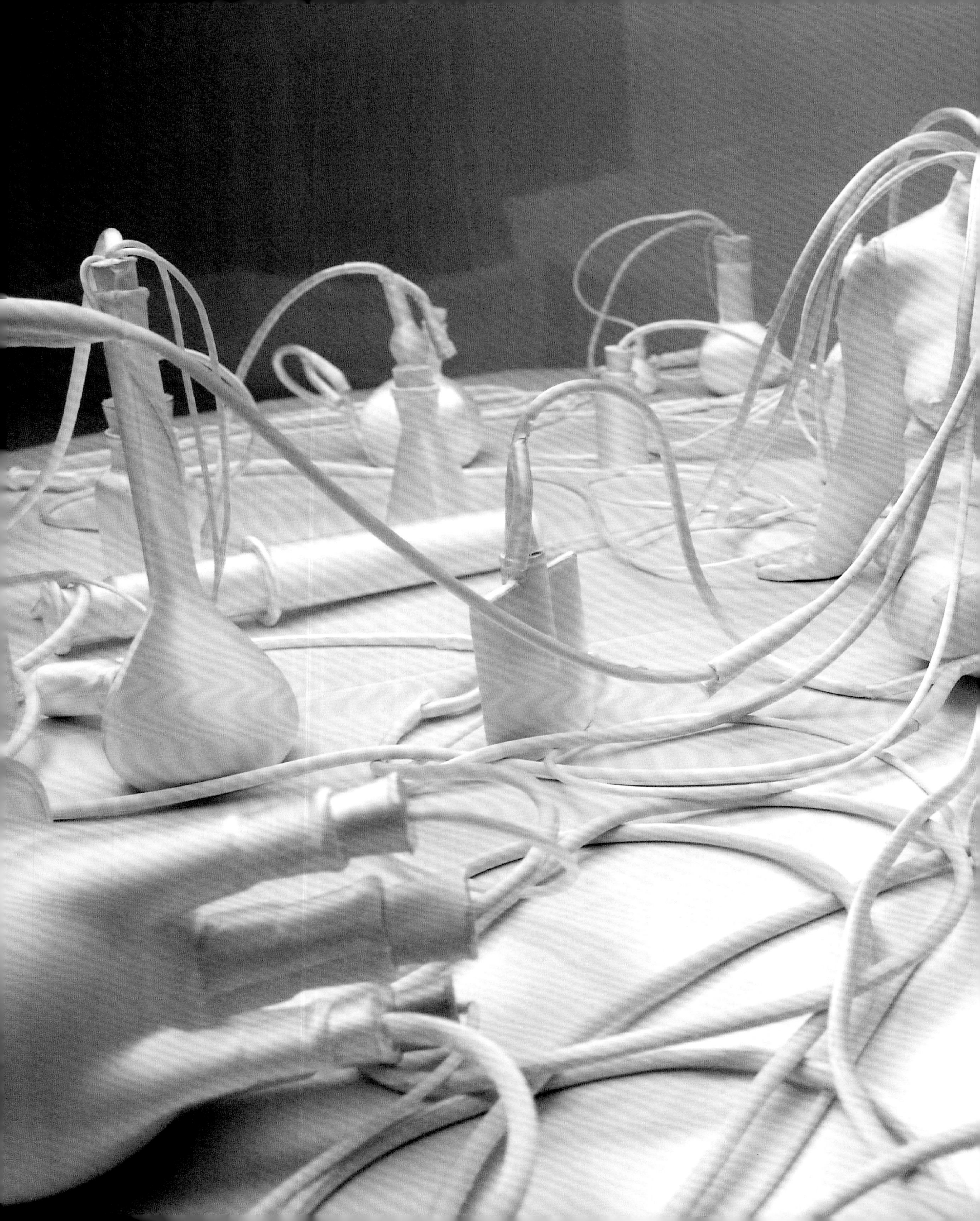

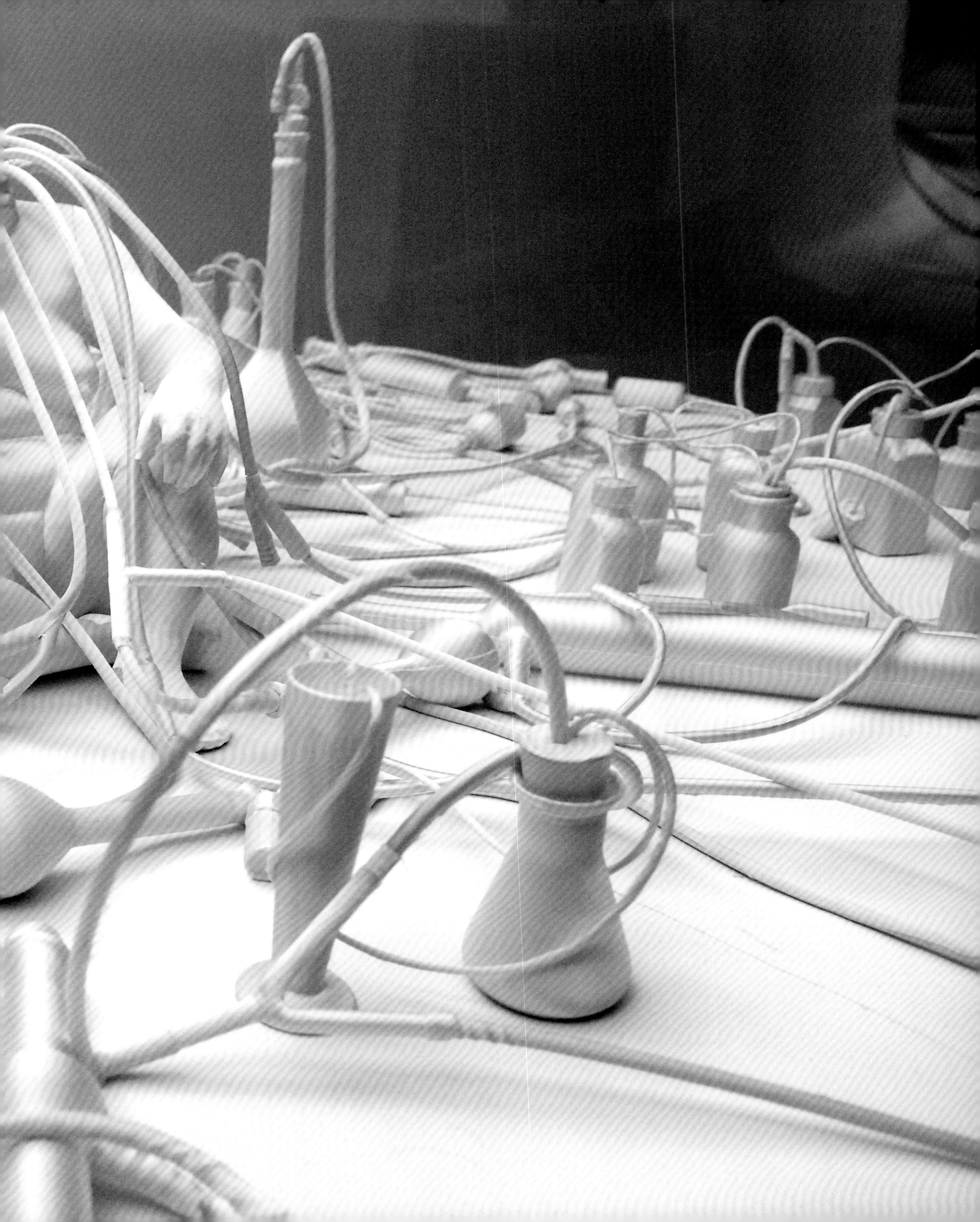

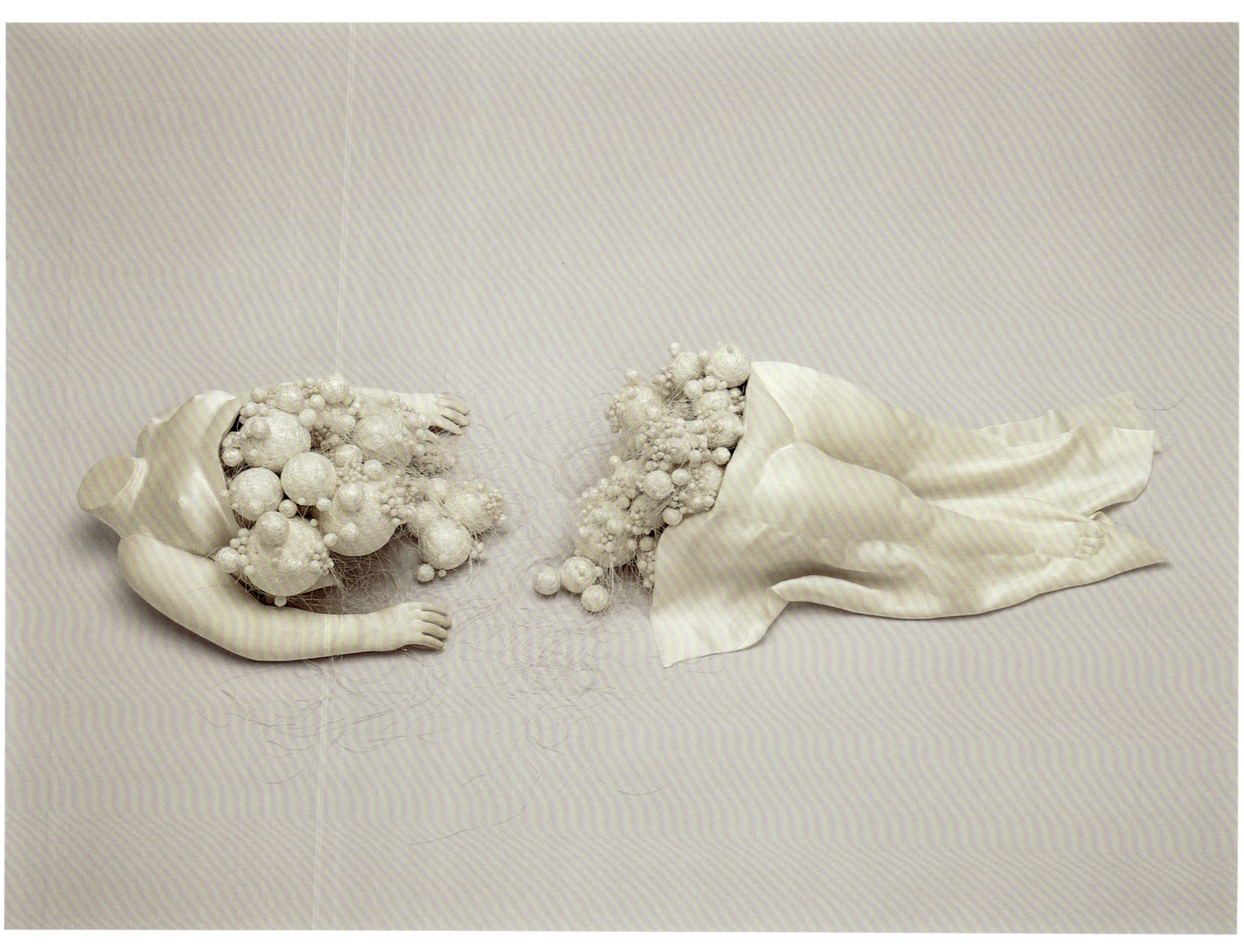

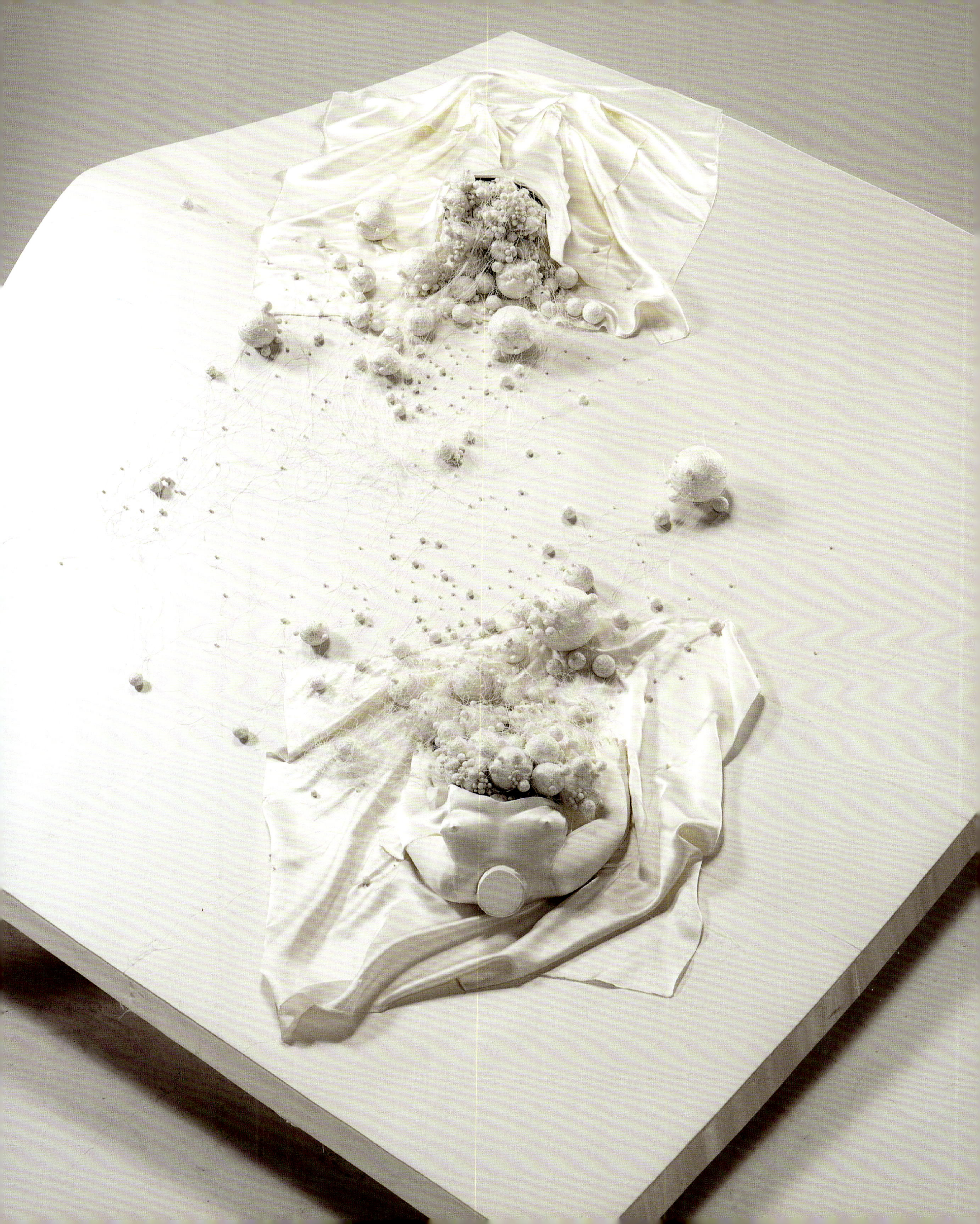

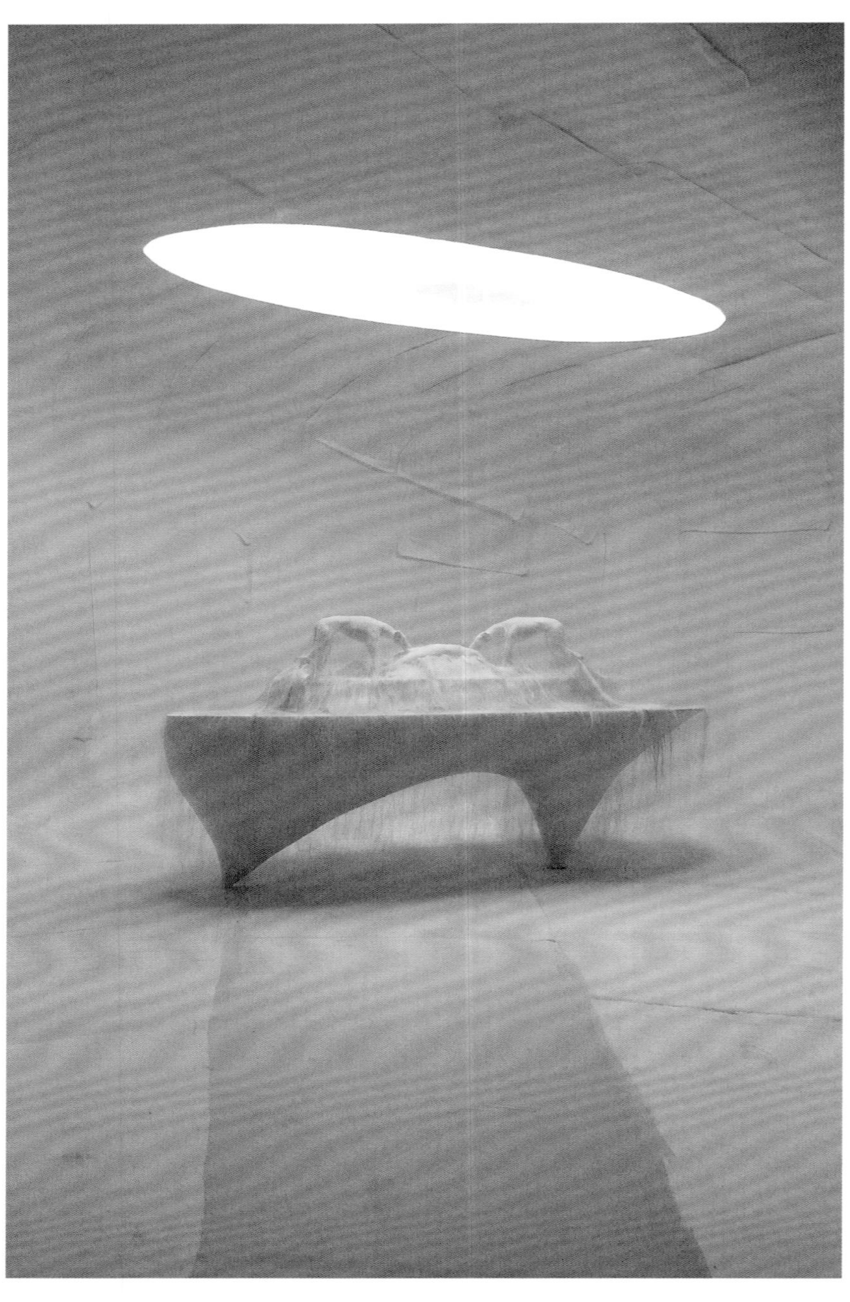

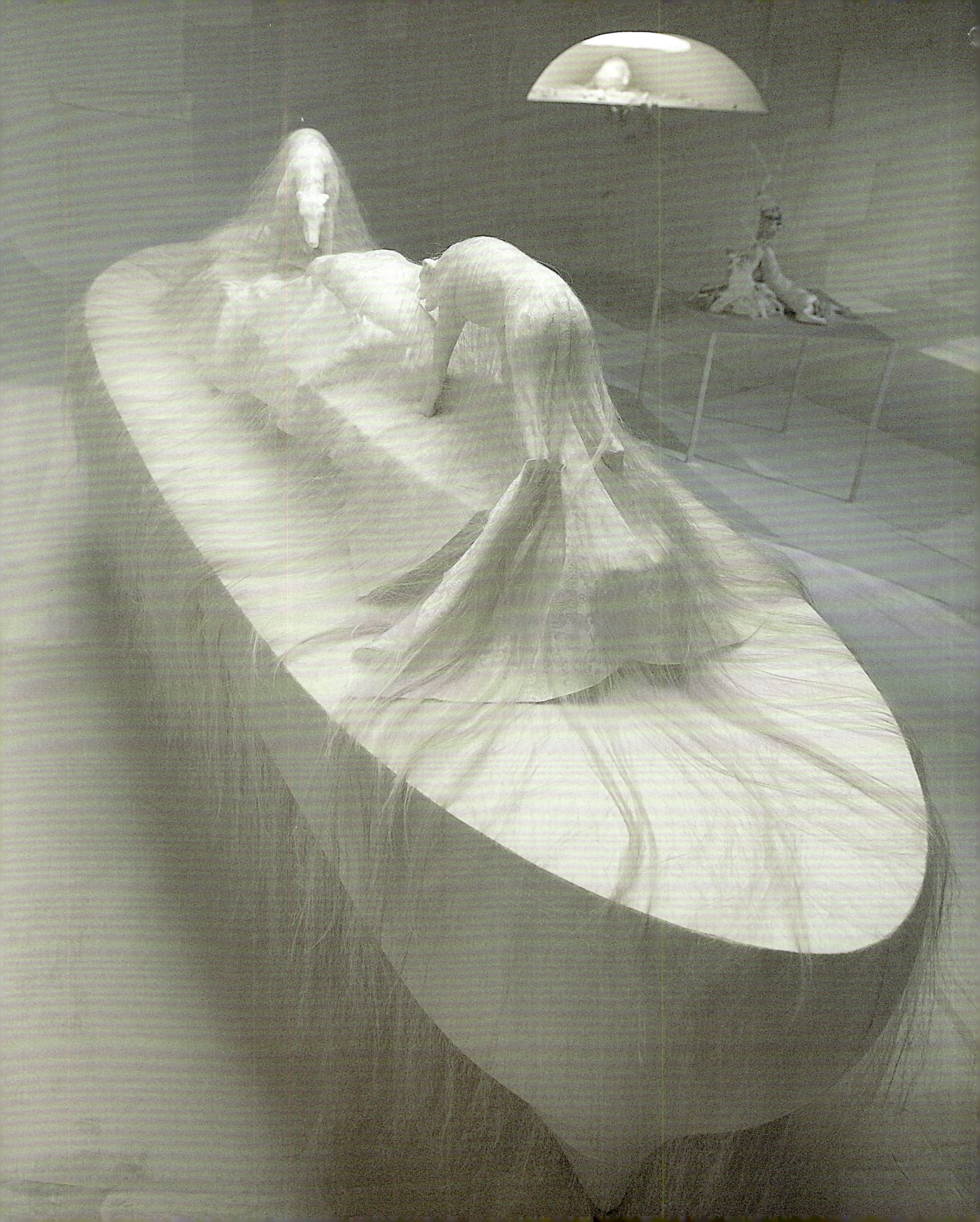

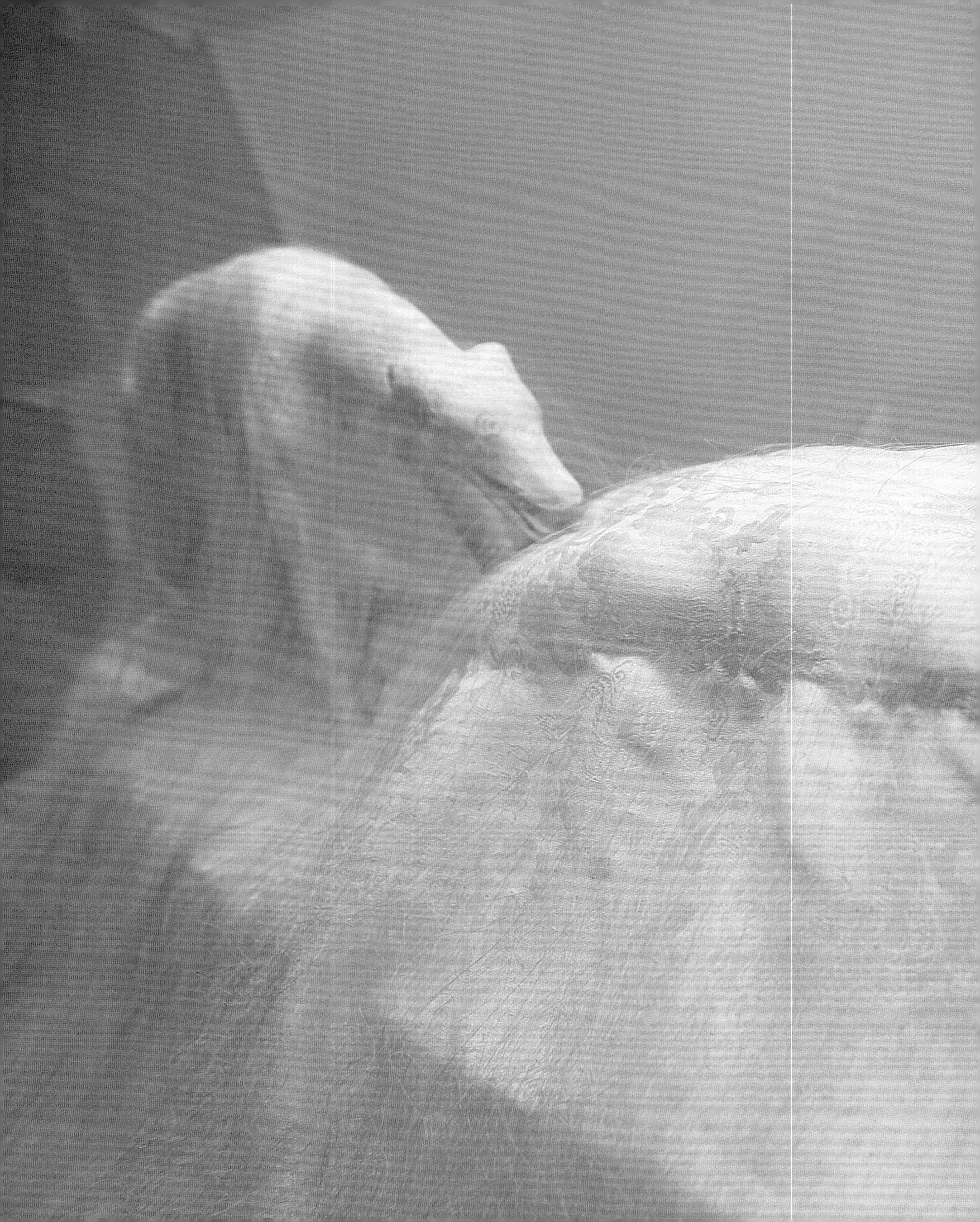

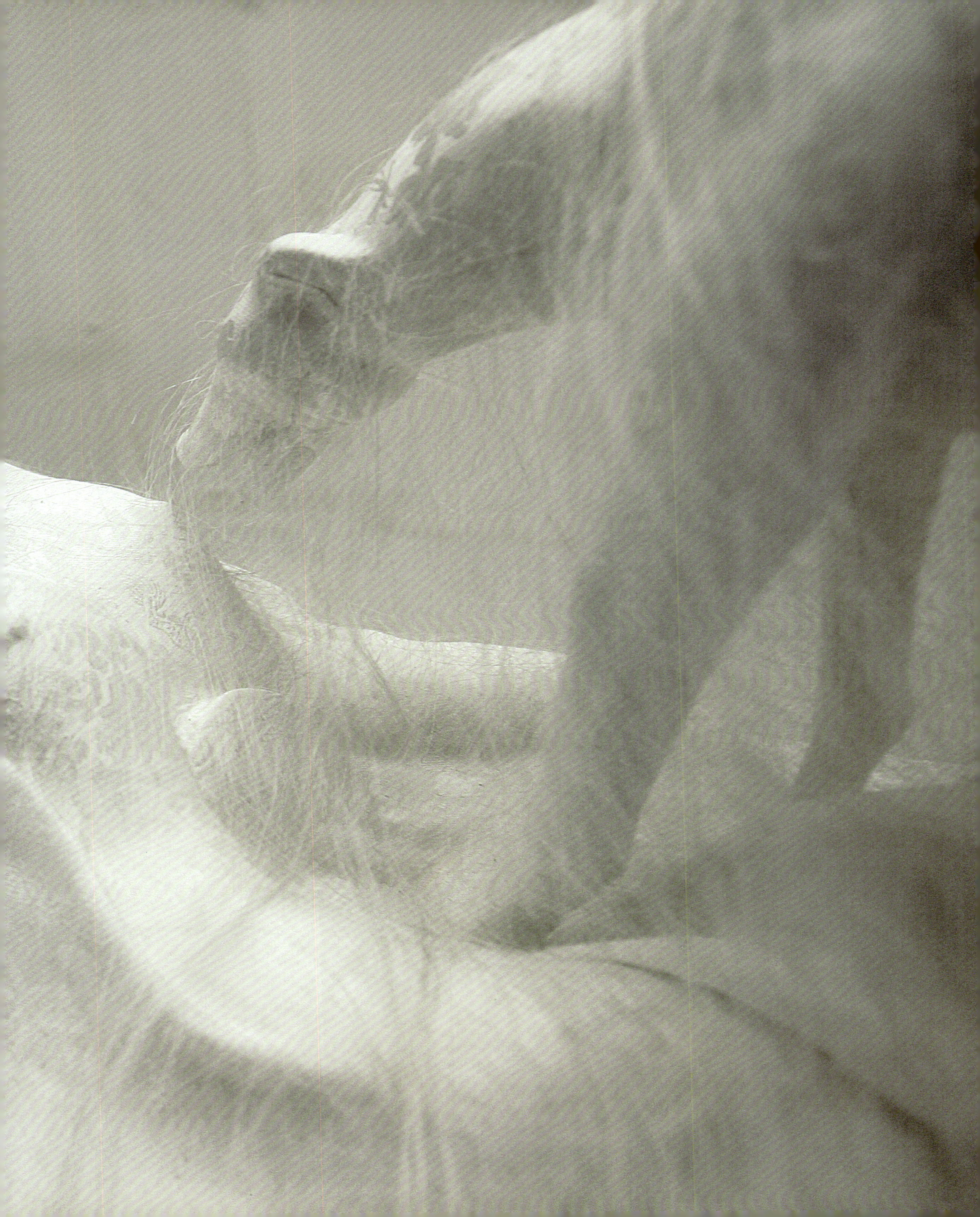

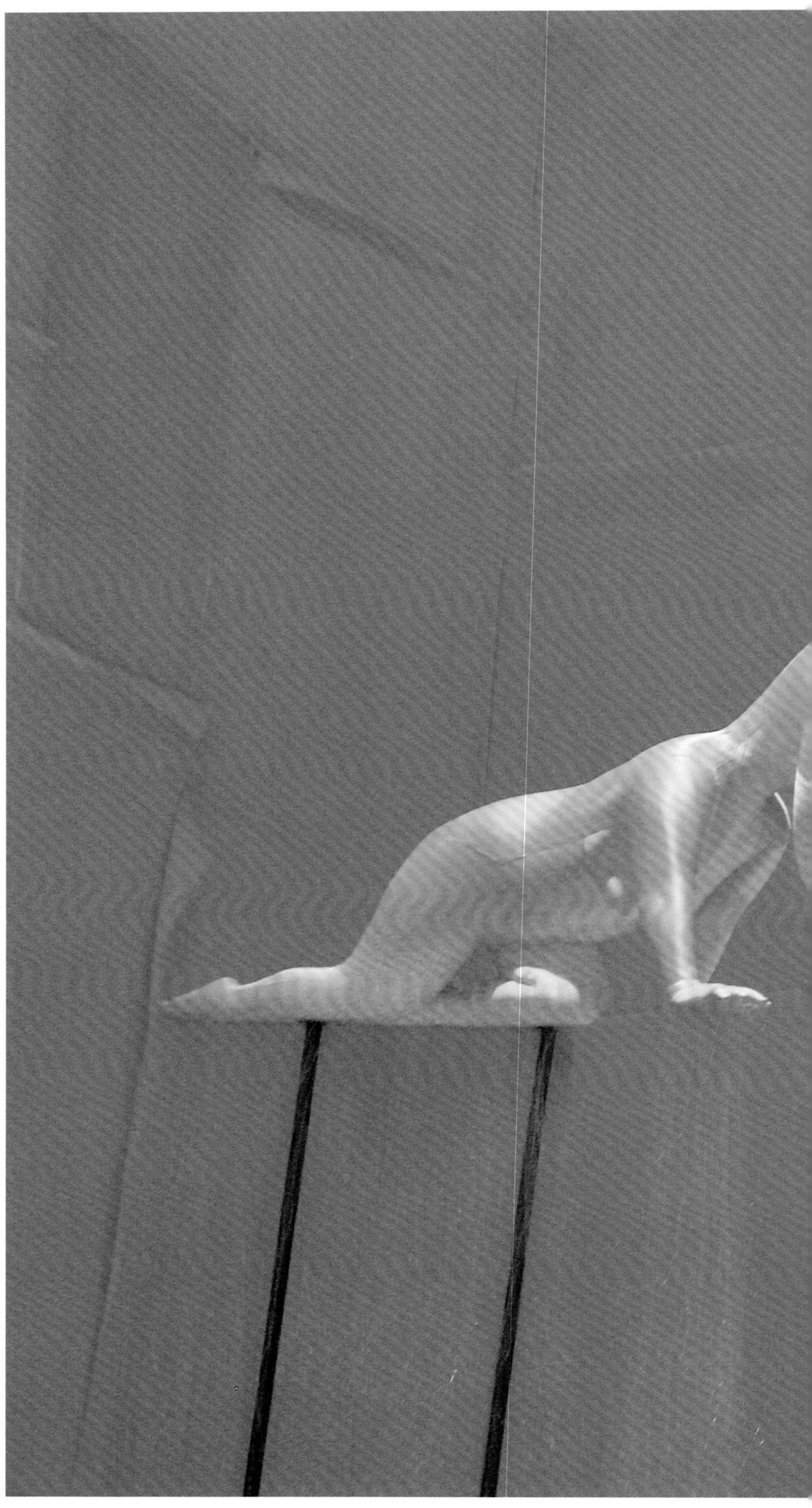

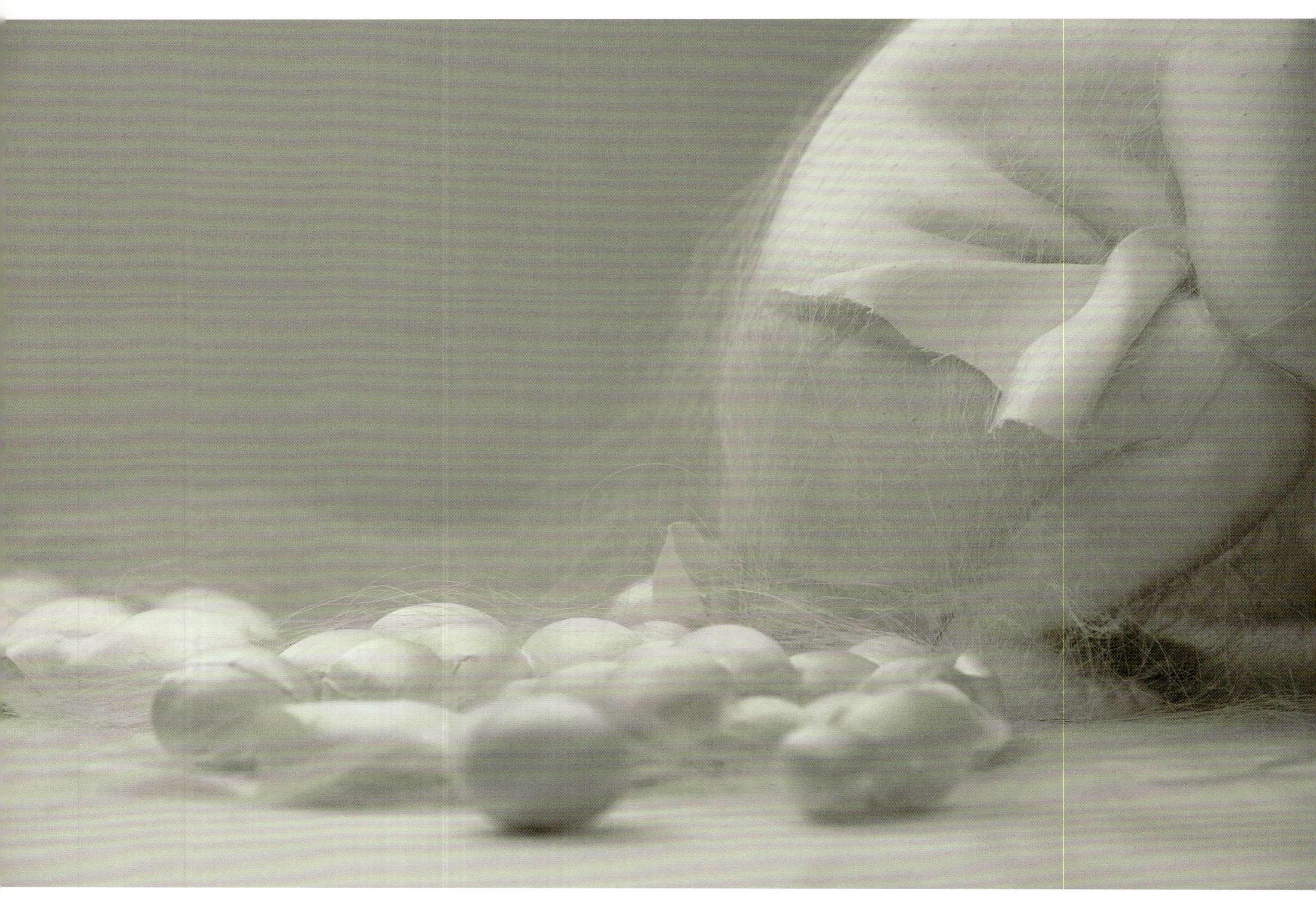

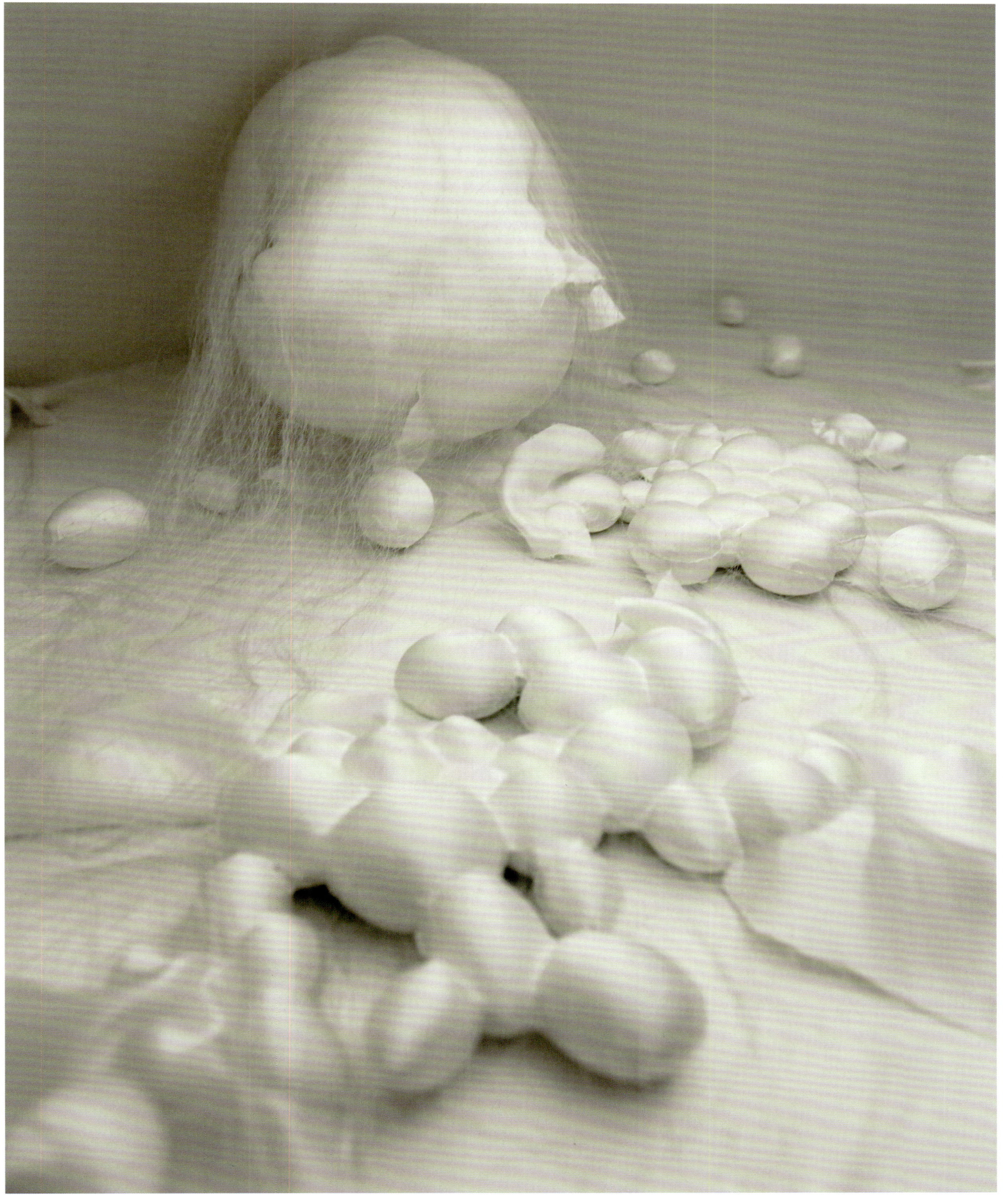

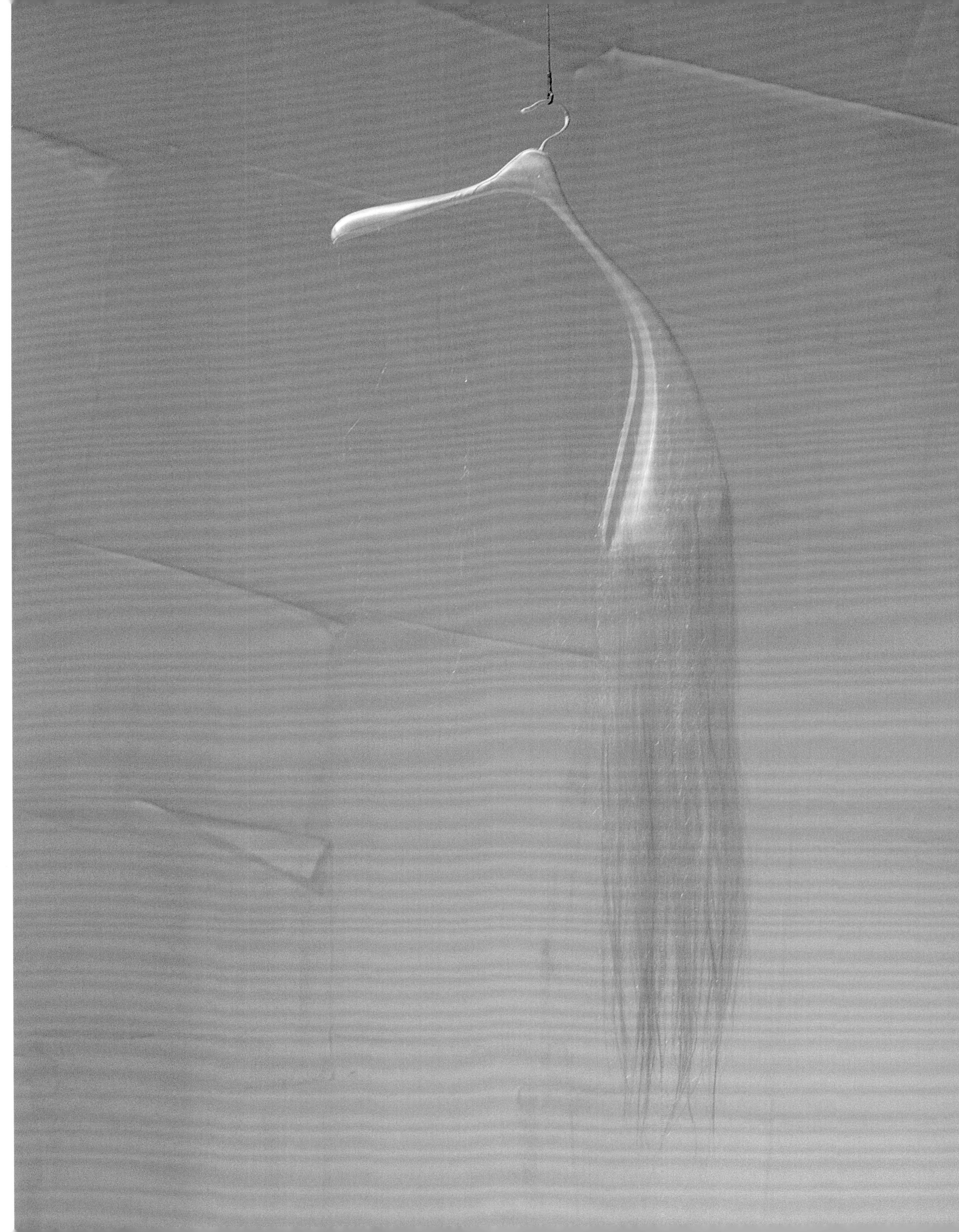

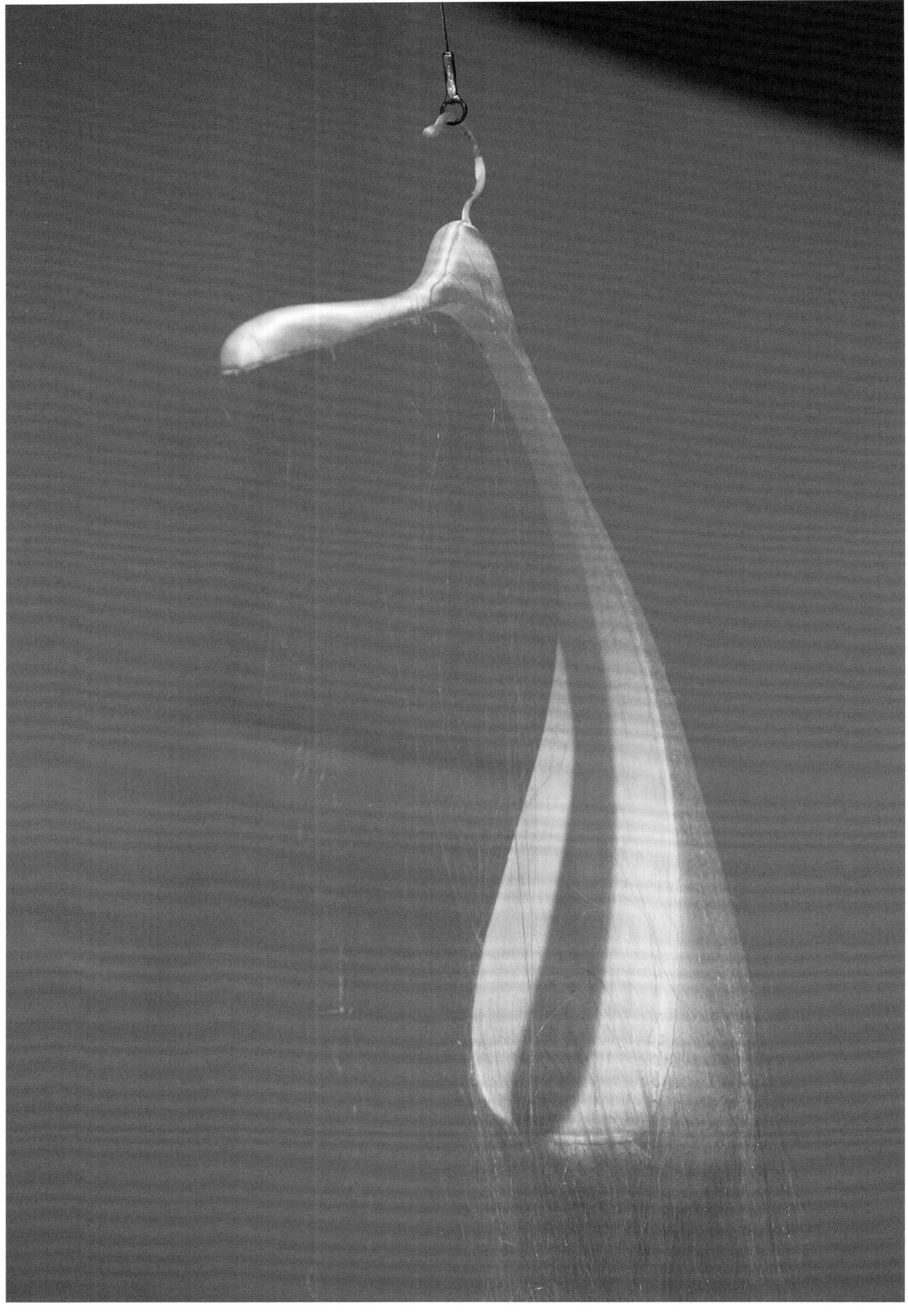

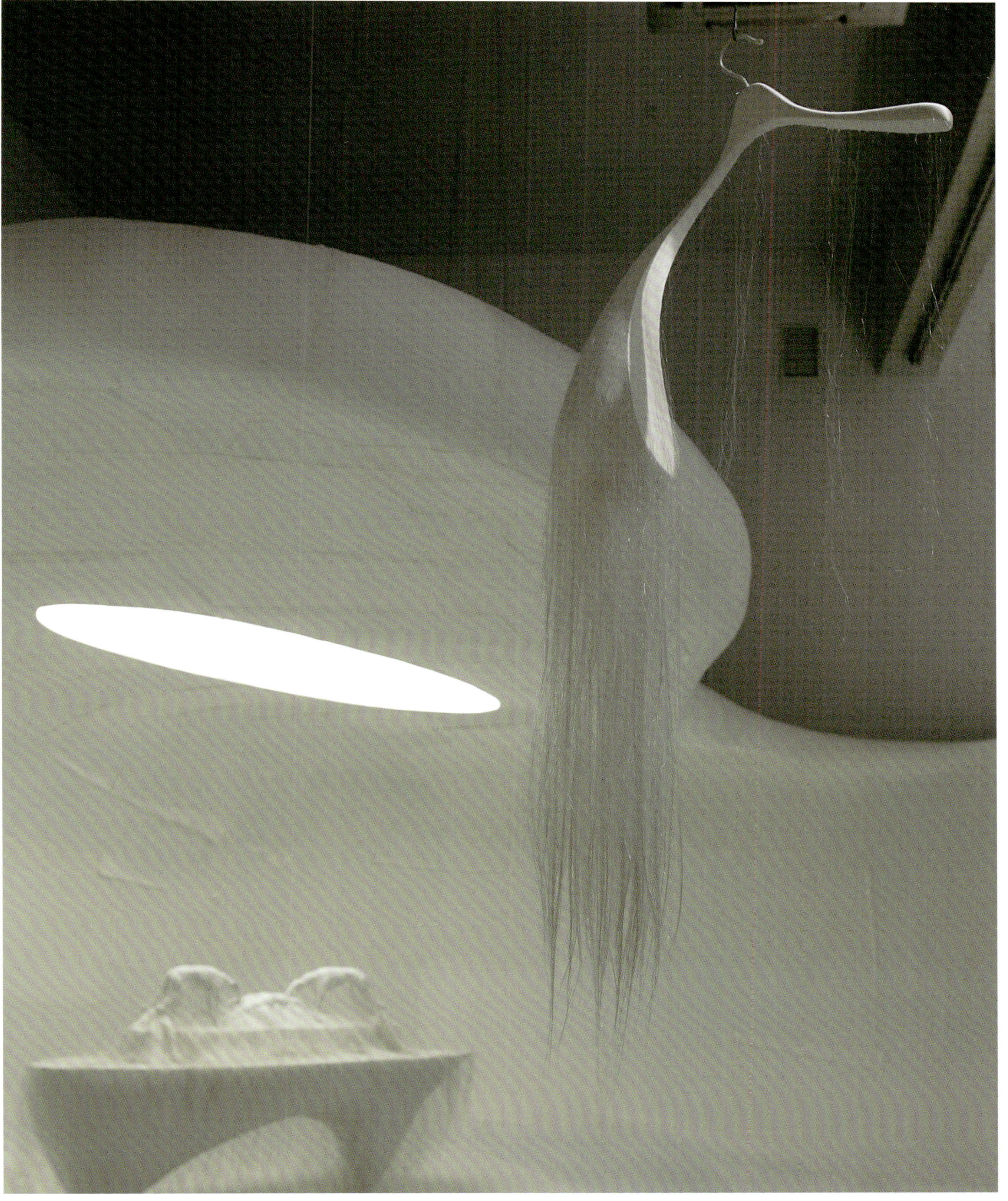

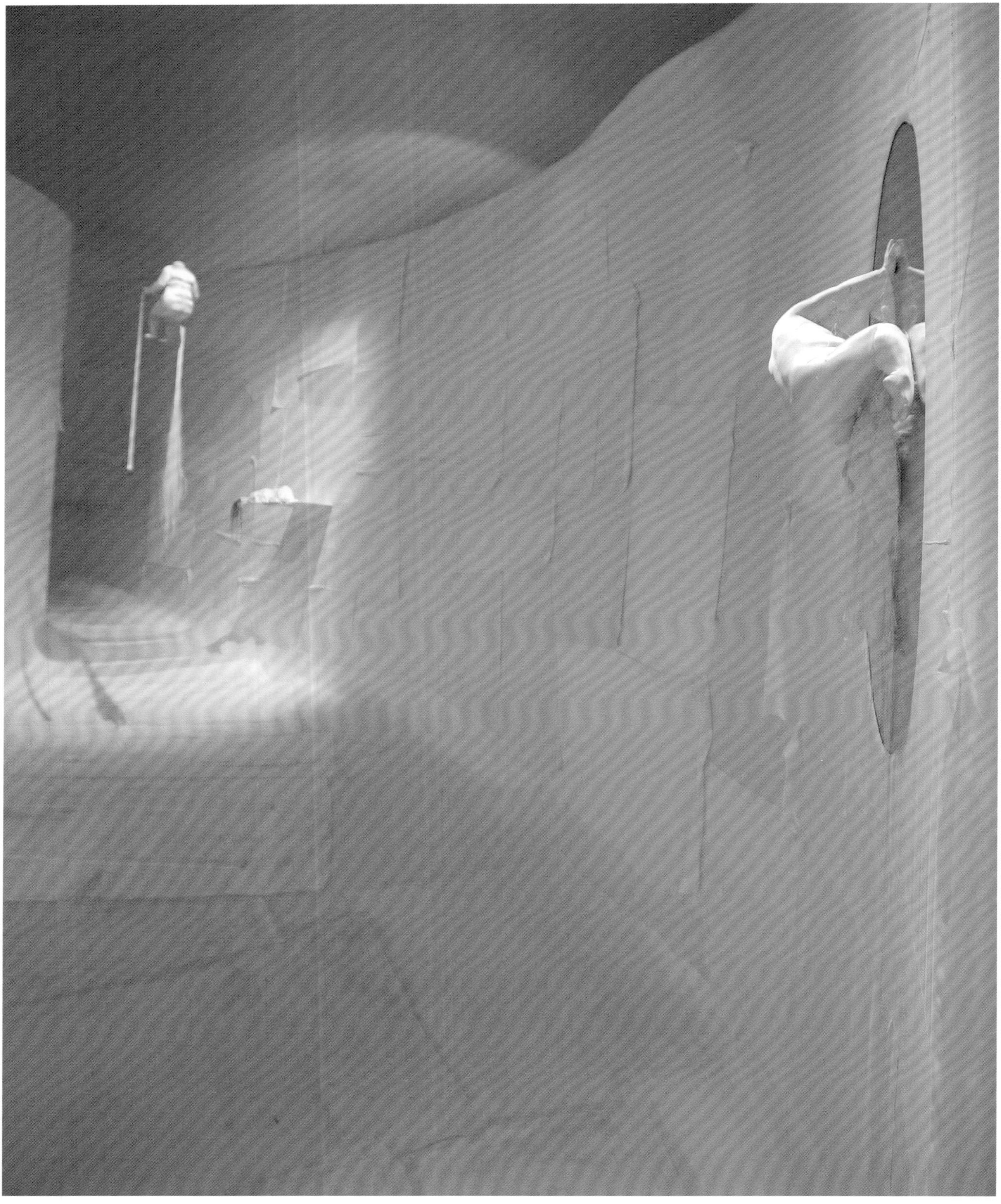

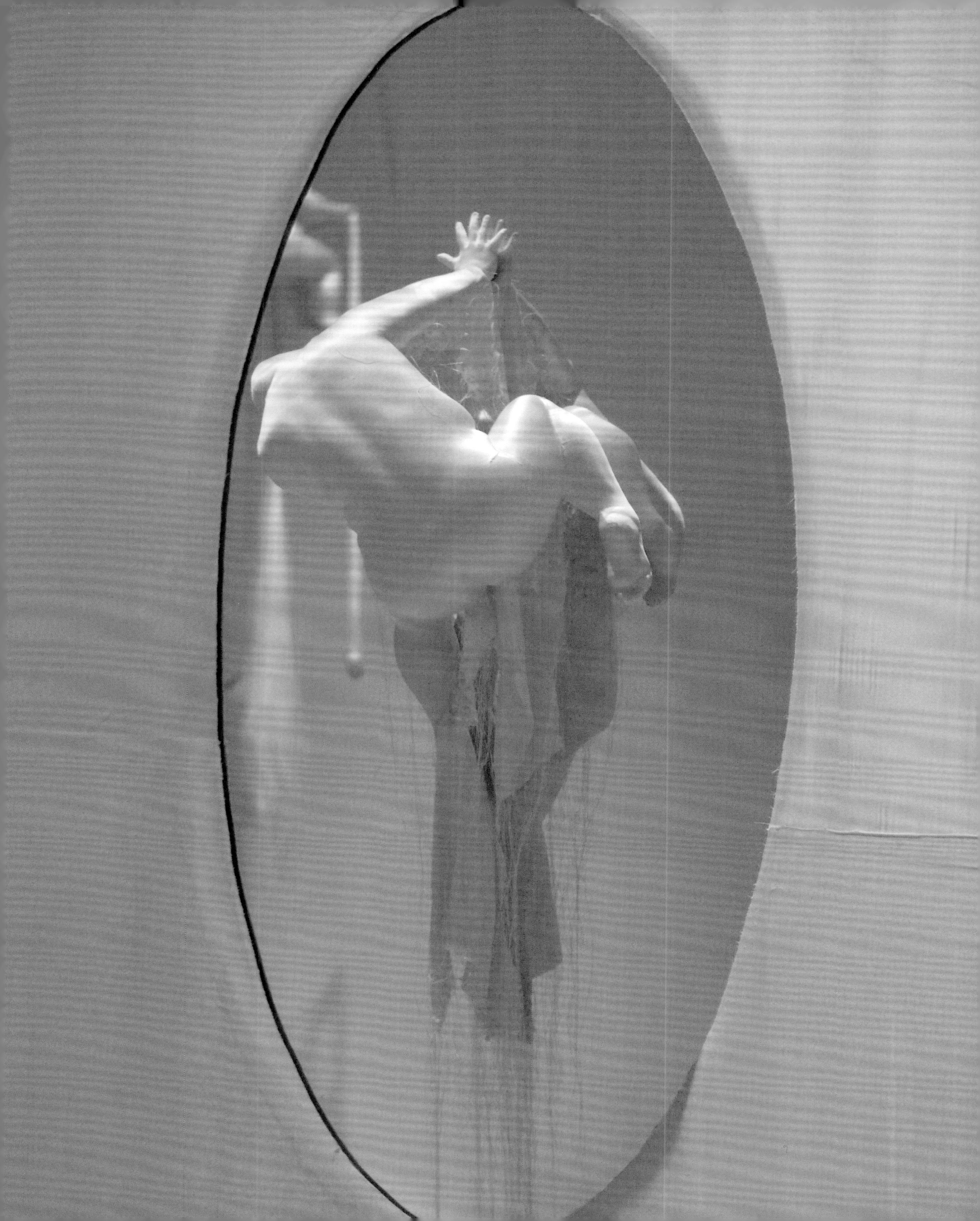

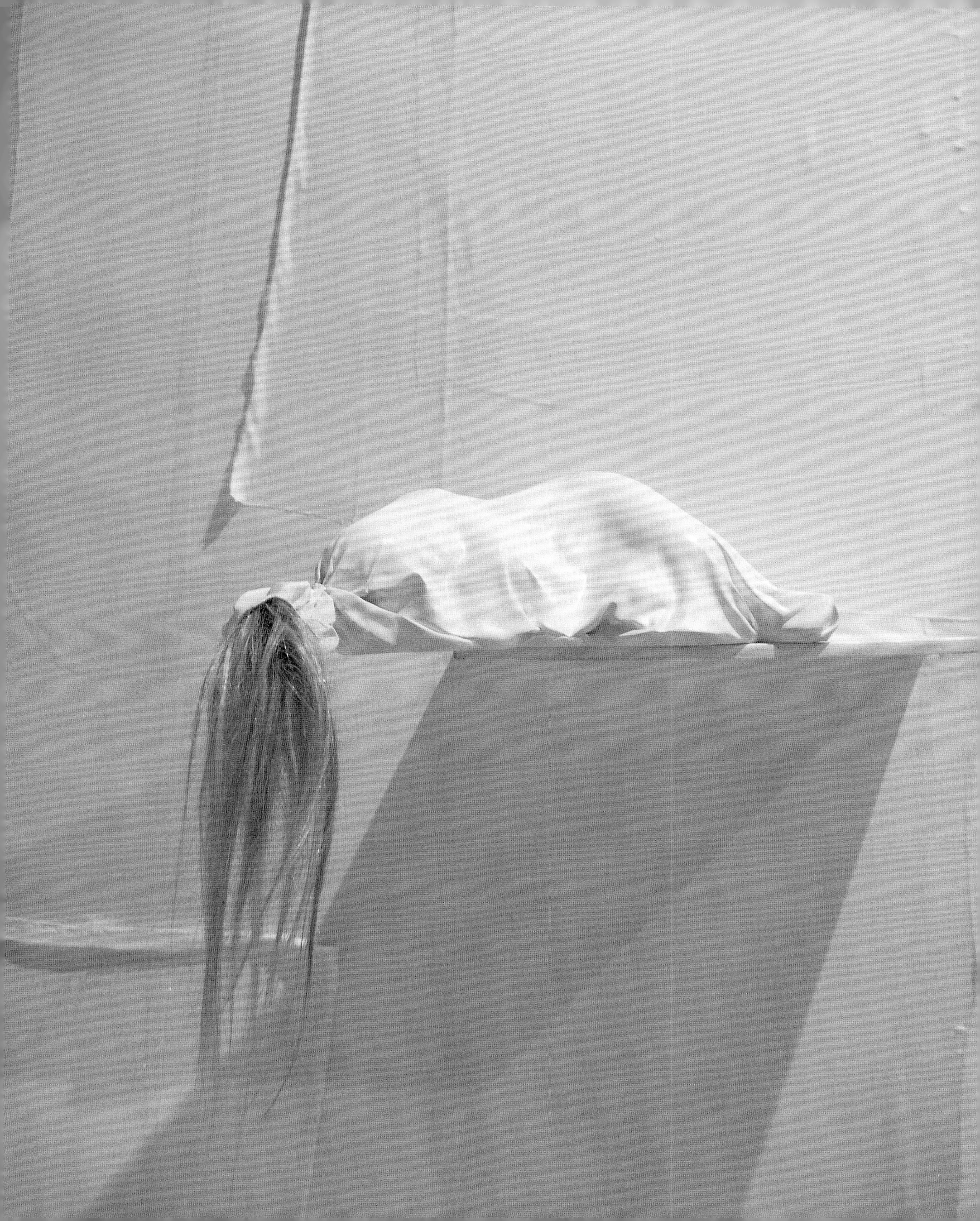

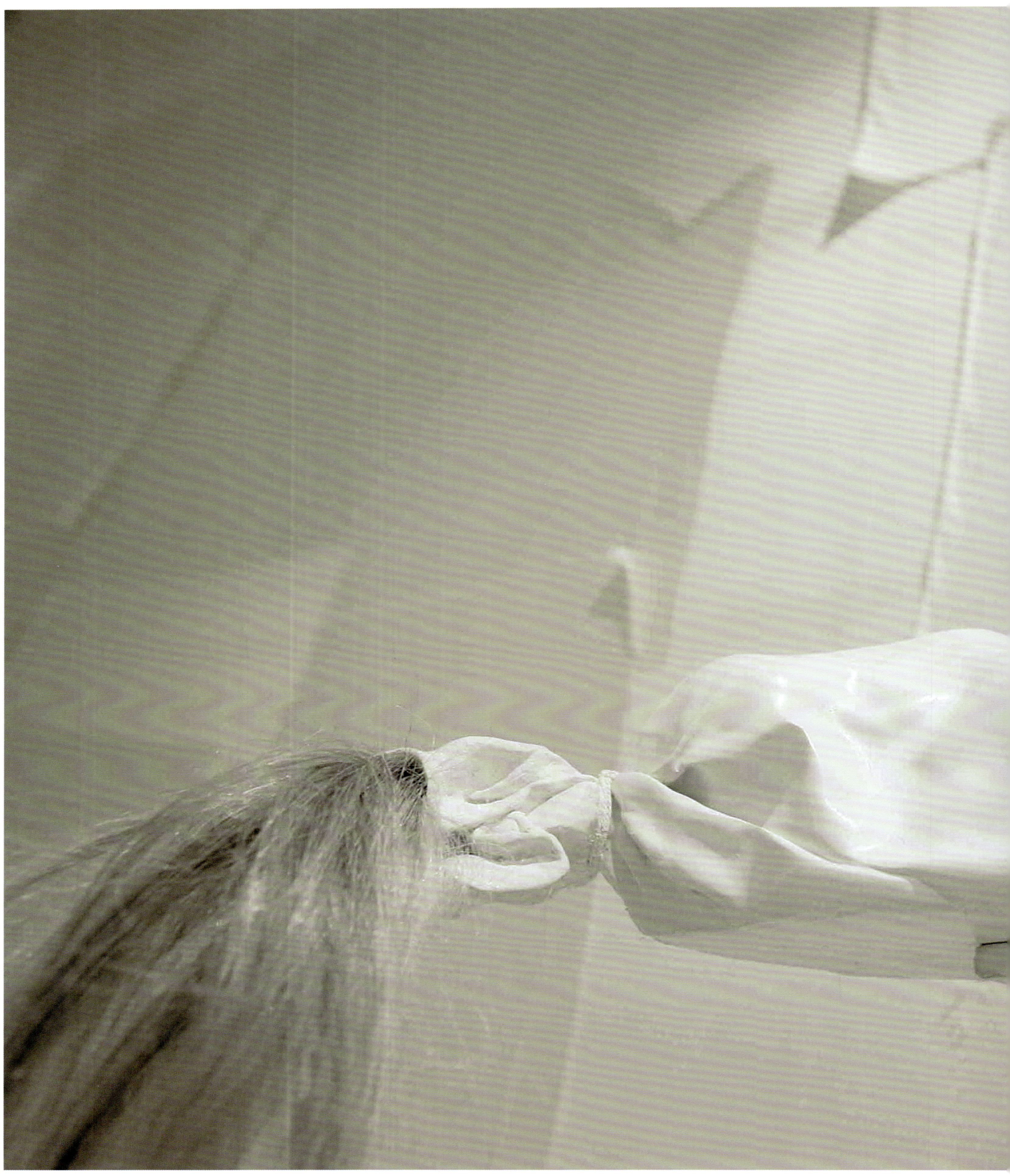

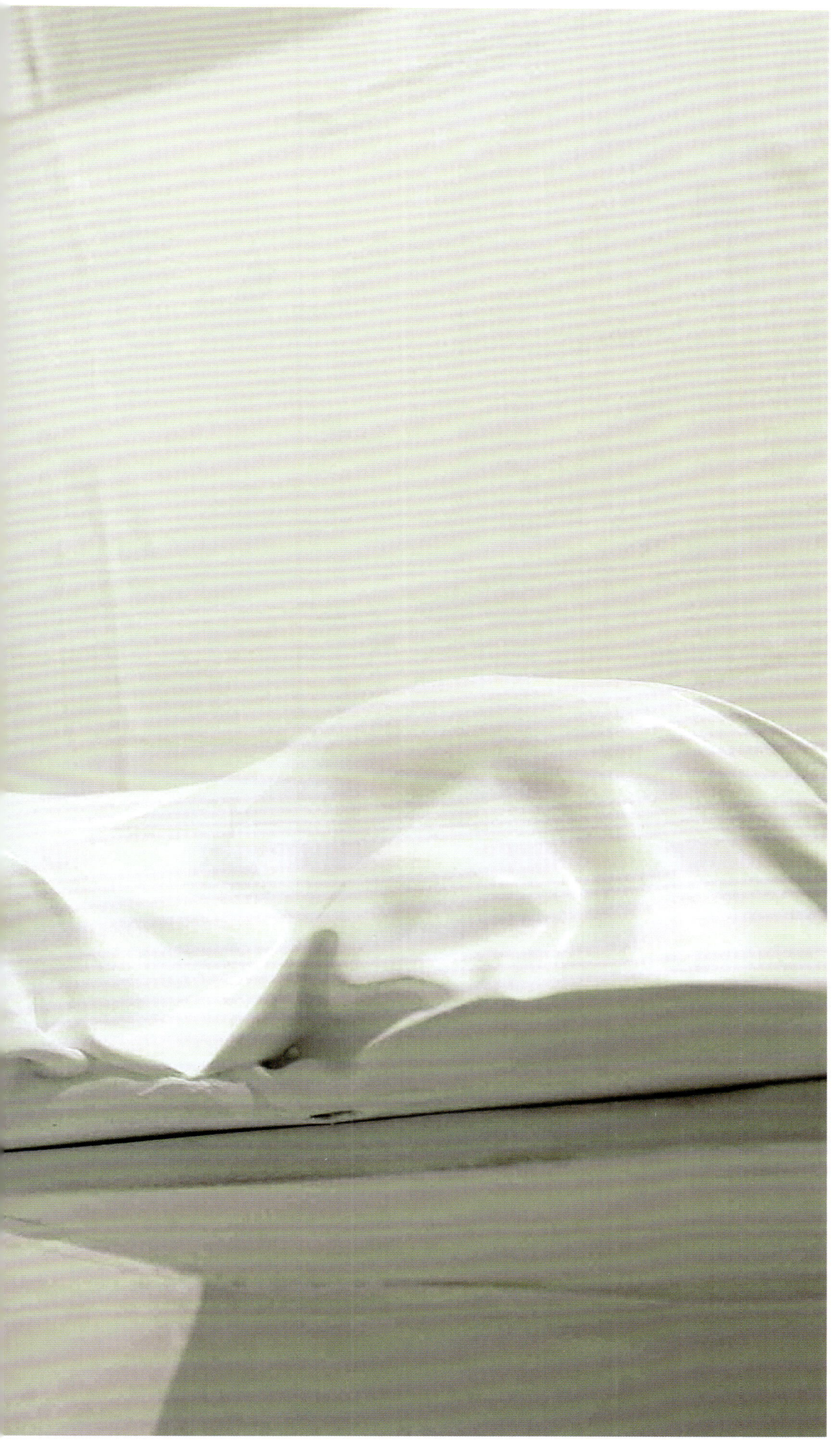

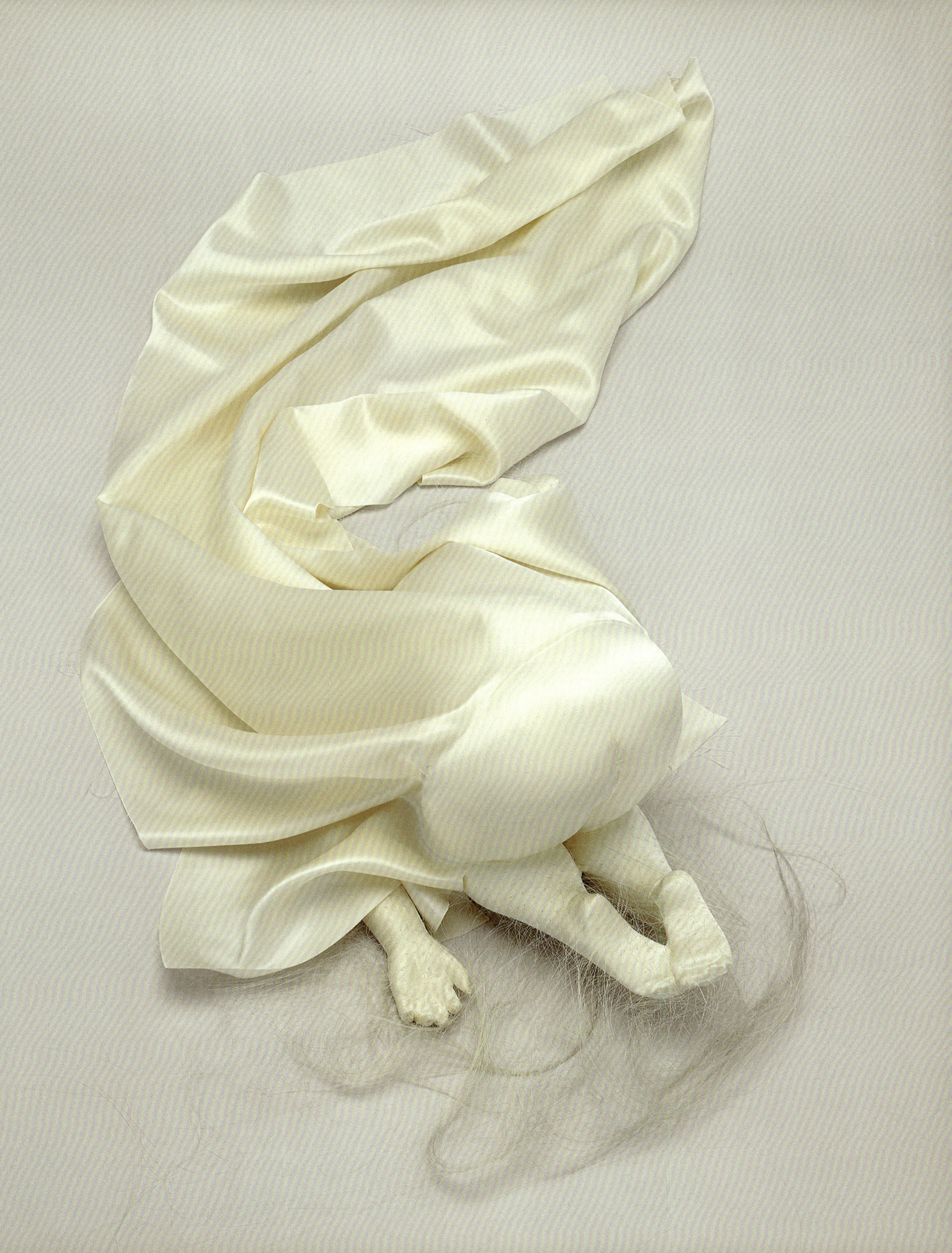

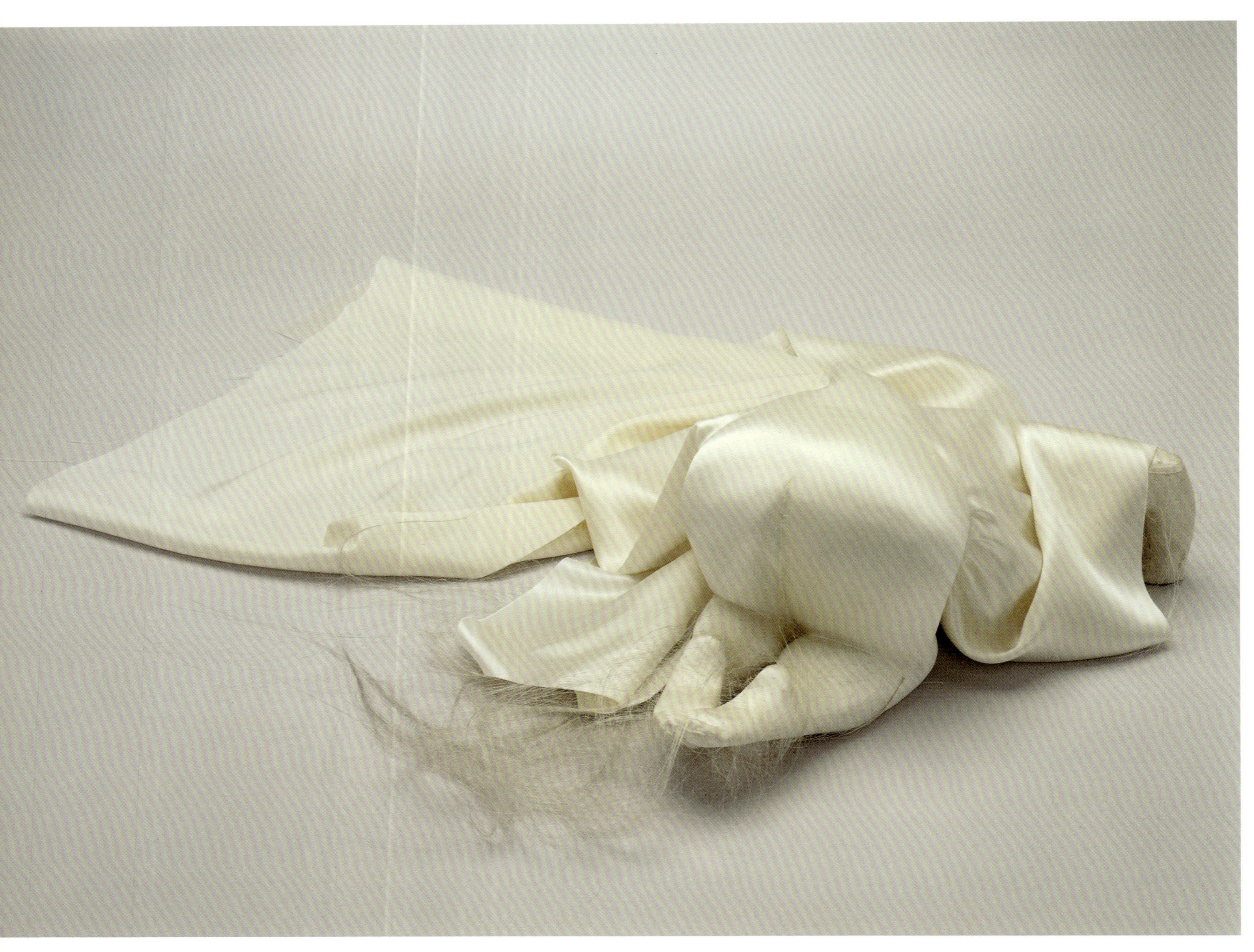

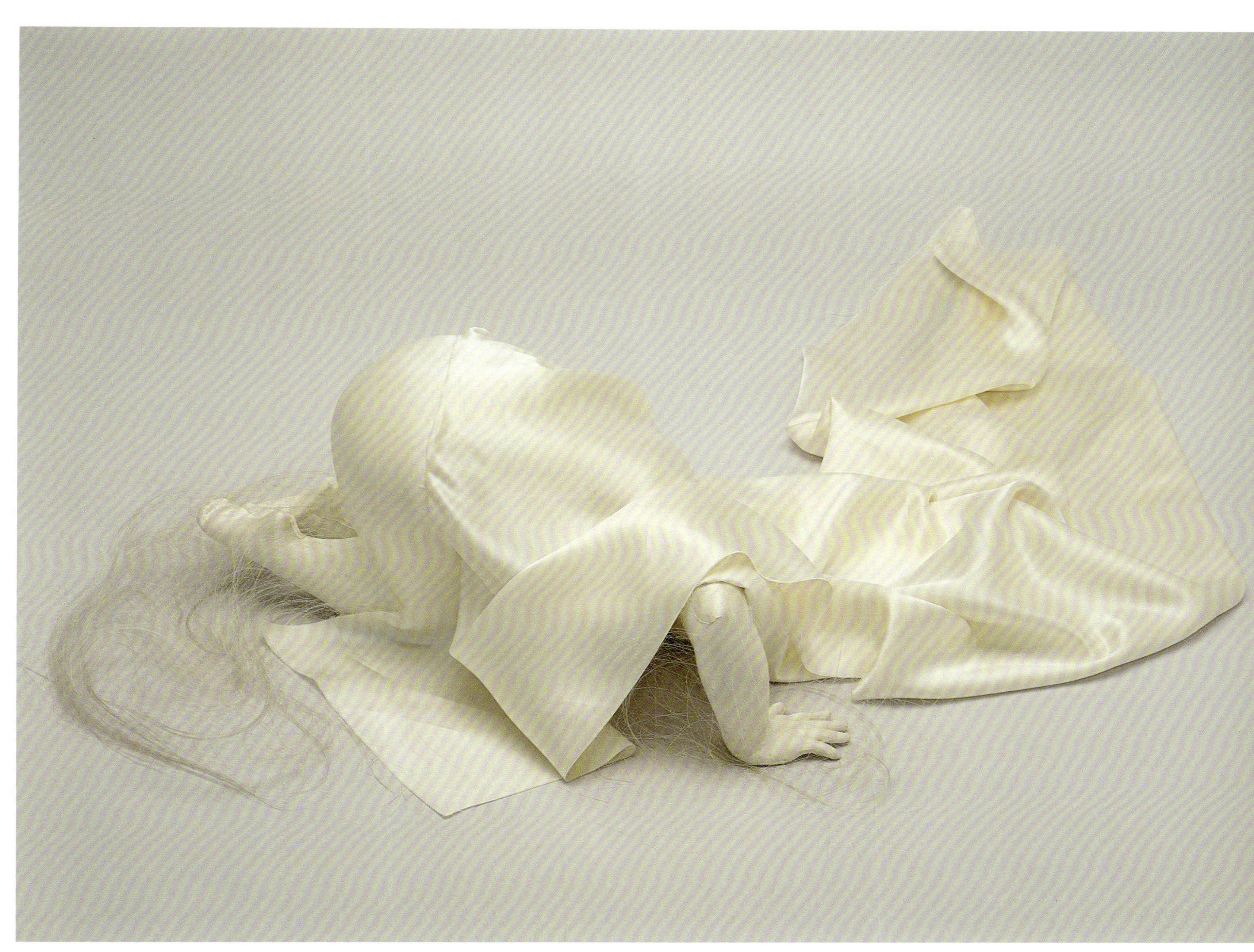

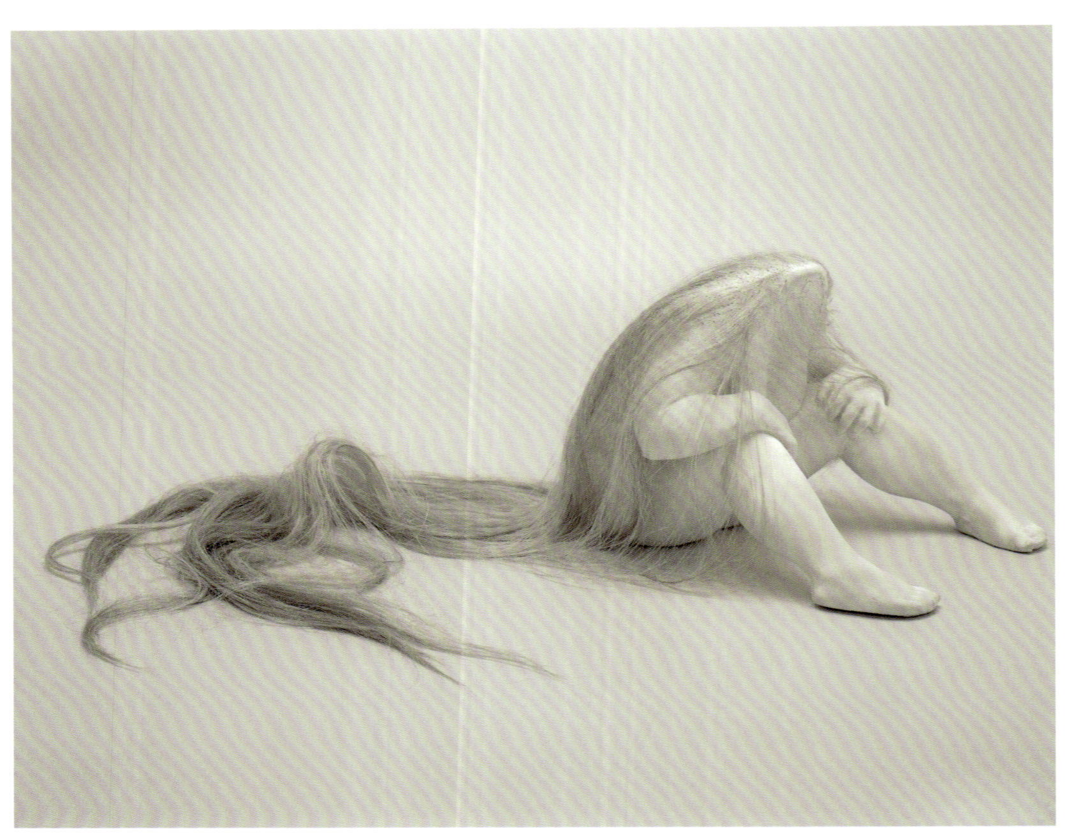

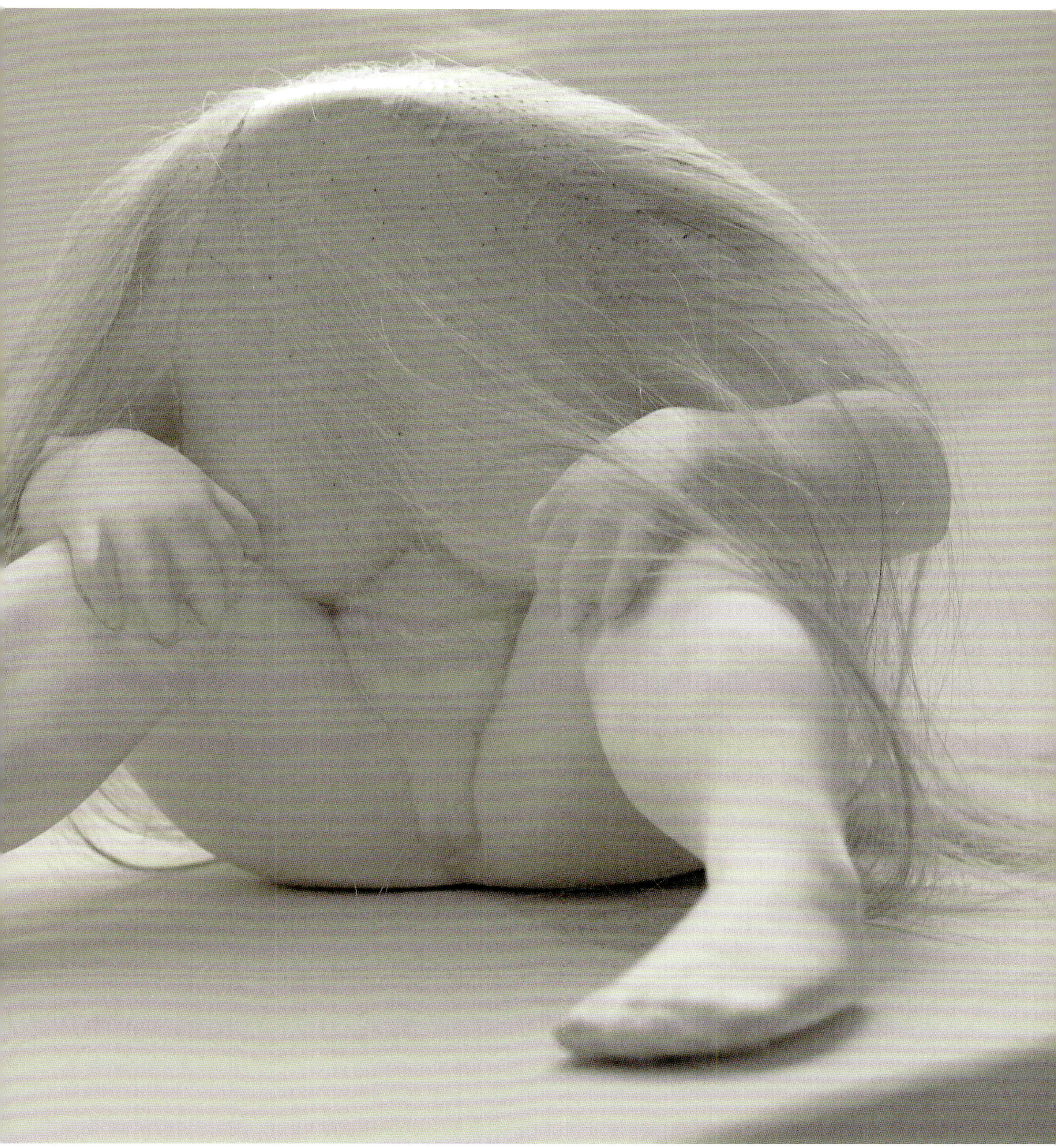

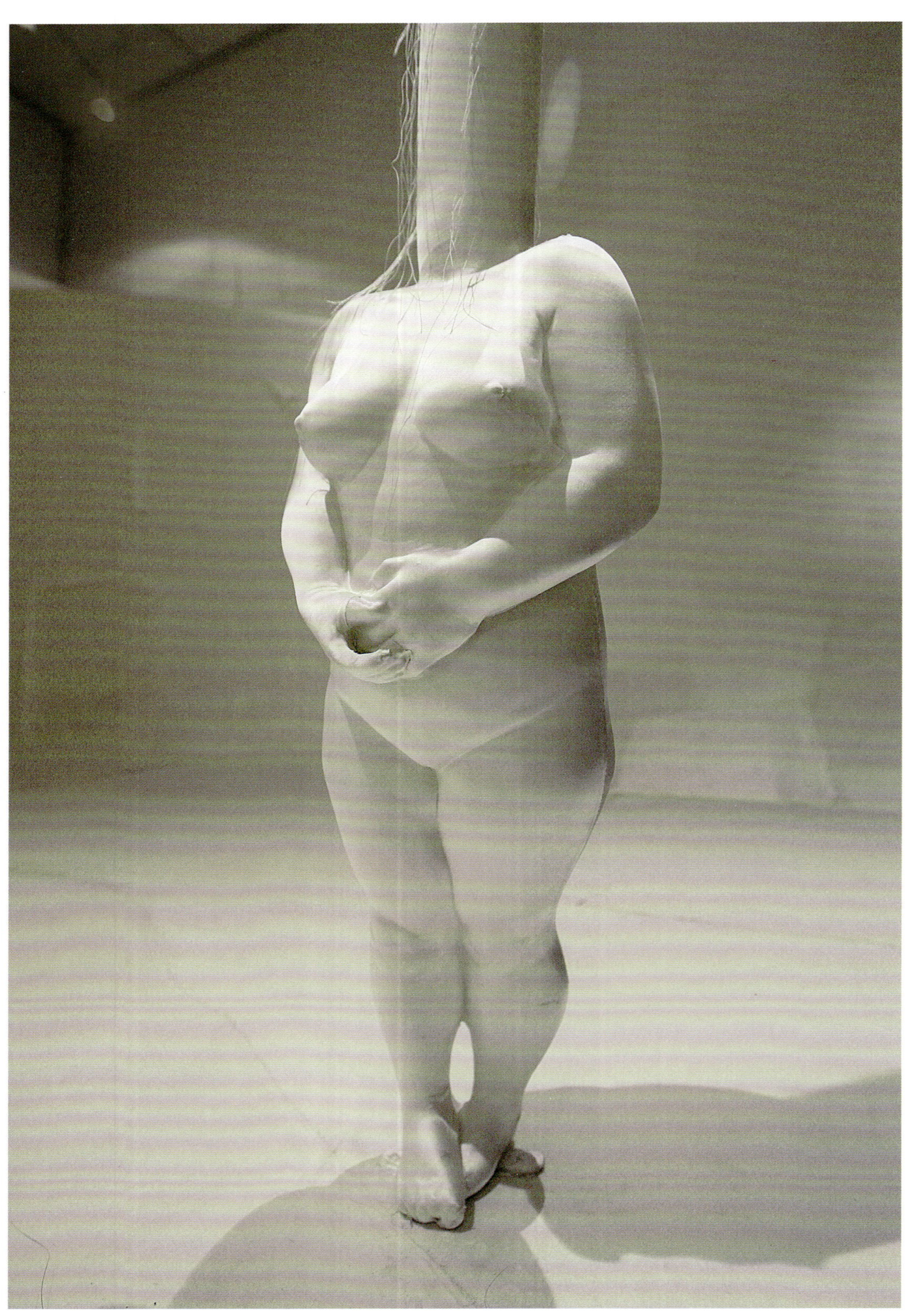

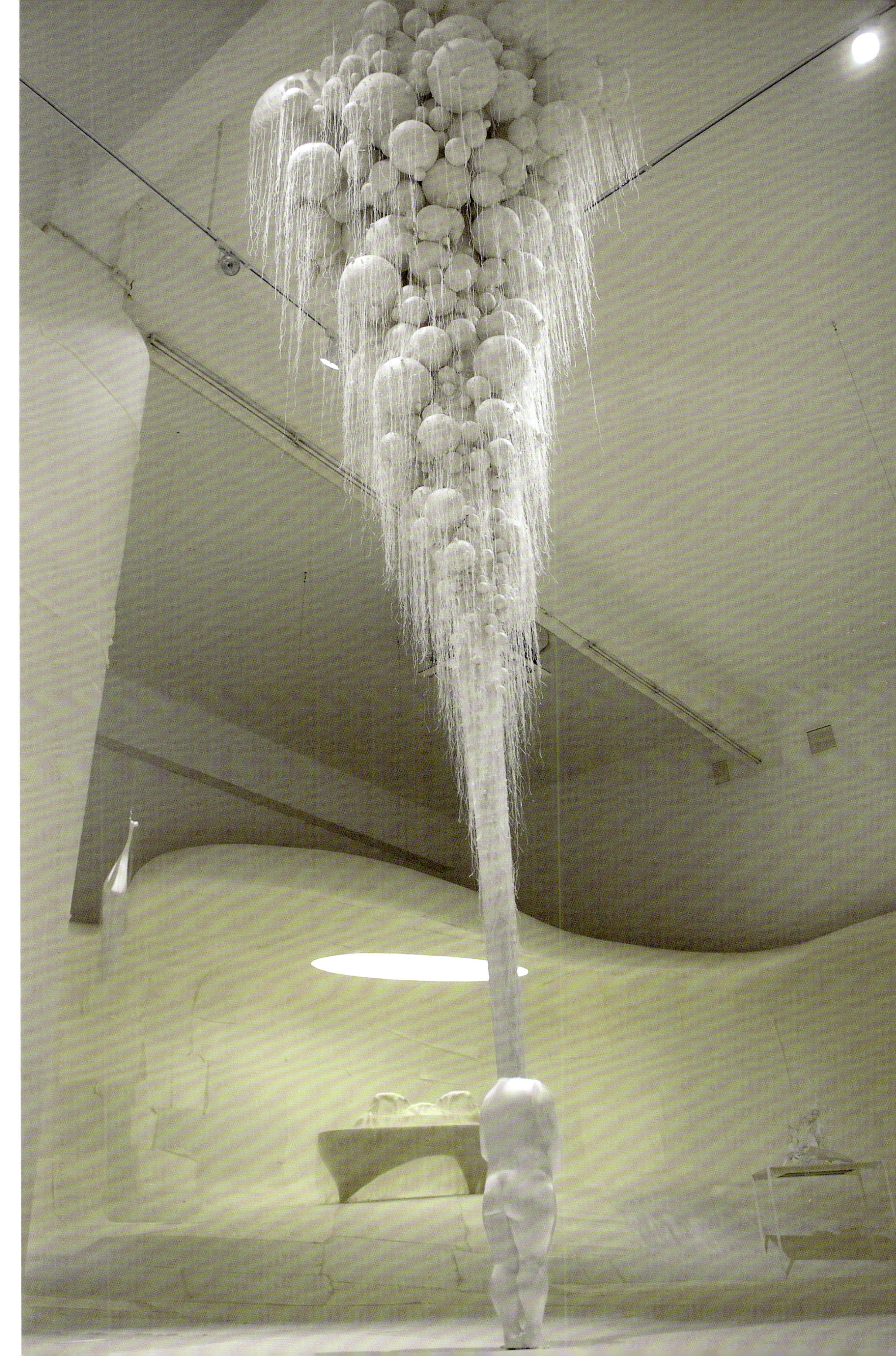

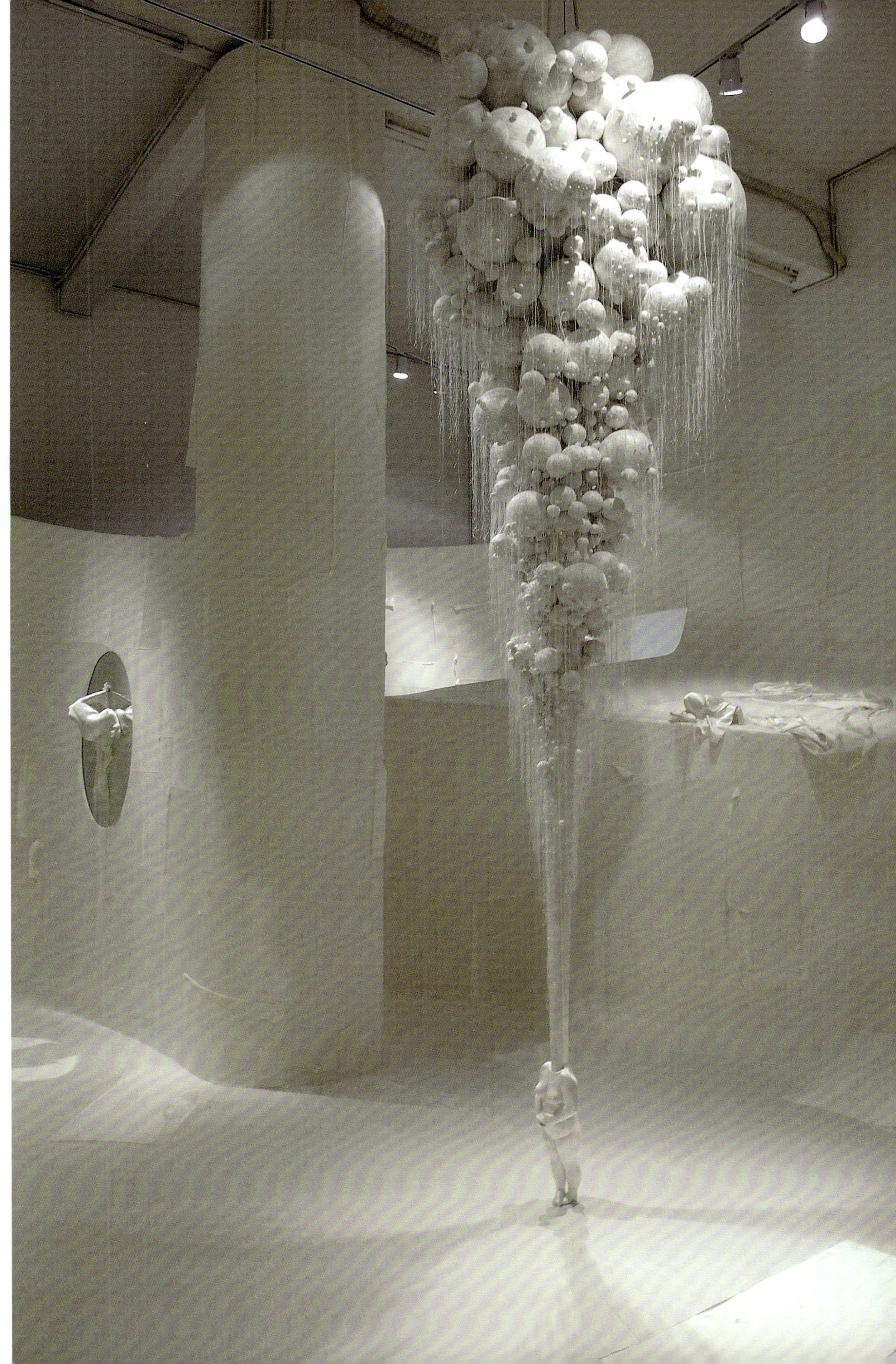

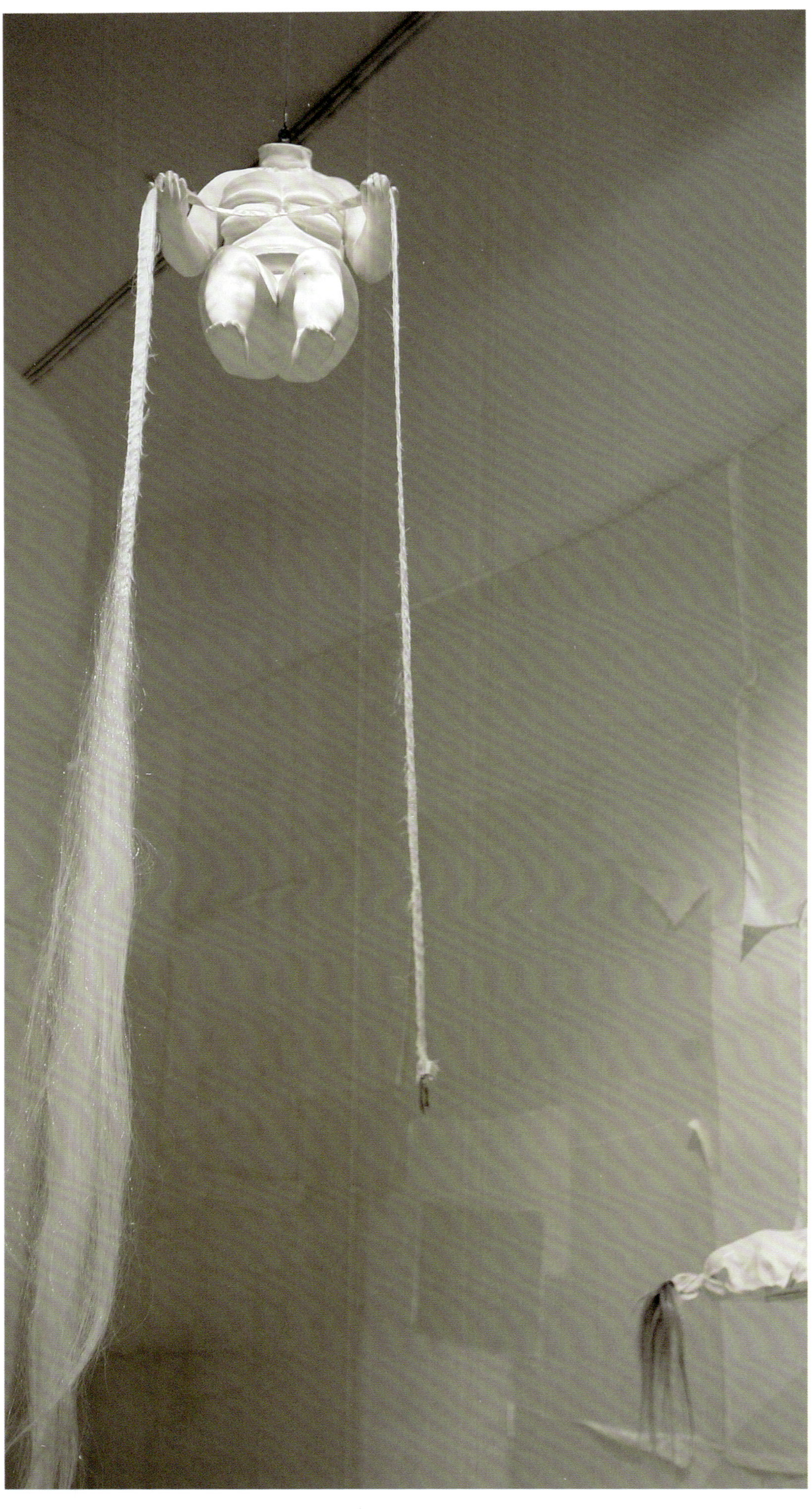

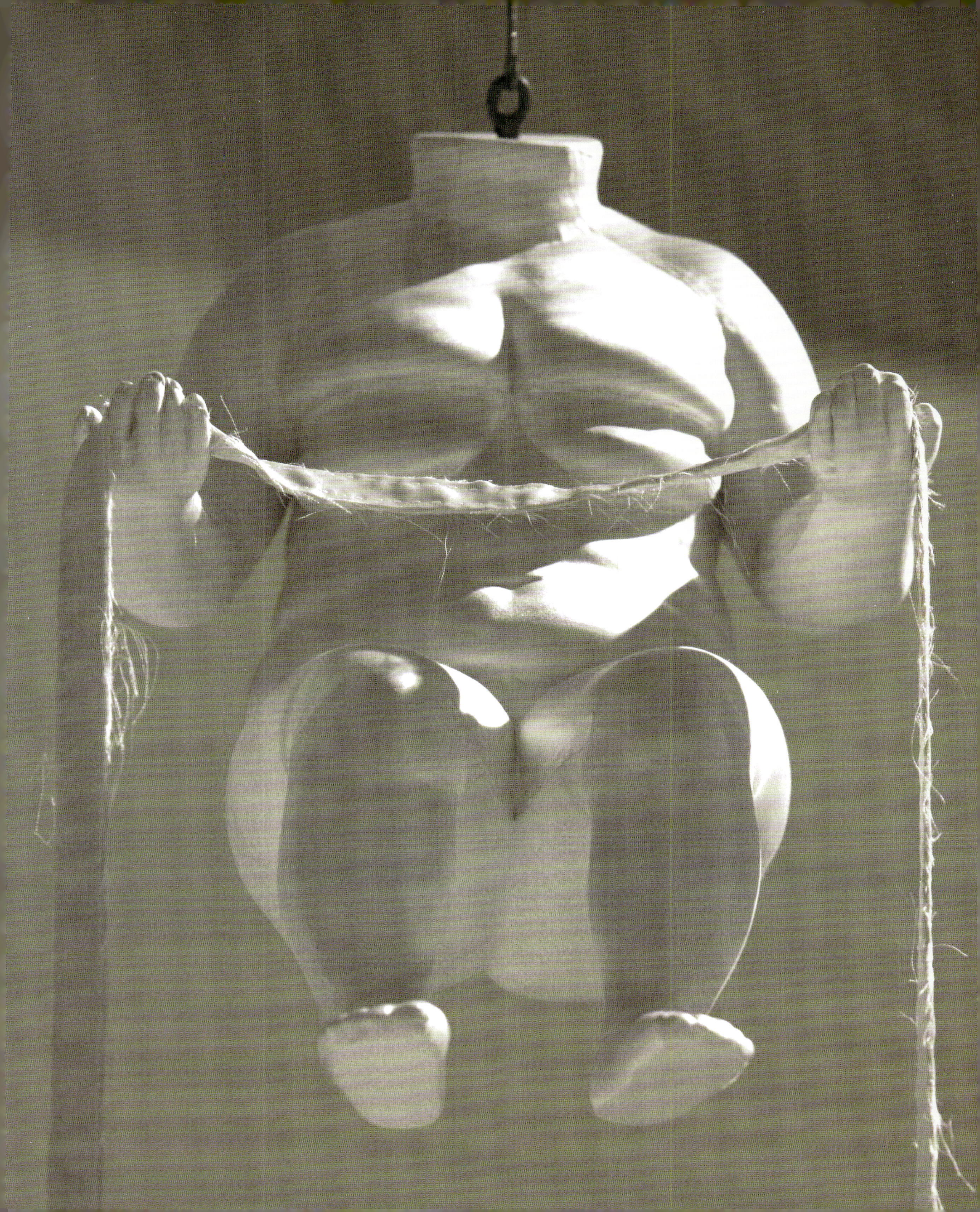

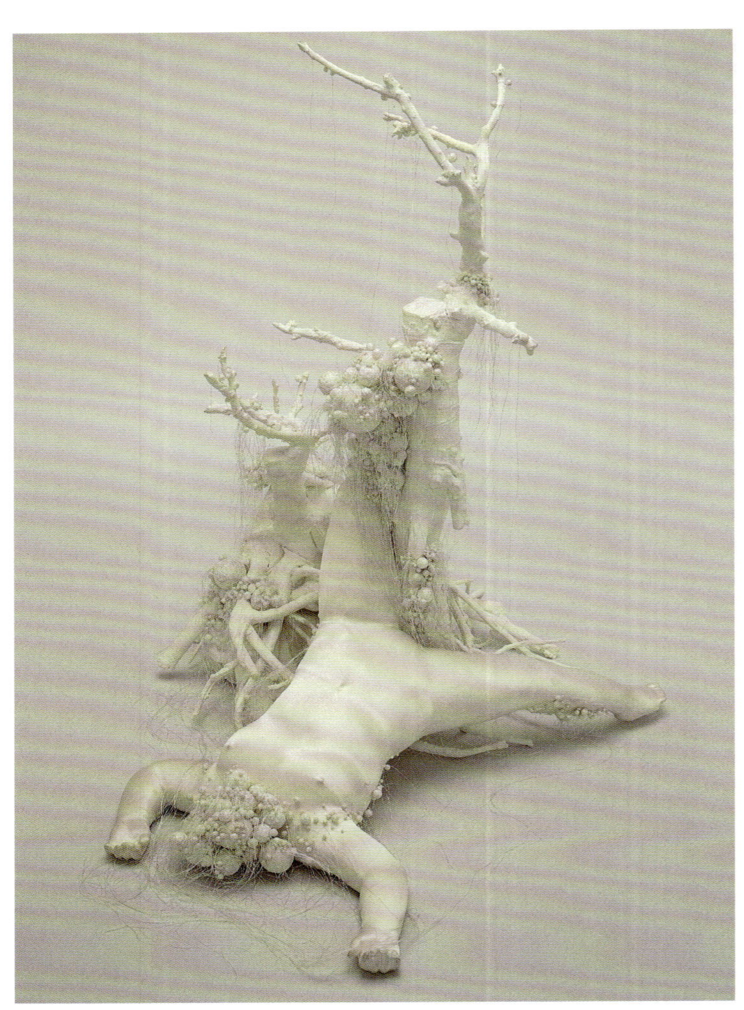

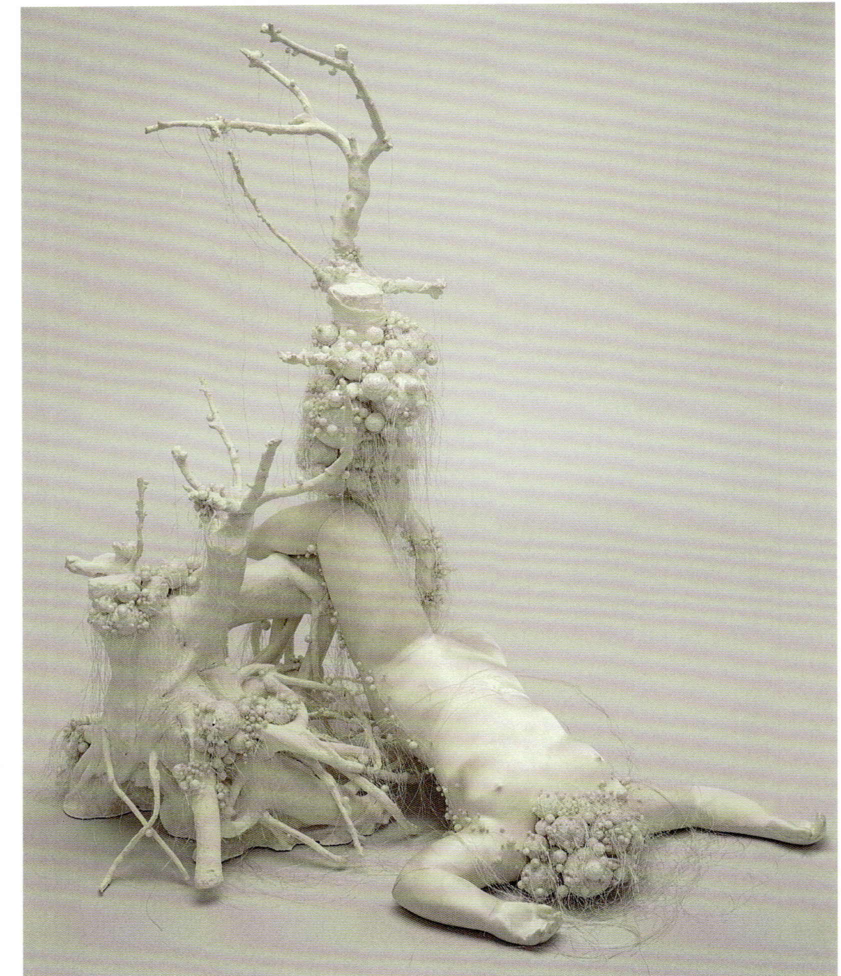

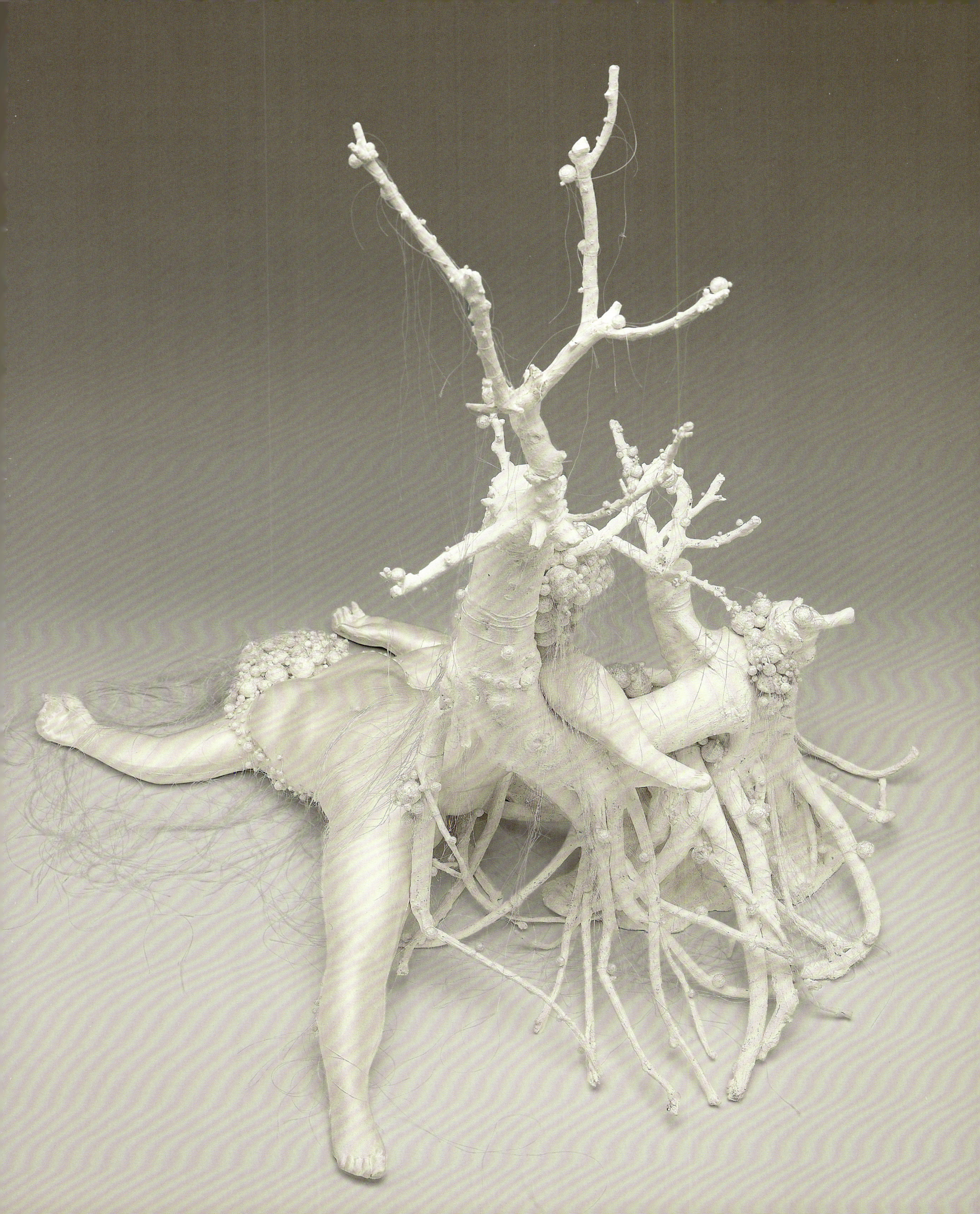

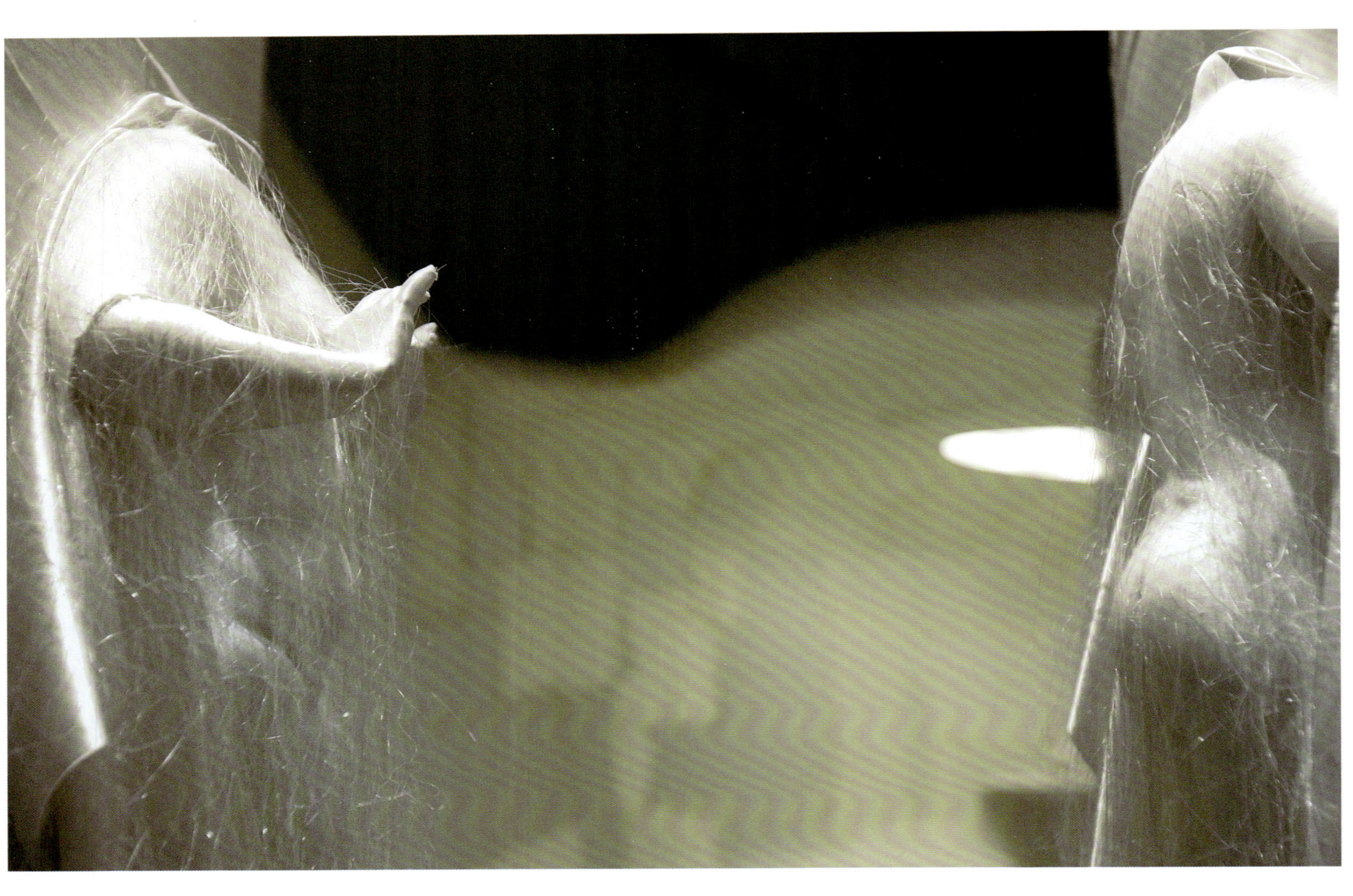

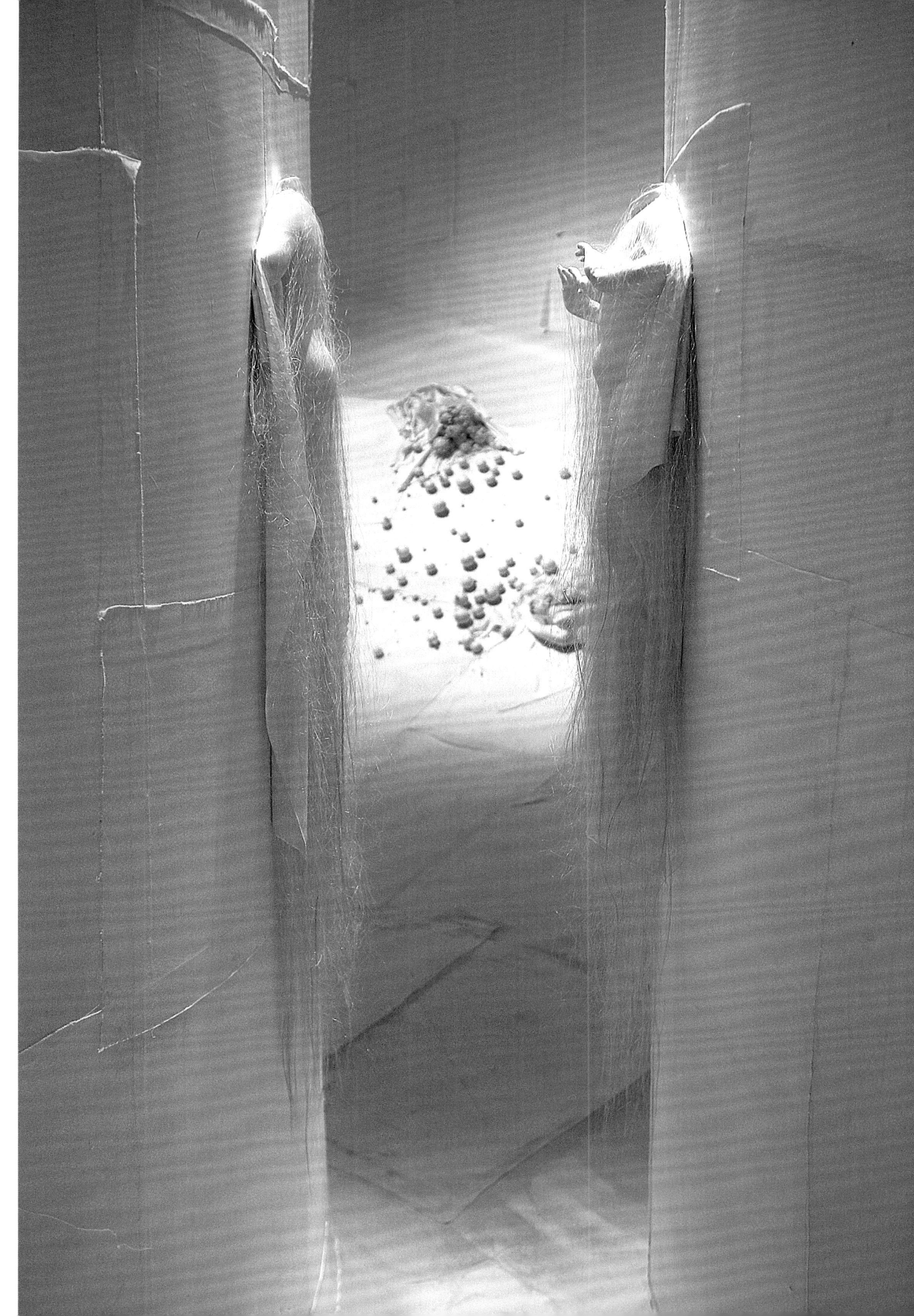

All the Same, 2011
Colored silk threads, synthetic skeletons, and metal constructions
Approximately 590 1/2 in. (1500 cm)
"The Same," Beijing Center for the Arts, December 18, 2011–March 10, 2012

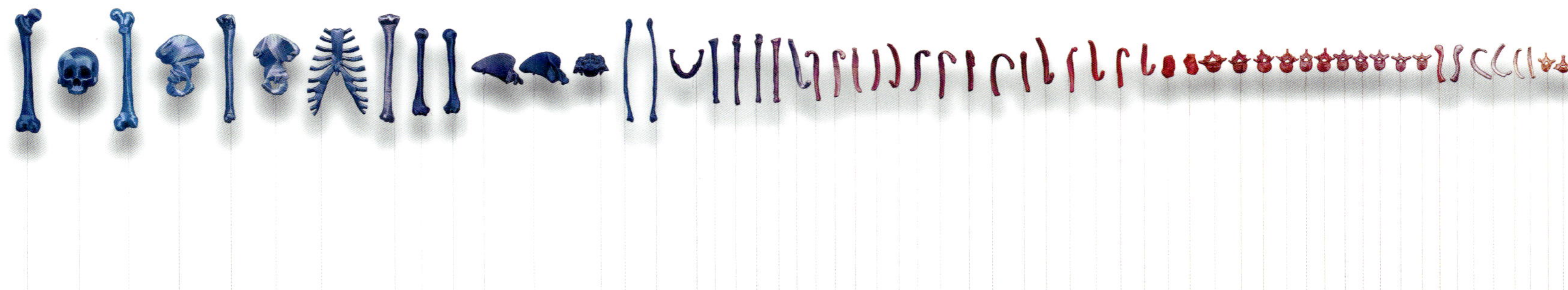

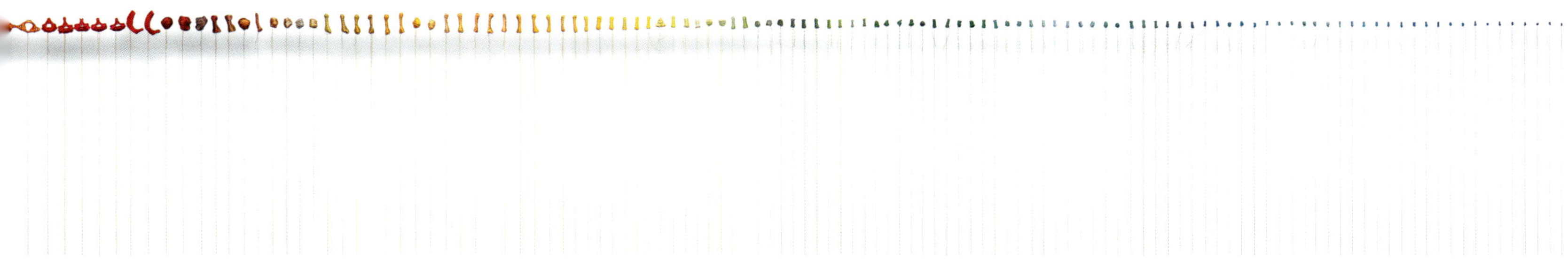

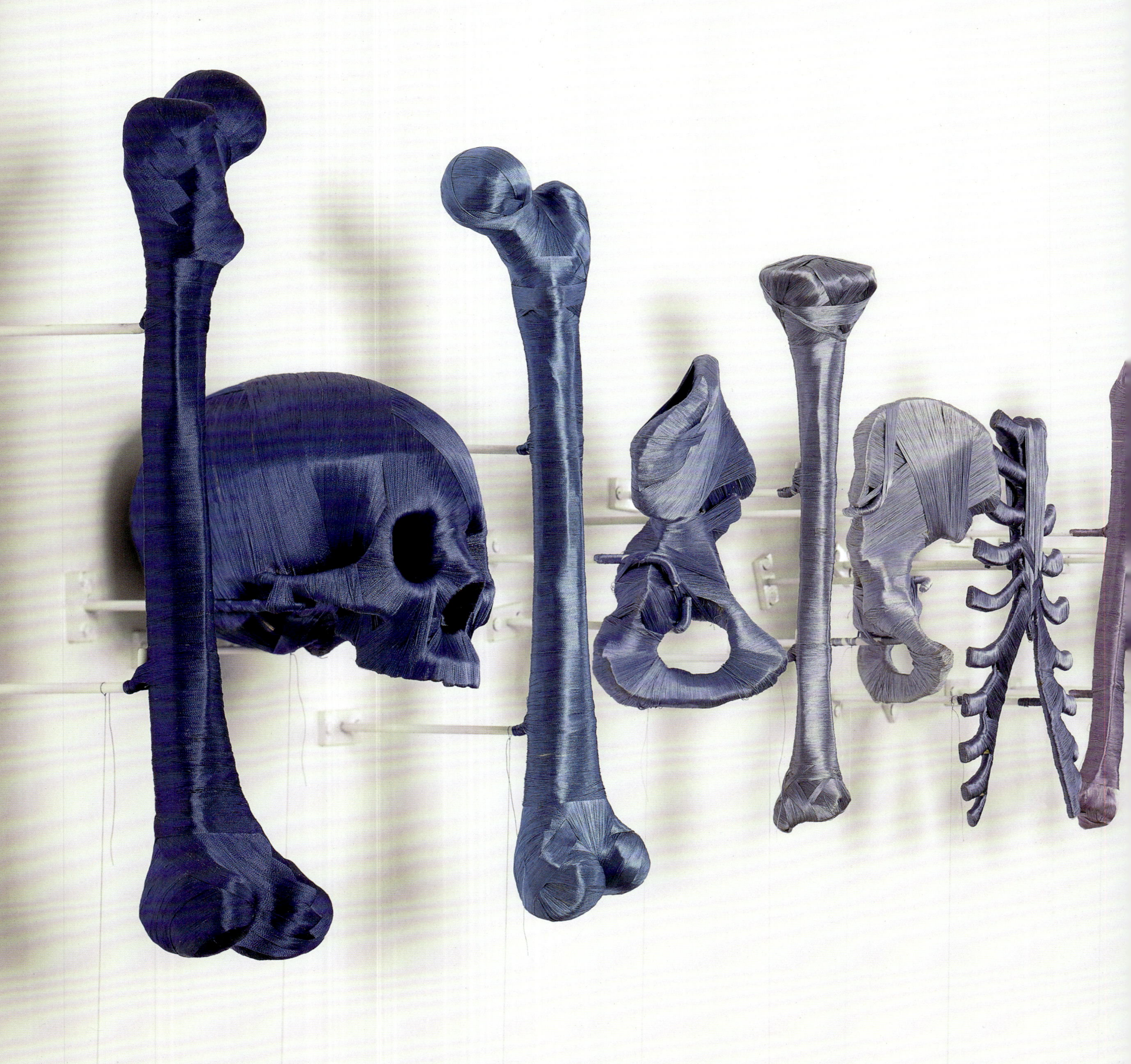

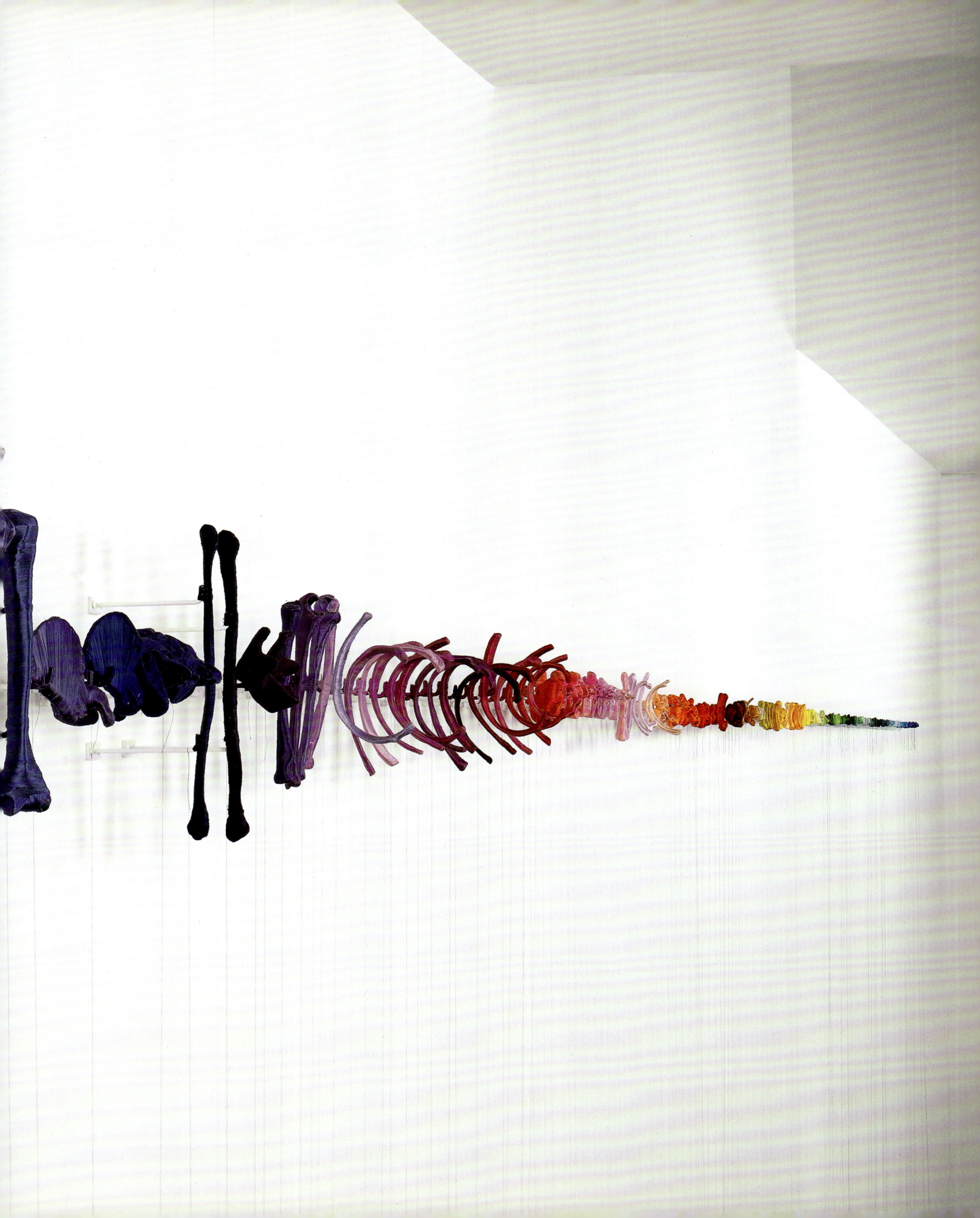

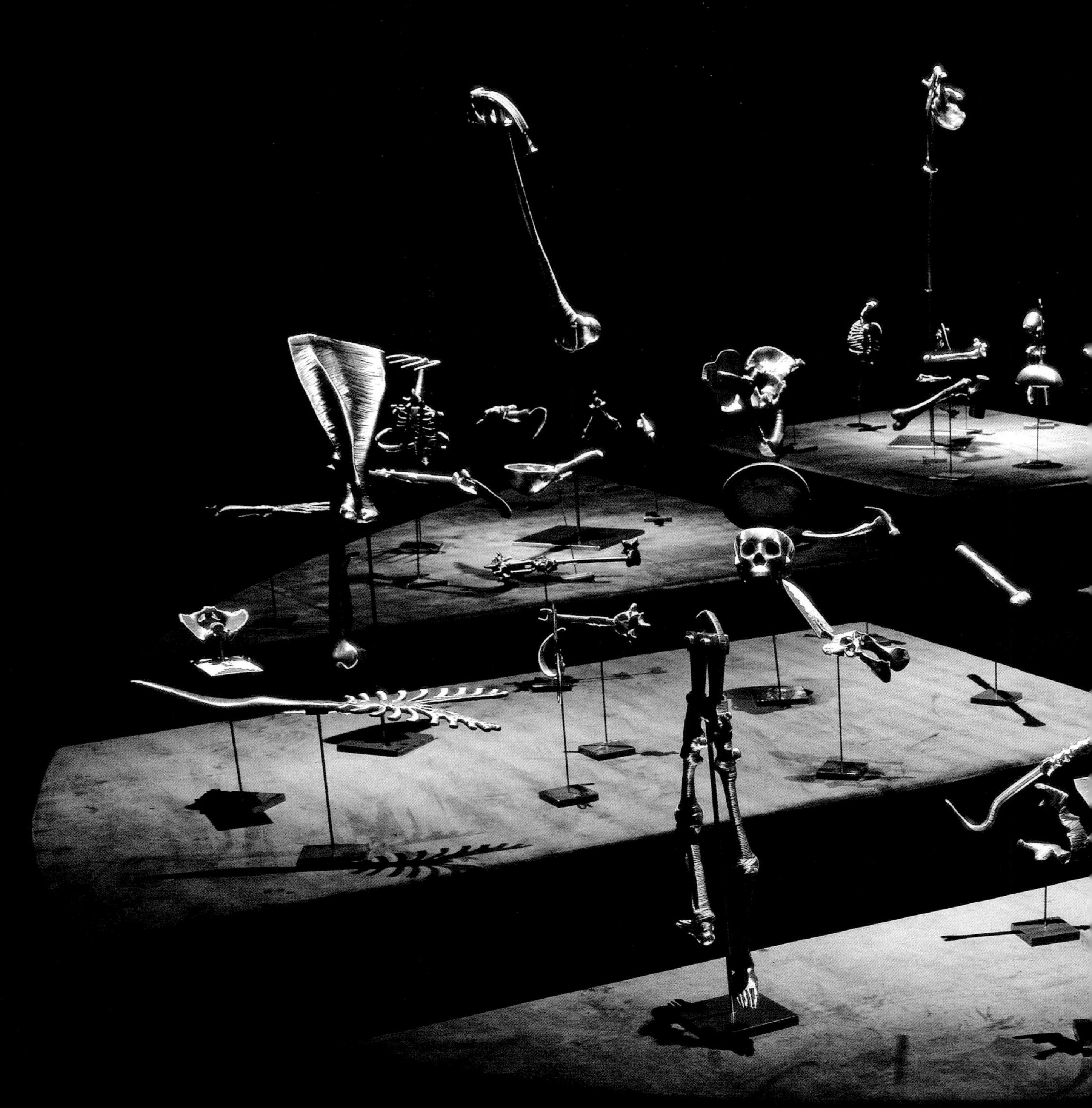

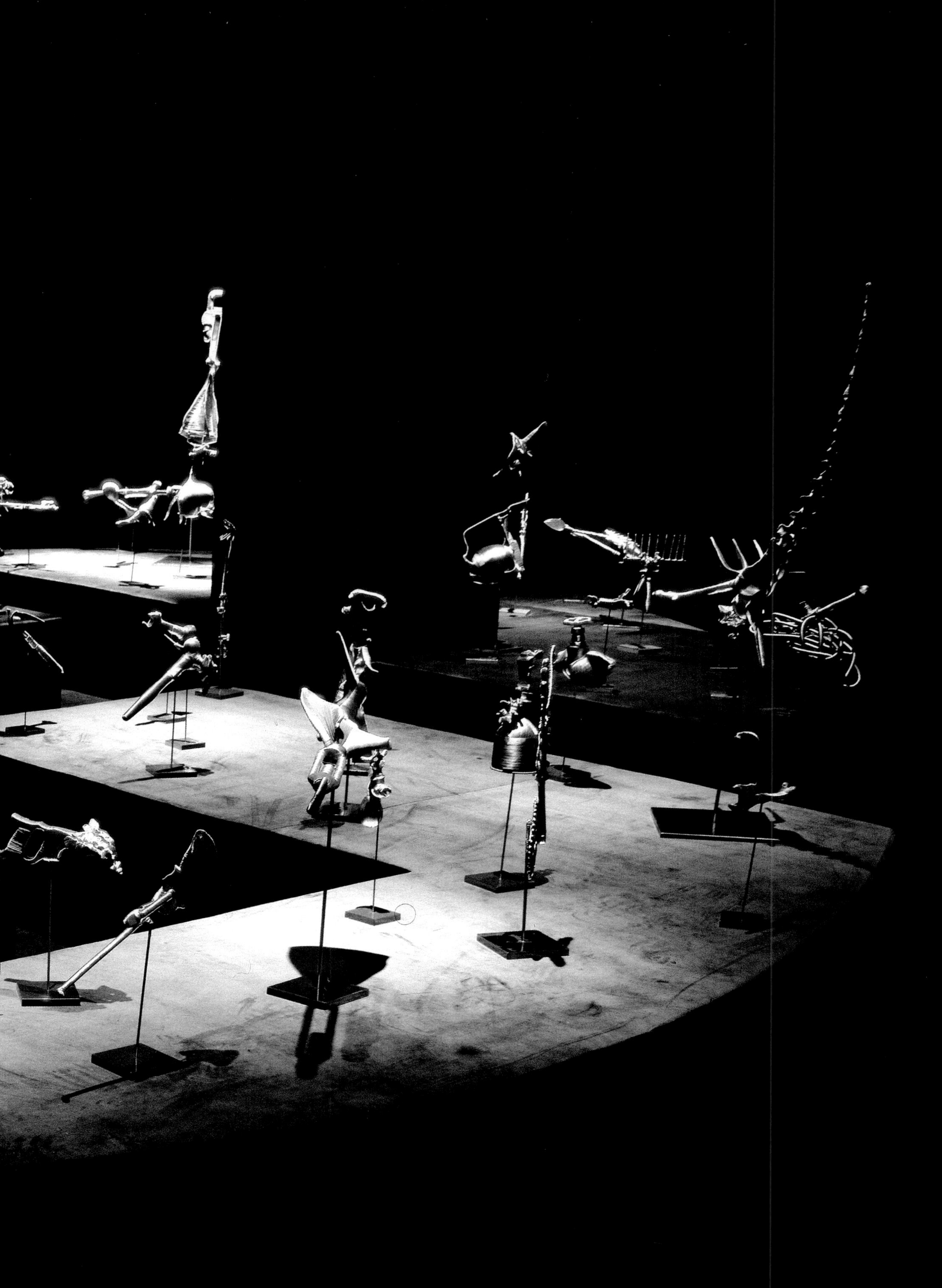

More or Less the Same, 2011
Polyurea, silk, cotton threads, and stainless steel stands
31 ½ x 393 ¾ in. diam. (80 x 1000 cm diam.)
"The Same," Beijing Center for the Arts, December 18, 2011–March 10, 2012
(from page 118)

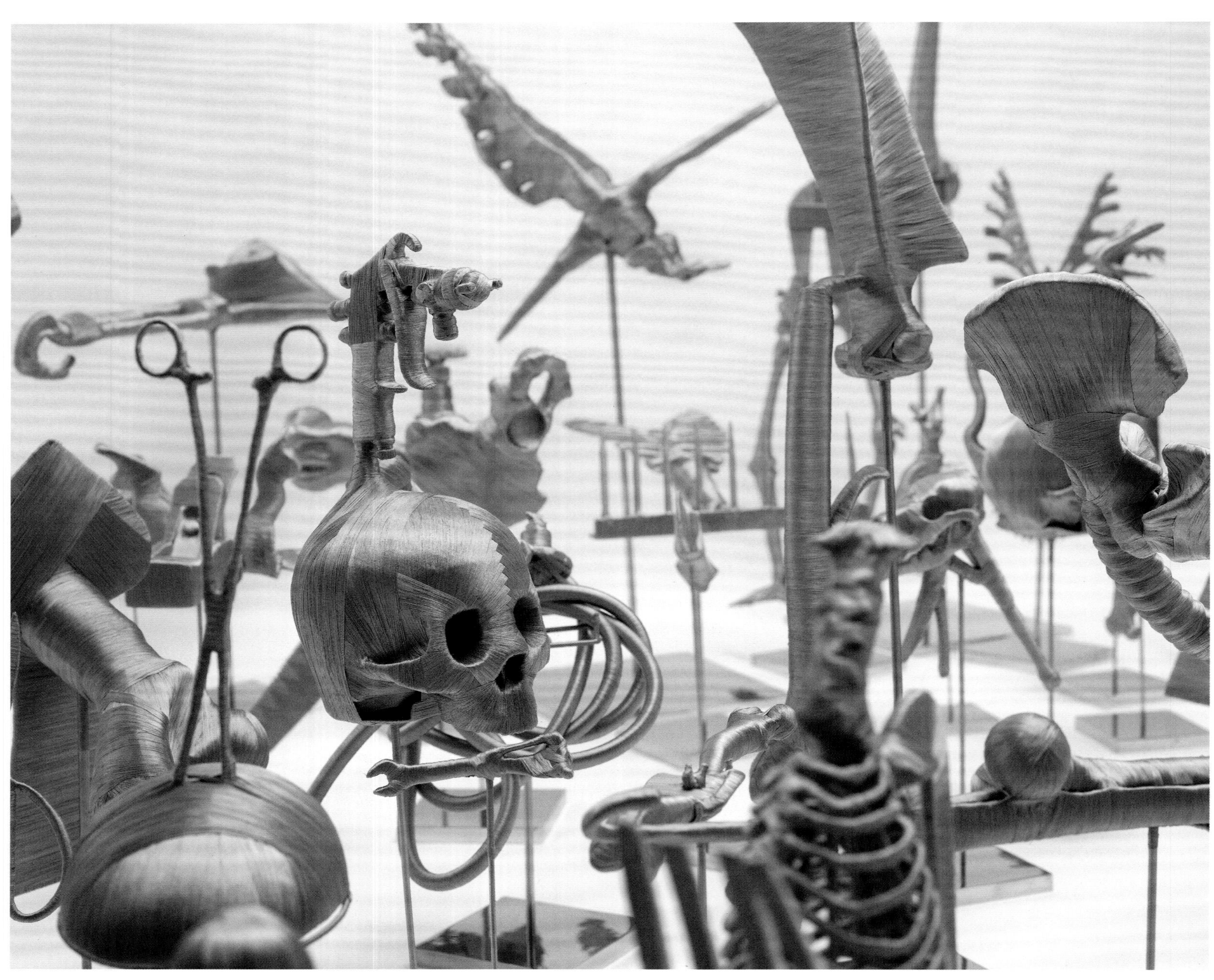

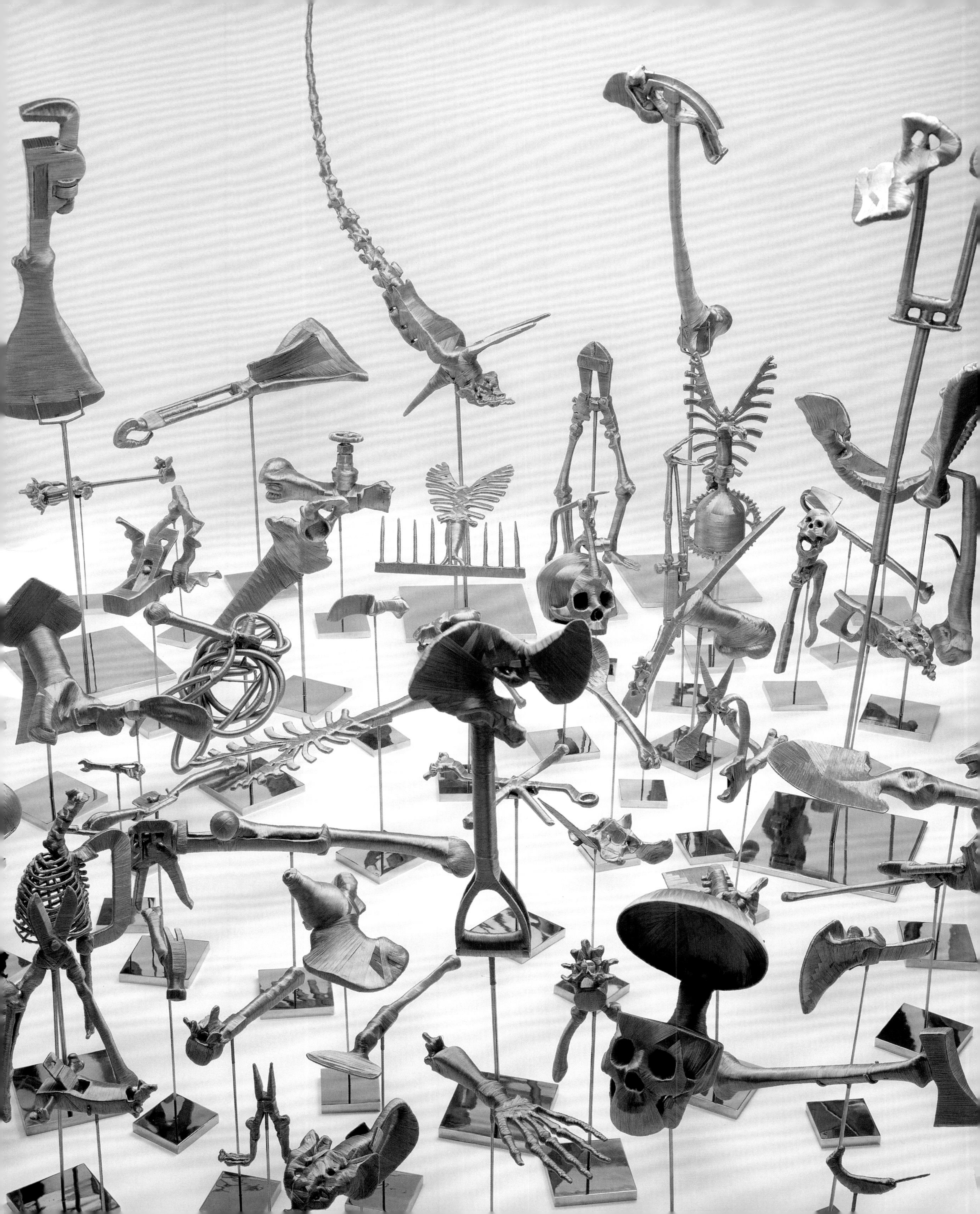

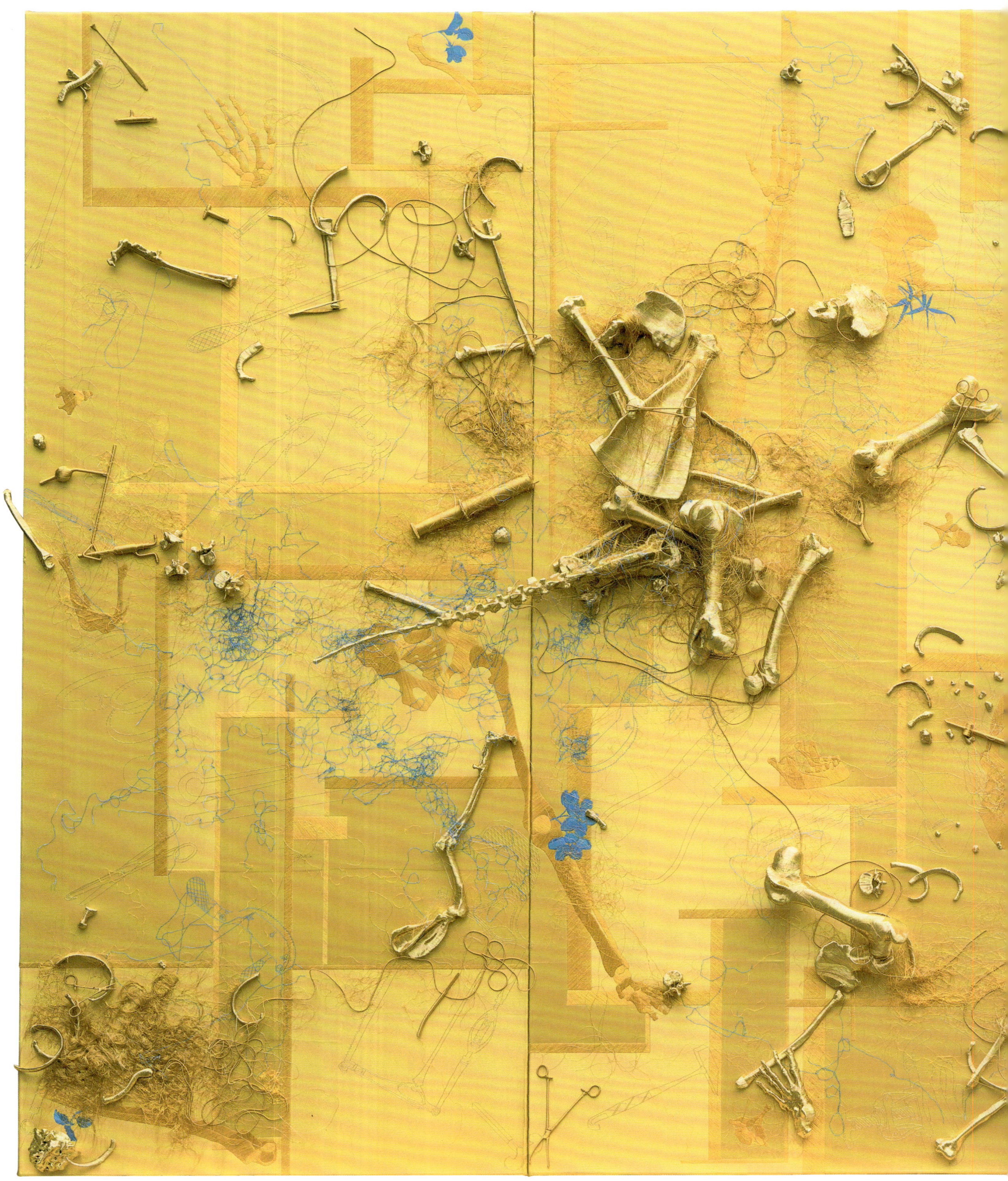

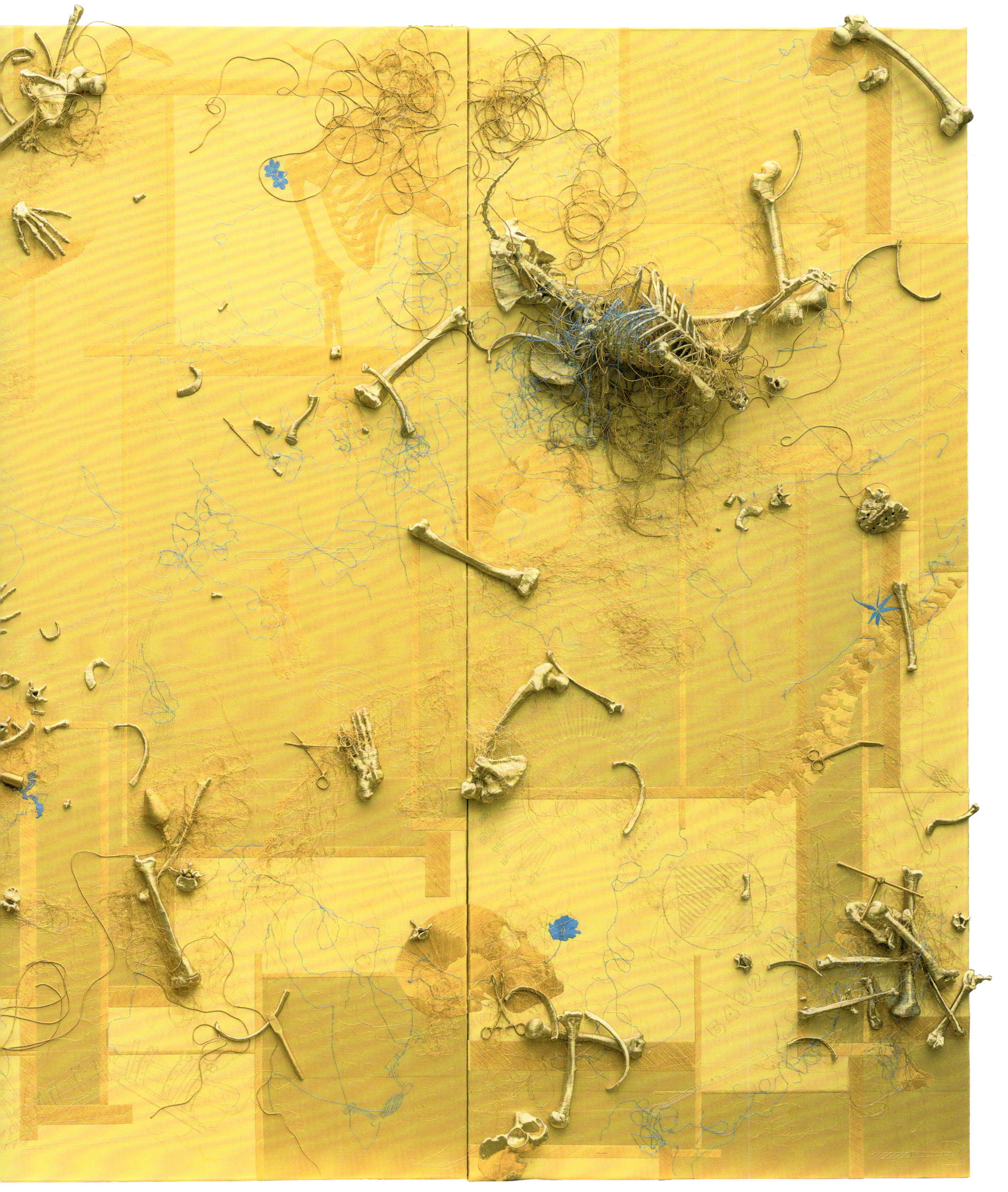

The Golden Mean, 2012
Synthetic resin bones wrapped in gold silk attached to panels
Approximately 185 ¾ x 110 ¼ in. (472 x 280 cm)
(pp. 122–123)

Bonsai Tree , 2012
Tree, threads, plastic figures and gold fcil
Approximately 30 ¼ x 22 x 39 in. (77 x 56 x 99 cm)

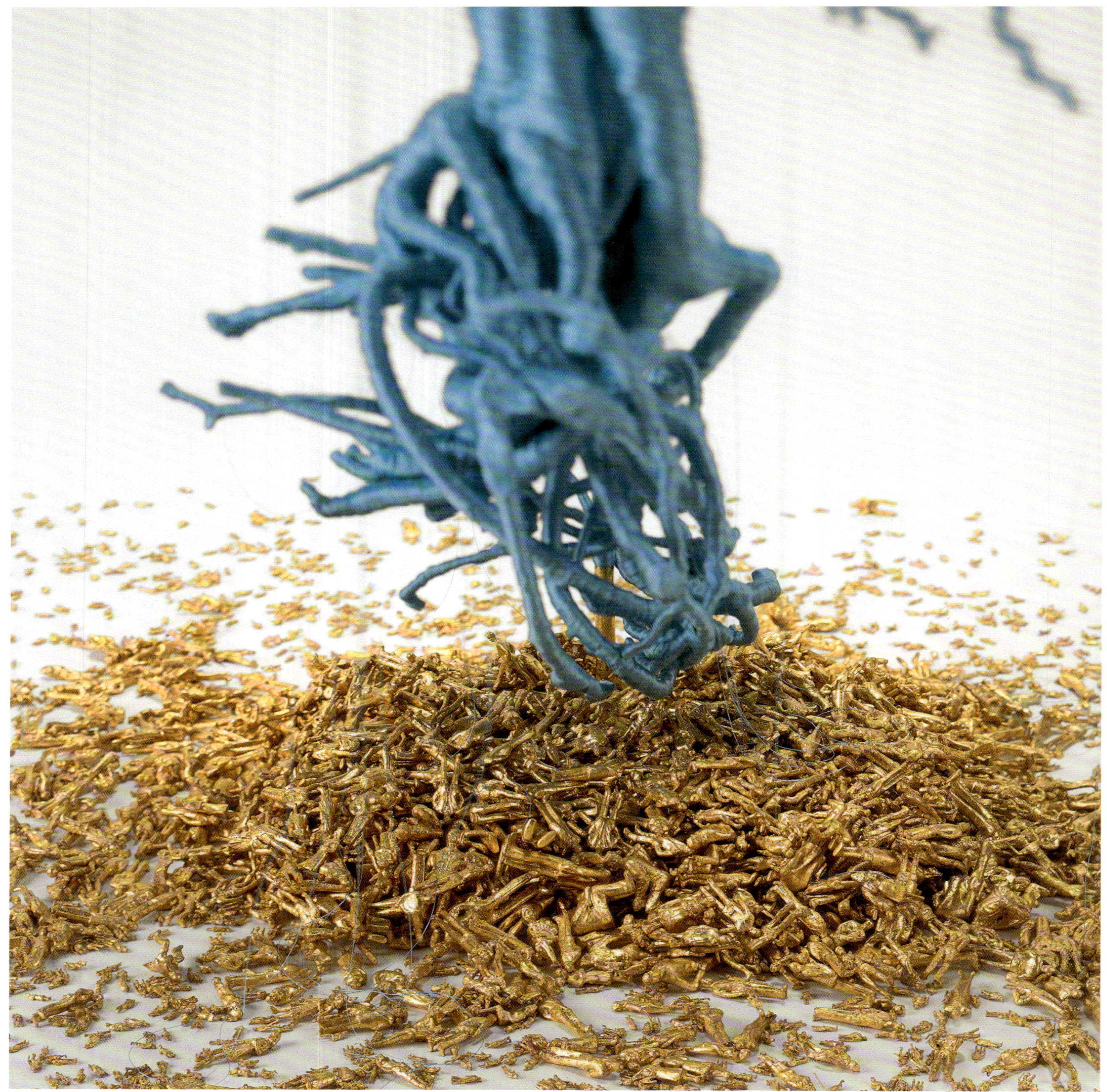

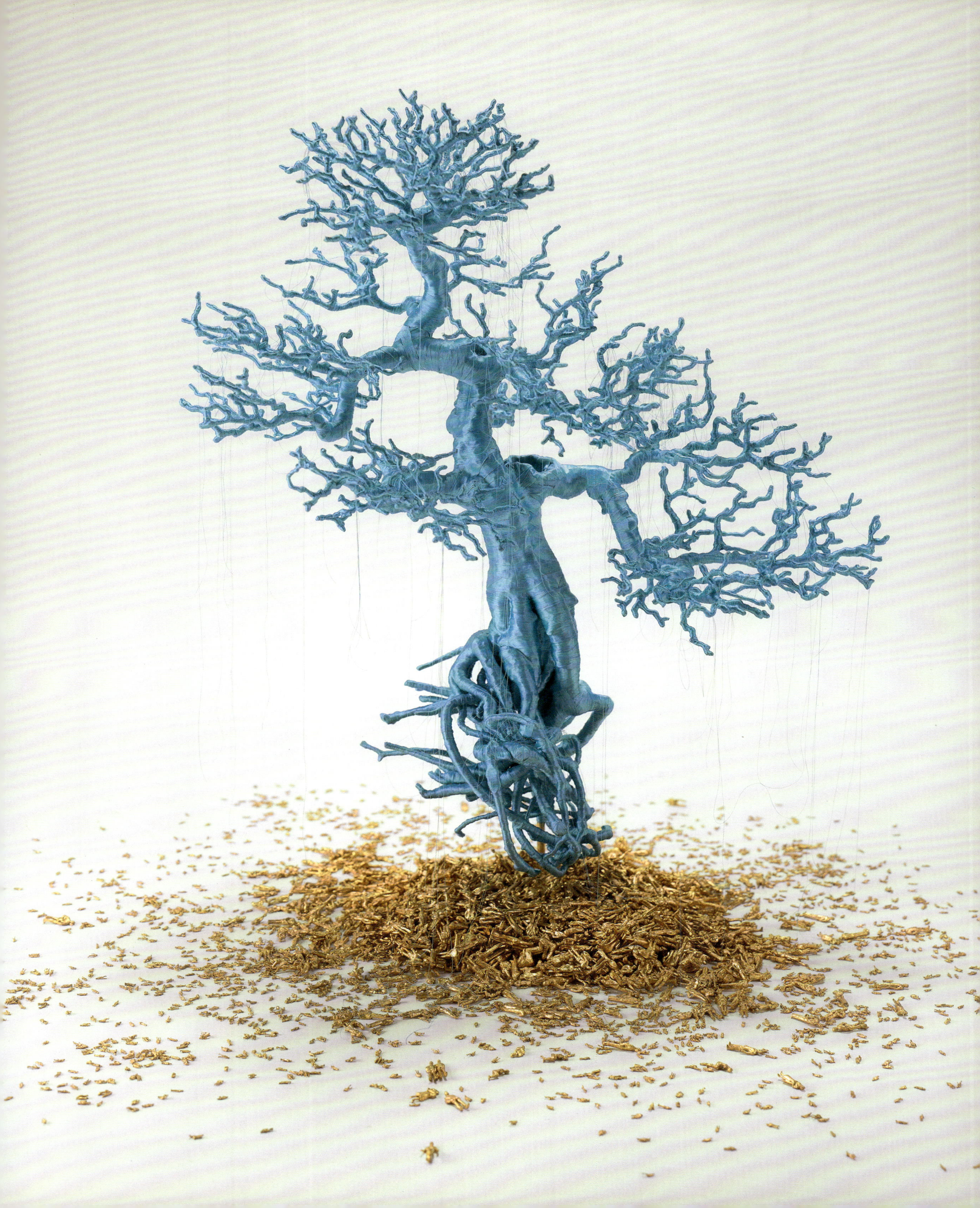

List of Works

The Proliferation of Thread Winding, 1995
White cotton thread, rice paper, 20,000 needles (12–15 cm in length), a bed, a video player, a television monitor
Dimensions variable

Bound and Unbound, 1997
White cotton thread, 800 pieces of household objects, video projection, sound
Dimensions variable
Hong Kong Museum of Art

Sewing, 1997
Sewing machine, white cotton thread, video projector, and speakers
35 ½ x 15 ¾ x 39 ¼ in. (90 x 40 x 100 cm)
Take a Step Back Collection

Day-Dreamer, 2000
White cotton threads, white fabric, digital photograph
59 x 86 ½ x 196 ¾ in. (150 x 220 x 500 cm)

Focus, 2001
Digital C-Type print on canvas, hair, silk threads, and cotton threads
95 ¼ x 5 x 69 ¾ in. (242 x 13 x 177 cm)

Spawn, 2001
Threaded and digital print on canvas
96 x 46 in. (393.8 x 166.8 cm)
Collection of Ethan Warsh

Here? Or There?, 2002
Fiberglass, fabric, thread, mixed media
Dimensions variable

Chatting, 2004
Fiberglass, silk threads, mixed media, sound
Dimensions variable

Endless, 2004
Fiberglass, silk, mixed media
Background wall: 55 ⅛ x 196 ¾ in. (140 x 500 cm); set area: Dimensions variable

Untitled No. 2, 2006
Felt, wig hair piece
Approximately 78 ¾ x 96 ½ in. (200 x 245 cm)

Mother's!!!, 2008
Polyurea, silk, cotton threads, etc.
Dimensions variable

All the Same, 2011
Colored silk threads, synthetic skeletons, and metal constructions
Dimensions variable

More or Less the Same, 2011
Polyurea, silk, cotton threads, and stainless steel stands
31 ½ x 393 ¾ in. diam. (80 x 1000 cm diam.)

The Golden Mean, 2012
Synthetic resin bones wrapped in gold silk attached to panels
Approximately 185 ¾ x 110 ¼ in. (472 x 280 cm)

Bonsai Tree, 2012
Tree, threads, plastic figures, and gold foil
Approximately 30 ¼ x 22 x 39 in. (77 x 56 x 99 cm)

Unless otherwise stated, all artworks are in the collection of the artist.

Biography

Born in 1961 in Taiyuan Shanxi Province, China.

Lin Tianmiao was born in Taiyuan Shanxi Province, China, in 1961. She studied Fine Arts at Capital Normal University in Beijing, and then at the Art Students League in New York. For nearly a decade she and her husband, artist Wang GongXin, lived in New York City, where she designed textiles until the couple moved back to Beijing in 1994. Working across installation, sculpture, photography, paper, and video, Lin Tianmiao's work has been included in numerous local and international exhibitions, such as: "Focus: Works on Paper," Long March Space, Beijing, China, 2008; "Global Feminisms," Brooklyn Museum, New York, 2007; "About Beauty," House of World Cultures, Berlin, Germany, 2005; "Mahjong: Works from the Sigg Collection," Kunstmuseum, Bern, Switzerland, 2005; "Between Past and Future," International Center of Photography, New York; Asia Society Museum, New York; Smart Museum, Chicago, 2004.

Education

1984, BFA, Capital Normal University, Beijing
1989, Art Students League, New York

Selected Solo Exhibitions

2011
"The Same," Beijing Center for the Arts, Beijing, China

2010
"The Constructed Dimension—2010 Chinese Contemporary Art Invitational Exhibition," National Art Museum of China, Beijing, China
"Audi A5 Popcorn—The Art of Lin Tianmiao," Audi Art Design Award Opening, Beijing, China

2009
"Gazing Back: The Art of Lin Tianmiao," OCT Contemporary Art Terminal of He Xiangning Art Museum, Shanghai, China

2008
"Mother's!!!," Long March Space, Beijing, China
"Focus," Long March Space, Beijing, China
"Visions de Paysages," JGM Gallery, Paris, France

2007
"Focus," Singapore Tyler Print Institute, Singapore
"Seeing Shadow," Art & Public Gallery, Geneva, Switzerland
Loft Gallery, Paris, France

2004
"Non Zero," Tokyo Art Project, Beijing, China

2002
"Focus," The Courtyard Gallery, Beijing, China

1997
"Bound and Unbound," The Central Academy of Fine Arts (CAFA) Gallery, Beijing, China

1995
Open Studio, Baofang Hutong 12#, Beijing, China

Selected Group Exhibitions

2010
"JUNGLE: A Close-up Focus on Chinese Contemporary Art Trends," Platform China, Beijing, China

2009
"Over Six Hundred Choices," Arrow Factory, Beijing, China
"Art in Use: Sculptural Objects," Hong Kong Arts Center, Hong Kong, China
"Metropolis Now! A Selection of Chinese Contemporary Art," Meridian International Center, Washington D.C.
"The State of Things—Brussels/Beijing," Center for Fine Art, Brussels

2008
"Our Future: The Guy and Myriam Ullens Foundation Collection," UCCA, Beijing, China
"Where Are We?," Beijing Center for the Arts, Beijing, China
"Four Season Group Exhibition," Zhejiang Academy of Art, Hongzhou, China
"Half Life of a Dream: Contemporary Chinese Art from the Logan Collection," San Francisco Museum of Modern Art, San Francisco
"Beijing–Athens: Contemporary Art from China," Grace National Contemporary Art Center, Athens, Greece

2007
"Multiplex: Directions in Art, 1970 to Now," Museum of Modern Art, New York
"Global Feminism," Brooklyn Museum, New York

2006
"Asian Contemporary Art in Print," Asia Society and Museum, New York
"Asian Contemporary Art in Print," The Gallery of Singapore Tyler Print Institute (STPI), Singapore
Martell Artist of the Year 2006, National Gallery of China, Beijing, China

2005
"Rapt: Austral-Asia Zero Five," Sherman Galleries, Sydney, Australia
"About Beauty," Haus der Kulturen der Welt, Berlin, Germany
"Shanghai Cool—Creative Reproduction," Shanghai Duolun Museum of Modern Art, Shanghai, China
"The New Works of Wang GongXin and Lin Tianmiao," Courtyard Gallery Annex, Beijing, China
"Mahjong: Works from the Sigg Collection," Kunstmuseum Bern, Switzerland
"Xianfeng! Chinese Avant-Garde Sculpture," Museum Beelden aan Zee, The Hague, The Netherlands
"Fairy Tales Forever," ARoS Aarhus Kunstmuseum, Denmark

2004
"Between Past and Future," International Center of Photographey, New York; Asia Society Museum, New York; Museum of Modern Art, Chicago
"Concrete Horizons," Adam Art Gallery, Victoria University of Wellington, New Zealand
"Officina Asia," Gallery d'Arte Moderna, Bologna, Italy
"Regeneration: Contemporary Chinese Art from China and the

US," Samek Art Gallery, Bucknell University, Otis College of Art and Design, Los Angeles
Gwang Ju Biennale, Gwang Ju, Korea

2003
Echigo-Tsumari Art Triennale, Japan
Arles Photography Art Festival, Arles, France
"New Zone Chinese Art," Zacheta National Art Gallery, Warsaw, Poland

2002
"Imagined Workshop: Second Fukuoka Asian Art Triennale," Fukuoka Asian Art Museum, Japan
"Pause: Fourth Gwang Ju Biennale," Gwang Ju, Korea
Ireland Biennale, Ireland
"Urban Creation: Shanghai Biennale," Shanghai Art Museum, China
Guang Zhou Triennale, Guang Zhou Art Museum, China

2001
"Shout on the Face," Earl Lu Gallery Lasalle-Sia College of the Art Singapore
"The New Media Art Festival: Non-Linear Narrative," The Gallery of National Academy of Art, Hong Zhou, China
"Threads of Vision: Toward a New Feminine Poetics," Cleveland Center for Contemporary Art, Ohio
"Floating Chimeras," Edsvik Konst Och Kultur, Sweden
"Translated Acts," Haus der Kulturen der Welt, Berlin, Germany; Queens Museum of Art, New York
"The New Works of Wang GongXin & Lin Tianmiao," The Loft New Media Art Space, Beijing, China
"The Digital Art Festival," The Loft New Media Art Space, Beijing, China

2000
"At the New Century 1979–1999: China Contemporary Art," Chengdu Museum of Contemporary Art, Chengdu, China
"Inside/Out New Chinese Art," National Gallery of Australia, New South Wales, Australia
"Home? Contemporary Art Project," Shanghai, China
"Inside/Out New Chinese Art," The Hong Kong Museum of Contemporary Art, Hong Kong, China
"Bed/Chair," Xuxian Art Center, Taipei, Taiwan

1999
"Beijing in London," Institute of Contemporary Art (ICA), London
"The Second Yearlong Contemporary Sculpture Exhibition," He Xiang Ning Art Museum, Shen Zhen, China
"Inside/Out New Chinese Art," San Francisco Museum of Modern Art, San Francisco
"Magnetic Writing / Marching Ideas: Works on Paper," IT Park Gallery, Taipei, Taiwan
"Cologne–Beijing/Beijing–Cologne: Exchange Exhibition," Gothaer Kunstforum, Cologne, Germany
"Inside/Out: New Chinese Art," The Mexico Museum of Contemporary Art, Mexico City, Mexico
"Food for Thought: An Insight in Chinese Contemporary Art," Mu Art Foundation, The Netherlands

1998
"Mark of Existence: Art Workshop in Process," Beijing, China
"Woman—Century," National Gallery of China, Beijing, China
"Life: Contemporary Chinese Art," Wan Fung Art Gallery, Beijing, China
"Neo Lagoon: Contemporary Art of North East Asia," The Niigata Prefectural Museum, Japan
"Inside/Out: New Chinese Art," Asia Society, New York; P.S.1 Contemporary Art Center, New York

1997
"Crack in the Continent," The Watari Museum of Contemporary Art, Tokyo, Japan
Fifth International Istanbul Biennale, Istanbul, Turkey
"Between Ego and Society," Artermesia Gallery, Chicago
"Another Long March," Chasse Kazerme, Breda, The Netherlands
"Against the Tide," The Bronx Museum of the Arts, New York
"Demonstration of Video Art," The Gallery of Central Academy of Fine Arts, Beijing, China

1995
"File NO.1—Conceptual Documents for Impossible Art," SoHo Biennale, New York
"Woman's Approach to Contemporary Art," Beijing Art Museum, Beijing, China
Chinese Women's Artists Invitation Show, National Gallery of China, Beijing, China
Group Show, Ground Gallery, Los Angeles
Group Show, City Gallery, Courtland, New York
Beijing Youth Painting Exhibition, National Gallery of China, Beijing, China
Youth Artist Association Show, National Gallery of China, Beijing, China
Beijing Youth Painting Exhibiticn, Liulichang, Beijing, China

Selected Bibliography

"All Good Things Are Frail: Lin Tianmiao in Conversation with Lu Jie," *Yishu: Journal of Contemporary Chinese Art*, November–December 2008.

Mother's!!!. Beijing: Long March Space, 2008.

Butler, Cornelia, Griselda Pollock, and Alexandra Schwartz. *Modern Women: Women Artists at the Museum of Modern Art*. New York: Museum of Modern Art, 2010.

Chiu, Melissa. "By a Thread," *Modern Painters,* September 2010.

Chiu, Melissa. "Thread, Concrete, and Ice: Women's Installation Art in China," *Art Asia Pacific,* 1998.

Goodman, Jonathan. "Lin Tianmiao Long March Space," *Sculpture Magazine*, May–June 2010.

Heartney, Eleanor. "Life after History," in *Half-Life of a Dream: Contemporary Chinese Art from the Logan Collection*. Berkeley: University of California Press, 2008.

Huang, Zhuan. "Gazing Back: A New Aesthetics of Gender," in *Gazing Back: The Art of Lin Tianmiao*. China: OCT Contemporary Art Terminal of He Xiangning Art Museum, 2009.

Li, Pi. *Here? Or There?: Wang GongXin and Lin Tianmiao*. China: Timezone 8 Ltd., 2005.

Li, Pi and Karen Smith. *Lin Tianmiao: Non Zero*. China: Timezone 8 Ltd., 2004.

Marcoci, Roxana. "Lin Tianmiao," in *Threads of Vision: Toward a New Feminine Poetic*. Cleveland: Cleveland Center for Contemporary Art, 2001.

Contributors' Biographical Notes

Melissa Chiu is museum director and senior vice president, Global Arts and Cultural Programs at Asia Society in New York, where she has worked since 2001. Previously, she was founding director of the Asia-Australia Arts Centre in Sydney, Australia. As a leading authority on Asian contemporary art, she has authored numerous publications, including two of the first comprehensive books on the subject (*Asian Art Now*, Monacelli Press, 2010, and *Contemporary Art in Asia: A Critical Reader*, MIT Press, 2011, with Benjamin Genocchio) and organized nearly thirty exhibitions of international art.

Guo Xiaoyan is a pioneer in the development of art institutions in China. From 2002 to 2007 she held the position of vice-director of the Guangzhou Triennial Office at the Guangdong Museum of Art. She is also one of the founders of the Shanghe Art Museum, the first nonprofit museum in Chengdu, China. In 2007, Guo Xiaoyan was selected as the curator of the Ullens Center for Contemporary Art (UCCA), and from 2008 she assumed the position as chief curator of UCCA. Since March 2010, she has been the chief operating officer of the Minsheng Art Institute and vice-director of the Minsheng Art Museum.

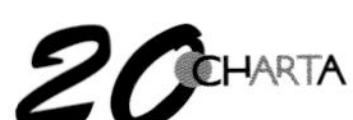

To find out more about Charta,
and to learn about our most recent
publications, visit

www.chartaartbooks.it

Printed in July 2012
by Bianca & Volta, Truccazzano (MI)
for Edizioni Charta